Carol McNicoll

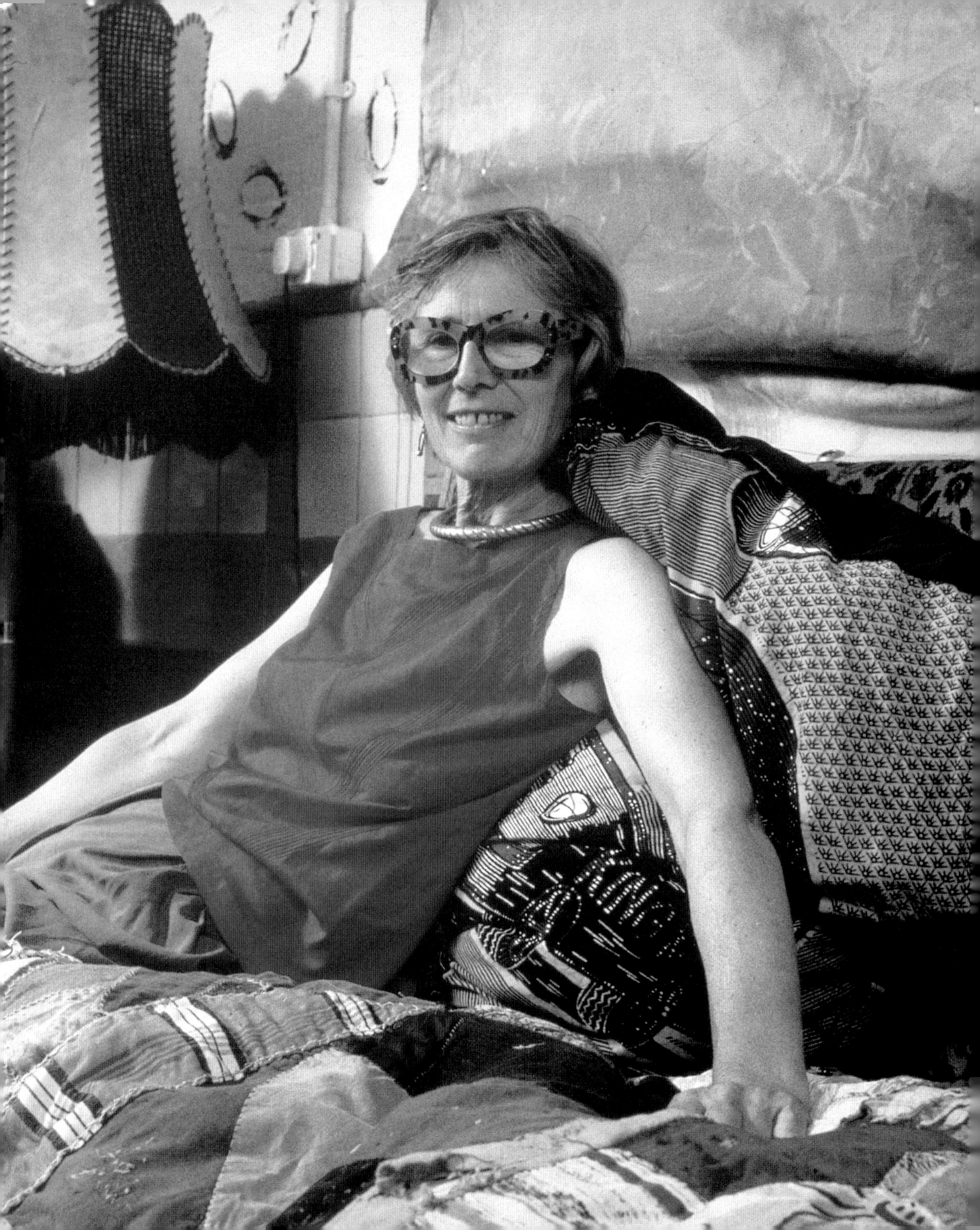

The City Gallery, Leicester
in association with Lund Humphries

Carol McNicoll

Tanya Harrod
and RoseLee Goldberg

The City Gallery, Leicester
90 Granby Street
Leicester LE1 1DJ
city.gallery@leicester.gov.uk

in association with

Lund Humphries
Gower House
Croft Road
Aldershot
Hampshire GU11 3HR

and

Suite 420
101 Cherry Street
Burlington
VT 05401
USA

www.lundhumphries.com

Lund Humphries is part of Ashgate Publishing

British Library Cataloguing-in-Publication Data
A catalogue record for this book is available from the British Library

ISBN 0 85331 883 2

Library of Congress Control Number: 2003104038

Designed by Chrissie Charlton & Company
Project Management by Rose James
Typeset by Tom Knott
Printed in Singapore under the supervision of MRM Graphics Ltd

frontispiece
1 Carol McNicoll 1999
Portrait and interior from 'Sources of Inspiration' by Tanya Harrod *Crafts Magazine* 1999 issue 161
Photograph: Nancy Honey

Contents

Show5 project initiated by
the Crafts Council

Funded by

Participating galleries

Birmingham Museums
& Art Gallery
The City Gallery, Leicester
Crafts Council, London
Manchester Art Gallery
The Potteries Museum
& Art Gallery, Stoke-on-Trent

Foreword

This book is one of a series of five developed as part of the *Show5* partnership initiated by the Crafts Council. *Show5* is the largest collaborative venture between five British museums and galleries, each focusing on the work of one of five leading makers who have helped define the territory of contemporary craft. The aim of this project is to celebrate the impressive achievements of these ground-breaking individuals who have both shaped and influenced the modern craft movement during the last 30 years. Their creative developments and innovative voices are documented and promoted here for an international readership.

The five artists invited to participate work with a wide range of craft media: Carol McNicoll's highly patterned and darkly humorous ceramics; Jim Partridge's pioneering woodwork, which ranges from vessels and furniture to large-scale architectural works; Michael Rowe's complex geometric metalwork; Richard Slee's 'Neo–Pop' ceramics; and Ann Sutton's innovative and experimental woven textiles.

What they do have in common is a desire to expand the boundaries of their craft and take it beyond the conventional and expected. They may, like Slee, McNicoll and Rowe, use traditional techniques to create a style of work that is instantly recognisable. Or, they may employ unusual techniques, like Partridge who uses blowtorches and chainsaws to sculpt his material or Sutton who utilises computer-driven looms.

Show5 is sincerely grateful to the National Touring Programme (Arts Council of England) and Esmée Fairbairn Foundation who have generously supported this creative project. Our thanks also go to Lund Humphries and the writers who had the vision to see the potential for this craft series and with whom we are very pleased to be working. *Show5* would like to thank the five partner galleries, the five artists, the lenders and all those who have contributed their time, ideas and support. A special mention to Kate Brindley and John Williams, without whose energy, commitment and support the project would not have been possible.

Louise Taylor
Director, Crafts Council

Introduction

The publication of this monograph, coinciding with a major retrospective solo show, celebrates the work of a unique and charismatic woman, Carol McNicoll. It also provides an opportunity to examine McNicoll's eclectic and diverse work from the late 1960s through to the dynamic new body of work emerging since 1998, placing McNicoll within an historical context and ensuring the future profile she deserves as one of Britain's leading ceramicists.

I first became aware of McNicoll's work on a visit to Next Interiors in the mid-1980s; they had commissioned a range of ceramics from the artist. I've been a huge fan ever since and curating the major retrospective exhibition of her career to date has been a pleasure.

McNicoll has been making ceramics for the domestic environment for around 28 years. She is one of a group of women artists such as Alison Britton, Jacqueline Poncelet and Jill Crowley who between them transformed the British ceramic scene. Her work embodies a quintessential form of English eccentricity resembling British domestic knick-knacks. McNicoll graduated in Fine Art in the late 1960s and studied an MA in Ceramics at the Royal College of Art, London in the 1970s.

She has also moved within another world. She worked as a machinist for Zandra Rhodes, who has collected McNicoll's work from the first. The architect Piers Gough commissioned work including 'The Architect's Teaset' (1984), later designing McNicoll a remarkable flat. She also designed and made stage costumes for Brian Eno and Andy McKay of Roxy Music fame.

She was born and raised in Birmingham, her aesthetic language formed through an upbringing in a Catholic home. The experiences of visiting churches filled with an array of eclectic objects both beautiful and gaudy are central to her work. Her father's collection of South Asian artefacts ignited a lifelong love for pattern and ornamentation.

Her work is functional and for the most part made from slip cast clay, important to McNicoll's work as it is mainly used to make mass-produced tableware. The replication

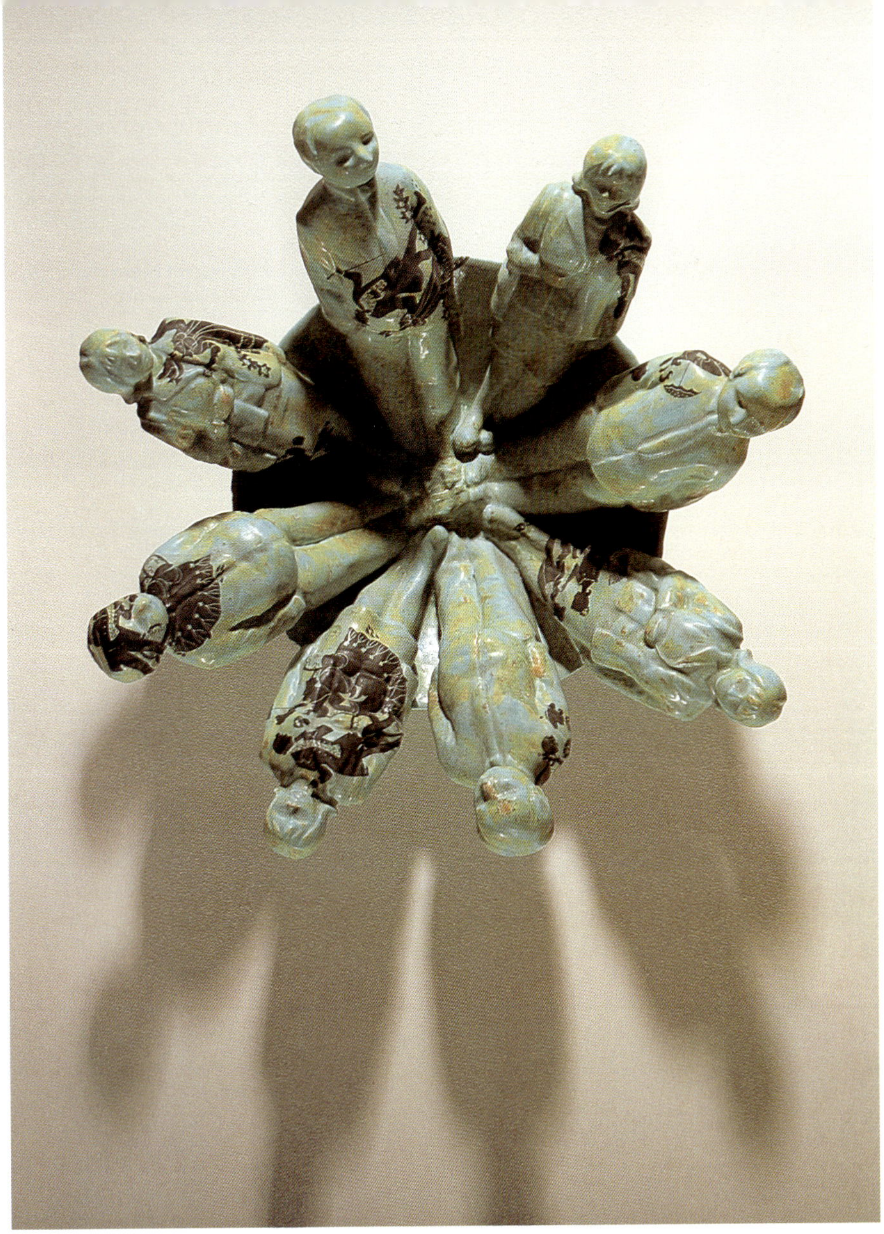

2 **Workplace Romance** 2002
Slip cast
One-off, mould made from a figure modelled by the artist, stoneware glaze, transfers
Diam. 33 cm; 13 in
Collection: the Artist
Photograph: David Cripps

possibilities of this technique are intrinsic to her work and are also a comment on ceramic tradition within the domestic context. McNicoll's creations are assemblages, hand built from individual cast elements and found objects. Objects are highly decorated, resulting in exotic and richly patterned surfaces.

Her current work has many complexities, is far more figurative and explores issues such as cultural identity, material culture, consumerism and socio-political ideas.

I would like to thank both Tanya Harrod and RoseLee Goldberg for their essay contributions, David Cripps for his photography, the Crafts Council for initiating this project and last but not least Carol McNicoll for her talent, energy, vitality and commitment. What next Carol?

Mark Prest
Acting Gallery Manager
The City Gallery Leicester

3 Still from *Musical,* 1968, 16mm film

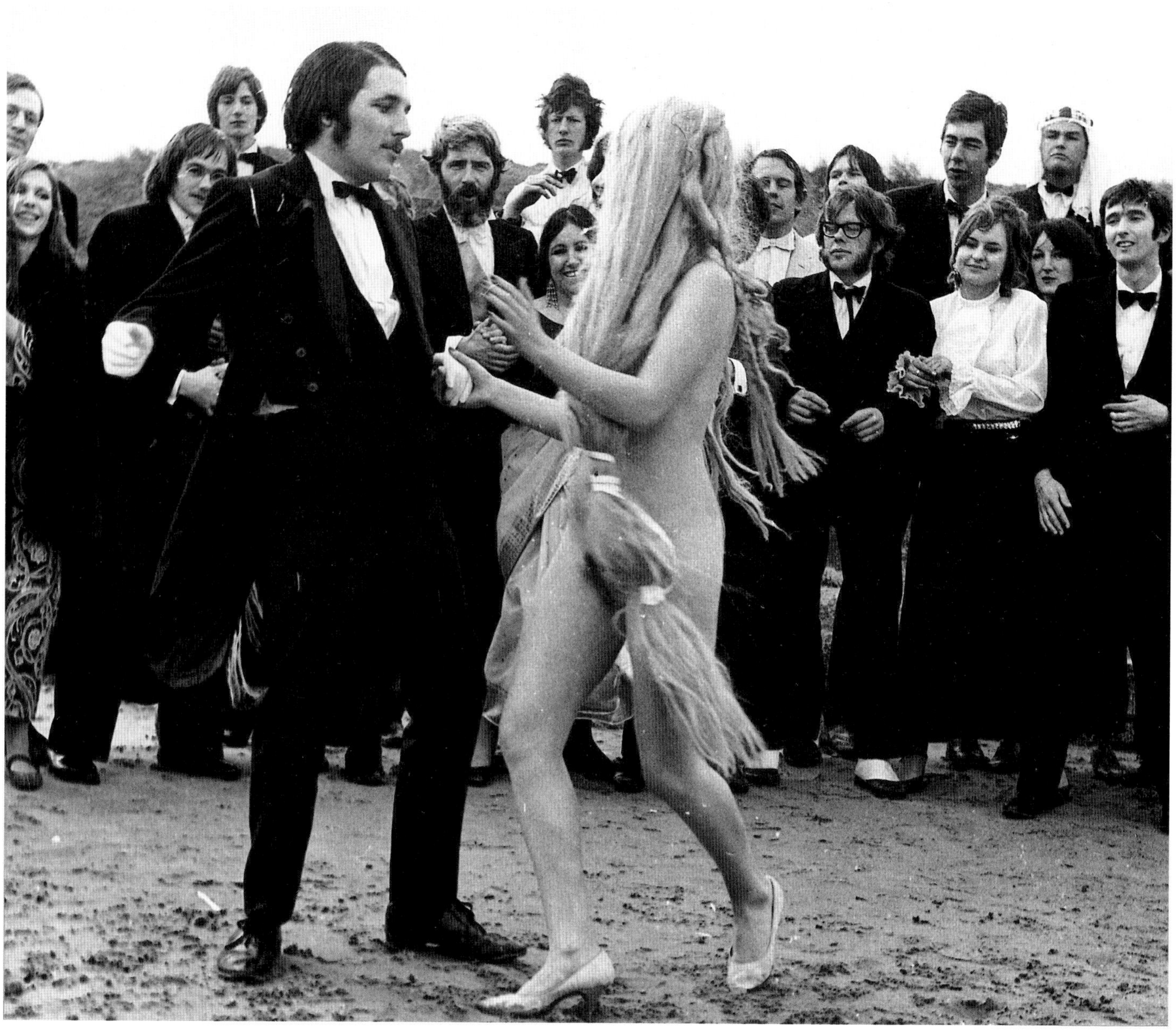

Carol McNicoll

Tanya Harrod

After she had made some exploratory moves in the areas of film-making, theatre design and painting, Carol McNicoll chose ceramics. That is to say, she decided to make objects to be used. In a statement made at the Northern Festival of Ceramics in 1994 she explained:

> *The tradition I work within is the vessel tradition. I make vessels because they have a long history of functioning both as 'sculpture' and utilitarian design. I am excited by the possibility of making objects that can both be used and be visually stimulating. I have always liked the idea of making ordinary everyday objects that make people think, that provide a moment of delight when it is least expected.*[1]

This modest statement is a trifle disingenuous, concealing an intimacy with the major conceptual debates about authorship and the procedures for making art that have characterised art practice since the late 1960s – the time when McNicoll embarked on her Diploma in Art and Design at Leeds Polytechnic.

Thinking back to that period McNicoll has noted: 'Making things to be used in a domestic context seemed, at that time, to be a truly revolutionary area to work in'.[2] The 'revolutionary' decision made in about 1970 was to take her into all manner of unexpected and, to an extent, conflicting worlds. During the 1970s she was the ceramicist who created contemporary versions of the eighteenth-century grand service for a loosely connected group of artists, designers and musicians who became famous partly through parodying and ironicising fame. By the 1980s she was being unexpectedly courted by the Crafts Council. They were interested in her first complex one-off pieces, but she was also going into limited mass production culminating in her collaboration with Next Interiors in 1985.

The 1990s saw a return to nuanced historicism in form and in decoration. On the eve of the millennium she embarked on a new body of work that has managed to be both highly ornamental and, in the loosest sense, political, touching on national identities, forgotten colonial ambitions and the paradoxes of Western consumption habits. They were first presented in a full array at her stealthily named exhibition, *Knick-Knacks*, held at the Yorkshire Sculpture Park in September–October 2000.[3]

Solihull

*Carol McNicoll of the Convent of the Holy Child, Birmingham passed the Inter-Collegiate Religious School Certificate Examination in April 1960 with Credit**

(Conference of Catholic Colleges Religious Examination)

But we need to begin in Birmingham, in the suburb of Solihull where Carol McNicoll grew up. Her Scottish father, David McNicoll, the son of a gamekeeper, was a successful engineer. Her Irish mother, Brigit O'Keefe, had trained as a nurse. Her family were farmers in County Waterford. Her father passed on cool rationalism, shyness and a love of gardening. He showed her how to use tools. Her mother was warm and gregarious. She dressed beautifully and taught McNicoll how to make clothes. She died in 1957 when McNicoll was 13.

Like all devout Roman Catholics in the 1940s, Brigit O'Keefe had married on the understanding that her daughter would be brought up in the faith and, accordingly, McNicoll was educated at two convent schools, at Olton and Edgbaston. As a result, her sense of 'habitus' – her framework of judgement and taste – was subtly and lastingly influenced by the Catholicism from which she was soon to lapse. On trips abroad with her parents she took in the dark, incense-laden interiors of churches in which objects of great beauty jostled with gaudier shrine offerings brought in by worshippers. Her father had worked abroad and the family home in Dove House Lane, Solihull was filled with the 'bric-a-brac of Empire' in the form of oriental carpets, Indian brassware and Chinese paintings. The carpets particularly attracted her and as a girl she pored over G. Griffin Lewis's *The Practical Book of Oriental Rugs*.

Retaking her science A-levels at Aston Technical College McNicoll began to work in the wardrobe at the Birmingham Repertory Company and later, for about a year, in London at the Theatre Royal, Stratford East. By then she had dropped out of a degree in Nutritional Science (a subject spotted in a book entitled *Careers for Girls*) and by 1966 had determined to go to art school. In 1967 she enrolled at Leeds Polytechnic to study Fine Art. On her Foundation Course at Solihull she had learnt that 'everything else was low status'.

Leeds

Letter to Carol McNicoll in 1970

Sorry I was so tired on the telephone, but I was so tired on the telephone, since the incredible keeps coming true so frequently these days that one can barely stand the pace.

Letter to Carol McNicoll, May 1970

Department of Fine Art
Leeds Polytechnic

Dear Friend,
How are you keeping? Well I trust. I am hoping you will be able to see your way clear to join me on Wed 27th of May at 9.30 am in the Big Studio. On that day it is my intention to start a little project which will proceed during three days. I have in mind to institute a period of 'Lent' to turn your life Topsy-Turvy. For example, those among us who smoke cigarettes might abstain. Those who do not might commence. Those who wear tatty garments might wear smart suits or pretty dresses, & vice versa. Those who restrict themselves to the disciplines of non-figuration might be persuaded to figurate & vice versa, etc, etc, (there's more to it.) Friends finding themselves unable to participate in such a project will please to be seen in the big studio pursuing a more individual course.
Trusting to find you on your right mettle ...
Yours
Tony Earnshaw
ARISE! ARISE! ETERNAL DEATH IS ABROAD – Wm Blake[4]

McNicoll recalls that at Leeds in the late 1960s Fine Art was broadly defined. The first Coldstream Report (1960) had signalled the change that was to sweep art schools: 'For many people the term "Fine Art" has too restrictive a connotation and it is not by any means accepted that all students, whatever subjects they are studying, should be required to take Fine Art in the sense, for example, of spending much of their time on "easel" painting.'[5] The 1970 Coldstream Report went further, noting that the fine arts derive from an 'attitude which may be expressed in many ways'.[6] In any case, from the late 1950s onwards Leeds College of Art (from 1970 Leeds Polytechnic and currently Leeds Metropolitan University) had been the seed ground for the transformation of British art education, initially under the guidance of Harry Thubron, Tom Hudson and Eric Taylor.[7] But the earnest promulgation of Basic Design at Leeds, derived in part from the *Vorskurs* taught at the Bauhaus, had by the late 1960s been significantly affected by reawakened interest in the life and work of Marcel Duchamp[8] and by developments in the United States - not least the various art practices of Andy Warhol. In addition, McNicoll recalls, the students combined home-grown northern humour with Dadaist strategies to attack anything they perceived as 'Establishment'.

The tutors at Leeds in the late 1960s were a varied group ranging from Robin Page, a performance artist, to Patrick Hughes, a highly literate creator of visual conundrums, to the sculptor Glyn Williams, a virtuoso carver whose work was to come into its own in the 1980s. Figures like the anarchist Tony Earnshaw and the poet and analyst of the counter-culture, Jeff Nuttall, were informally on hand. There was a shift in sensibility (as yet only narrowly chronicled) at Leeds and other art schools from formulaic modernism to a reactionary, poetic postmodernity. Thus McNicoll's big project at Leeds, sparked off by a Saturday afternoon visit to *The Sound of Music*, was a film, *Musical* (3), made (in 1968) with three fellow students. It reads as a lexicon of postmodern practices. The conventions of the classic musical were sent up, alternative happy endings were offered, the soundtracks of existing musicals were collaged and big set-piece scenes defiantly tackled on tiny budgets. The comedian Roy Hudd was invited to open the premiere, unaware that he had wandered onto a minefield of irony, parody and camp.

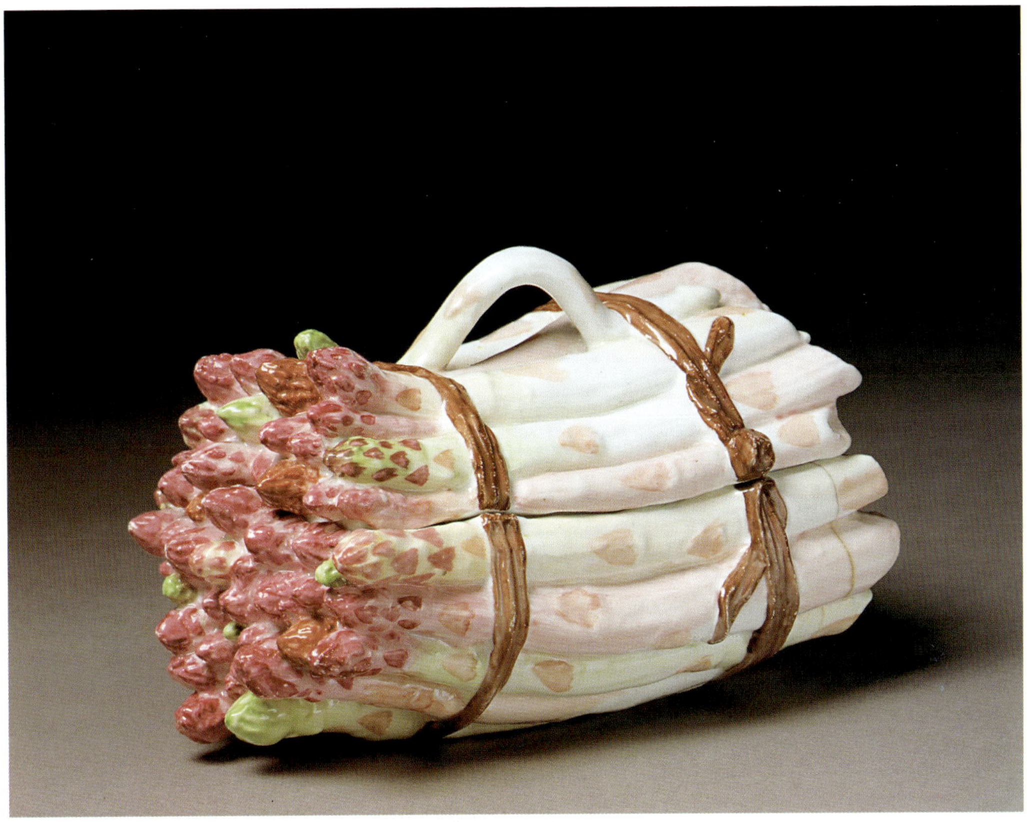

4 **Asparagus box and cover**
c. 1756
Soft-paste porcelain, painted in enamels
Made at the Chelsea porcelain factory, London
Collection: Victoria and Albert Museum, London
Photograph: Victoria and Albert Museum
© V&A Images

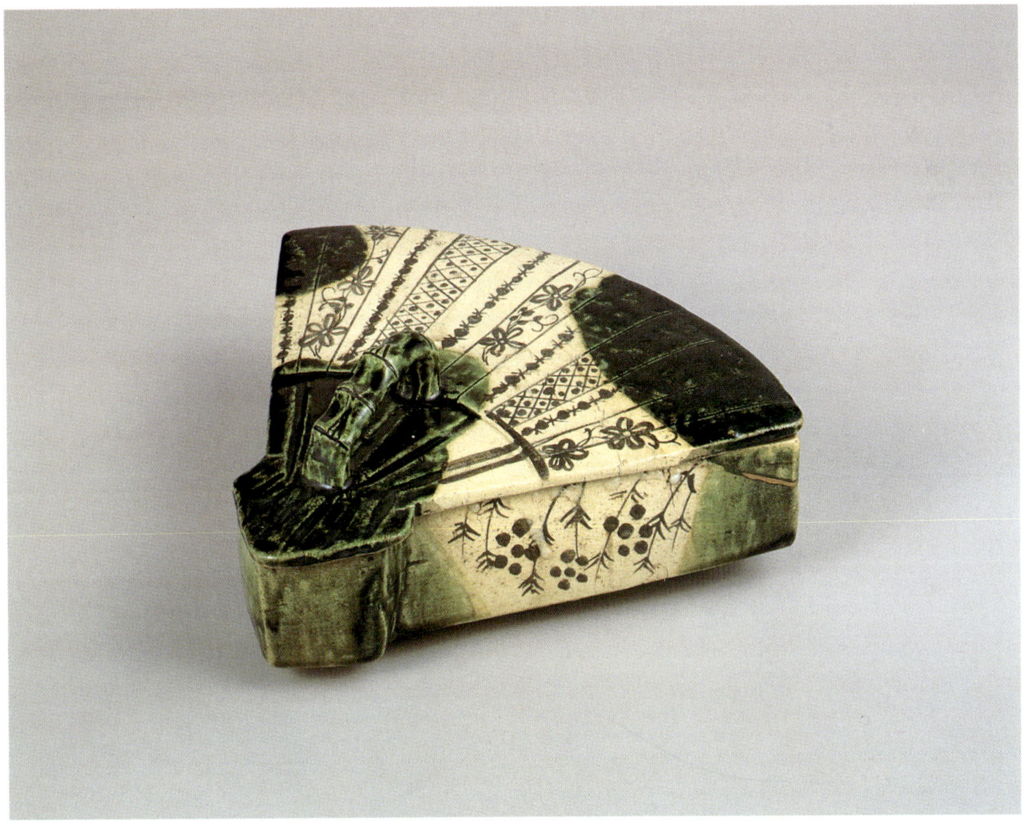

5 **Fan-shaped Food Container with Lid**
Oribe ware, Momoyama period, 16th century 11.3 x 29.7 x 24.8 cm; 4.5 x 11.75 x 1.75
Kyoto National Museum, Japan

Roger Coleman taught at Leeds in those years. In his autobiographical manifesto *The Art of Work*[9] he describes the setting up of 'The Welfare State', a collective rock/theatre group, followed by 'YOW!' (Yorkshire Open Workshop), which staged events at Halifax and Hebden Bridge. These groupings and events were intended to critique the Arts Council's limited, elitist funding of alternative art forms designated by the Council 'New Activities'. Thus the all-inclusive nature of *Musical* (with its huge cast, massed choirs and orchestra) linked to another characteristic of art practice at Leeds – an emphasis on community.

McNicoll painted too – badly she recalls – and later made a shorter film in an 'unknown foreign language' to be shown three times with different subtitles. She also investigated ceramics, inspired by one of her tutors, David Seeger, who had cast a teapot using a crab shell that he decorated with willow-pattern transfer. He sent her down to the Victoria and Albert Museum to study the source of his inspiration, the exquisite artificialities of eighteenth-century porcelain and faience (4). He also introduced her to an abiding future influence, Japanese Oribe ware (5), with its characteristic square or faceted shapes decorated with monochrome abutting eccentric passages of pattern. However, making ceramic objects on the Fine Art course at Leeds in 1970 certainly did not indicate any sympathy with the existing studio pottery movement, whether art school or workshop based. Leeds was the place where, McNicoll recalls, anything could be art and, more specifically, where the students believed they were at the cutting edge of whatever art might be.

McNicoll made a few ceramic objects, most memorably *Chips, Chops and Peas* (6) – three little containers on a tray, each with a lid carrying a slip cast replication of the item it was intended to contain.[10] As Richard Deacon pointed out in an essay of 1985, the piece signalled two themes that have run through much of her subsequent work. One was to do with rules of making in which slip casting from existing objects operated as a distancing device. The other was to do with making objects that held things – liquids, light bulbs, food.[11] The particular ethos of Leeds had served McNicoll well. But at the same time, like

6 **Chips, Chops and Peas** 1969
Cast from life, slip cast earthenware,
clear glaze and onglaze enamels
Plate diam. 27 cm; 10.5 in

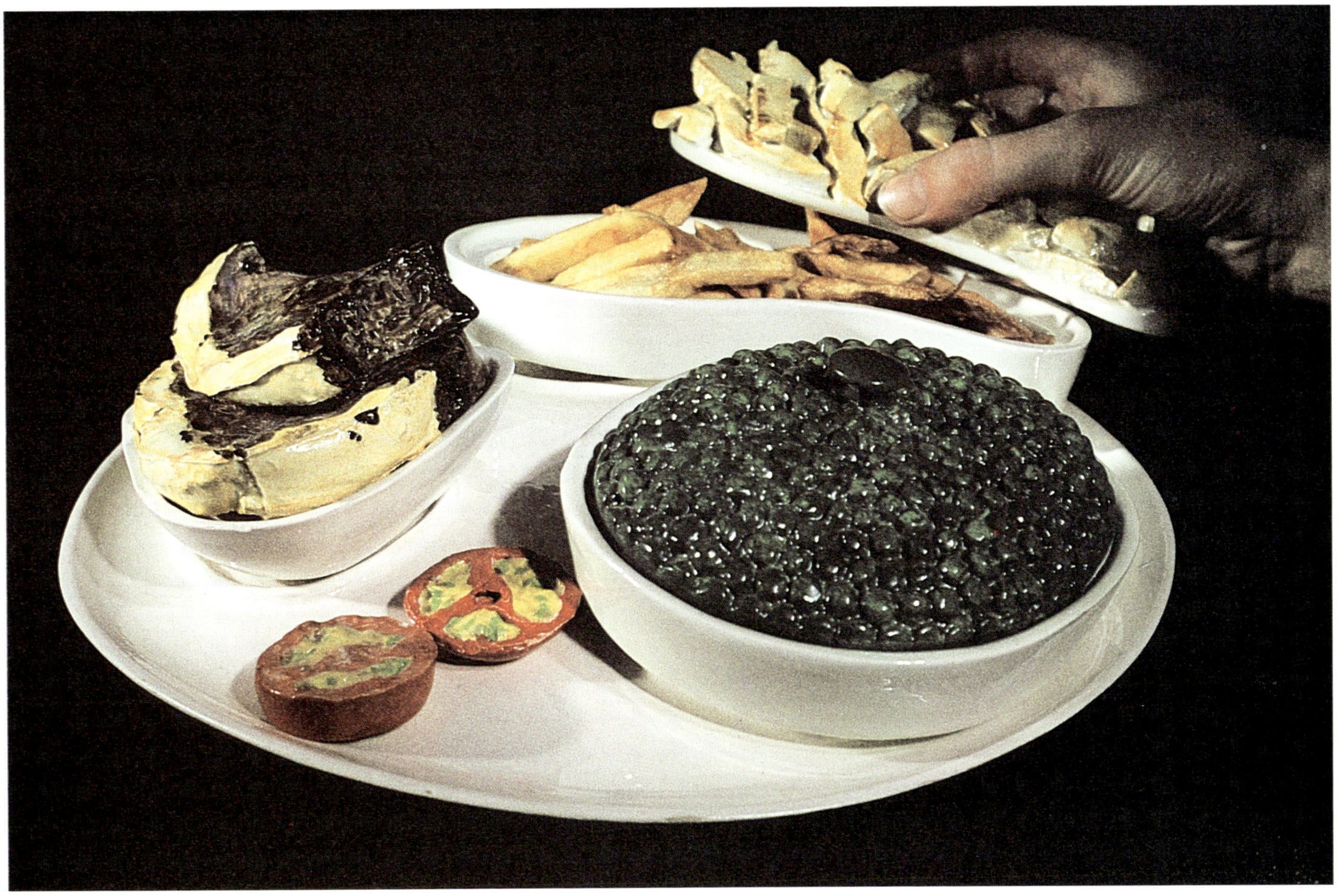

Coleman, she ended up finding fine art practice hard to justify.[12] Childhood memories of functional and beautiful oriental rugs and hours spent dressmaking with her mother came to stand for something important. In 1970 she applied to the Royal College of Art (RCA) to do a Master of Arts in either Film or Ceramics. She was accepted by the School of Ceramics and Glass.

Urban pastoral

Camp sees everything in quotation marks. It's not a lamp, but a 'lamp'; not a woman but a 'woman'. To perceive Camp in objects and persona is to understand Being-as-Playing-a-Role. It is the farthest extension, in sensibility, of the metaphor of life as theatre.

(Susan Sontag, *Notes on 'Camp'*, 1964, reprinted in *A Susan Sontag Reader*, Penguin Books, Harmondsworth, 1983, p.109)

In 1970 the RCA awarded McNicoll a Princess of Wales Scholarship, given to 'the most distinguished female students of all the Schools of Art throughout the United Kingdom'. It was worth £27 a year. After the idealism and inclusivity of Leeds, the RCA seemed a place of hierarchies, emphasised by the fact that each School occupied a different floor of the austere block designed by Jim and Betty Cadbury-Brown alongside the Royal Albert Hall. That hardly mattered. McNicoll was living in a commune in Camberwell with her then boyfriend Brian Eno.[13] The summer before starting at the College she worked for the fashion designer Zandra Rhodes in her cramped workshops in Porchester Road, West London, silk-screening her textiles on the first floor, or cutting and sewing in the attic. Rhodes had started her career as a textile designer and working for her was an informal introduction to the beauties of pattern. Rhodes was to become a loyal friend and patron of McNicoll's work. She was establishing herself as an increasingly high profile dress designer who also created a series of remarkable interiors for living and entertaining. These were much photographed and practically every image would include ceramics by McNicoll. In 1972 Roxy Music

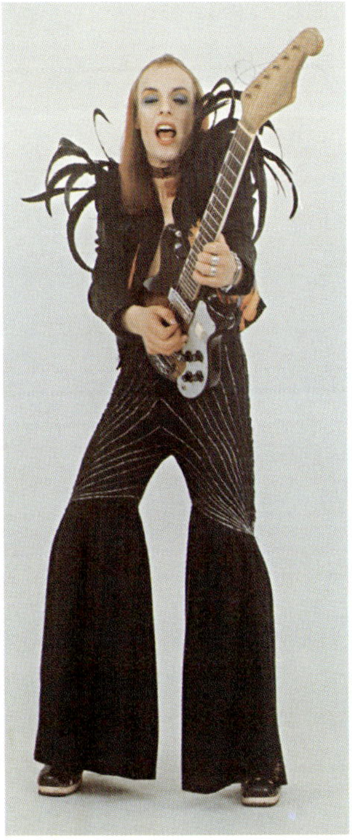

7 Brian Eno of Roxy Music wearing a costume designed by Carol McNicoll, 1973

produced their first LP with Eno as a brilliant 'untutored synthesiser player'.[14] Carol designed Andy McKay and Eno's costumes, including Eno's memorable outfit with cockerel feathers coming out of heavily padded shoulders (7). Some of her friends were, therefore, from the more cerebral end of rock and roll. But through Rhodes she became part of a rather different, if overlapping, world, that functioned like a court, a small urban clique governed by an esoteric set of aesthetic values.

By virtue of 'guilelessly straddling a number of heavily contested boundaries – such as those between art and craft, between art and decoration, between pop and fine, between profane and sacred'[15] this grouping has been mostly overlooked in conventional accounts of the visual art of the 1970s and 1980s. No wonder – to analyse such an evanescent world is to betray it.[16] Susan Sontag's 1964 essay *Notes on 'Camp'* scrutinises the sensibility in an American context. In an acute ethnographic article – one of a series of penetrating studies of contemporary mores that appeared in *Harpers & Queen* – Peter York characterised the London group as 'Them!' after the cult 1950s sci-fi film.[17] The writer Michele Hanson, who had a stall in the Portobello Market in the 1970s, dubbed them 'The Drapes' – subtly startling in appearance to the extent that appearance became their language. Both Carol McNicoll and Michele Hanson were at a seminal gathering of the clan in March 1972 – Andrew Logan's (First) Alternative Miss World, held in the artist's studio in Hackney – 'a competition where no one was jealous'.[18] Logan, who disarmingly set great store by 'music, jumbles, crochet and chat' was a crucial figure. At the heart of his art (and that of another key figure, the painter Duggie Fields) was the creation of Utopian interiors formed from a plethora of abandoned, unloved objects, magically transformed. In some ways their activities resembled a latter-day Arts and Crafts Movement, albeit stripped of overt politics, in which life and art are seamlessly merged.[19]

McNicoll's work developed rapidly in this milieu, which had far greater influence than the tutoring she was receiving at the RCA, whether in the form of intelligent discussions with

8 **Zip Cup and Saucer, Plate** 1972

One-off, factory-made cup, saucer, zips

Plate diam. 17 cm; 6.5 in

Photograph: Robyn Beeche

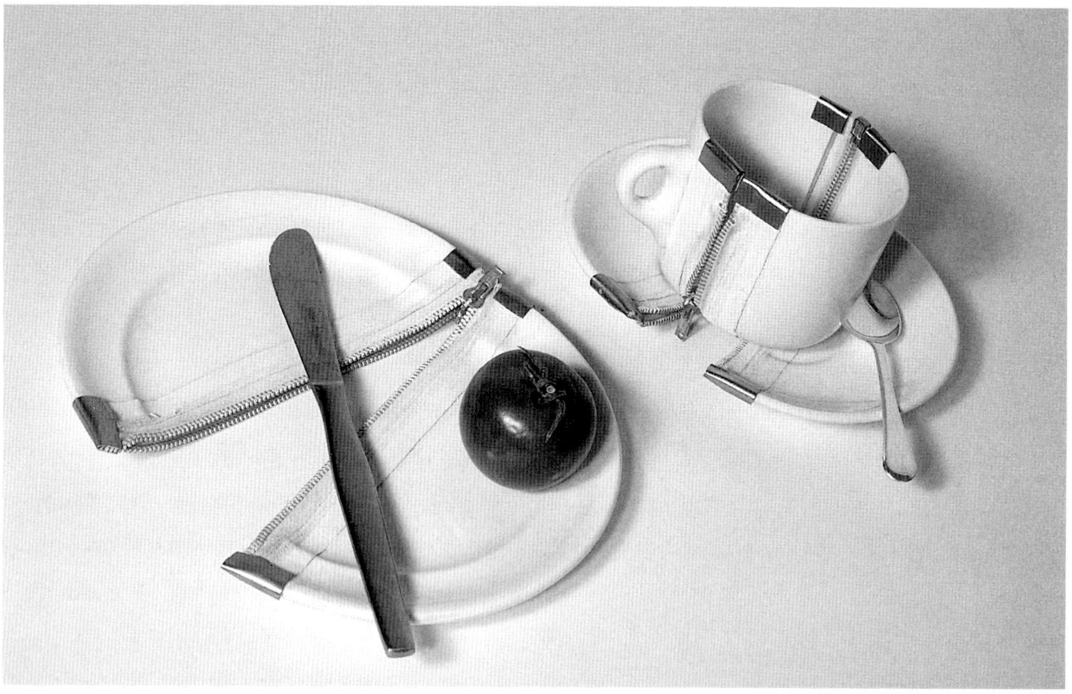

9 **Mobile Lawn** 1973

Mixed media, one-off

H. 13 x l. 24 x w. 19 cm; 5 x 9.5 x 7.5 in

Private collection

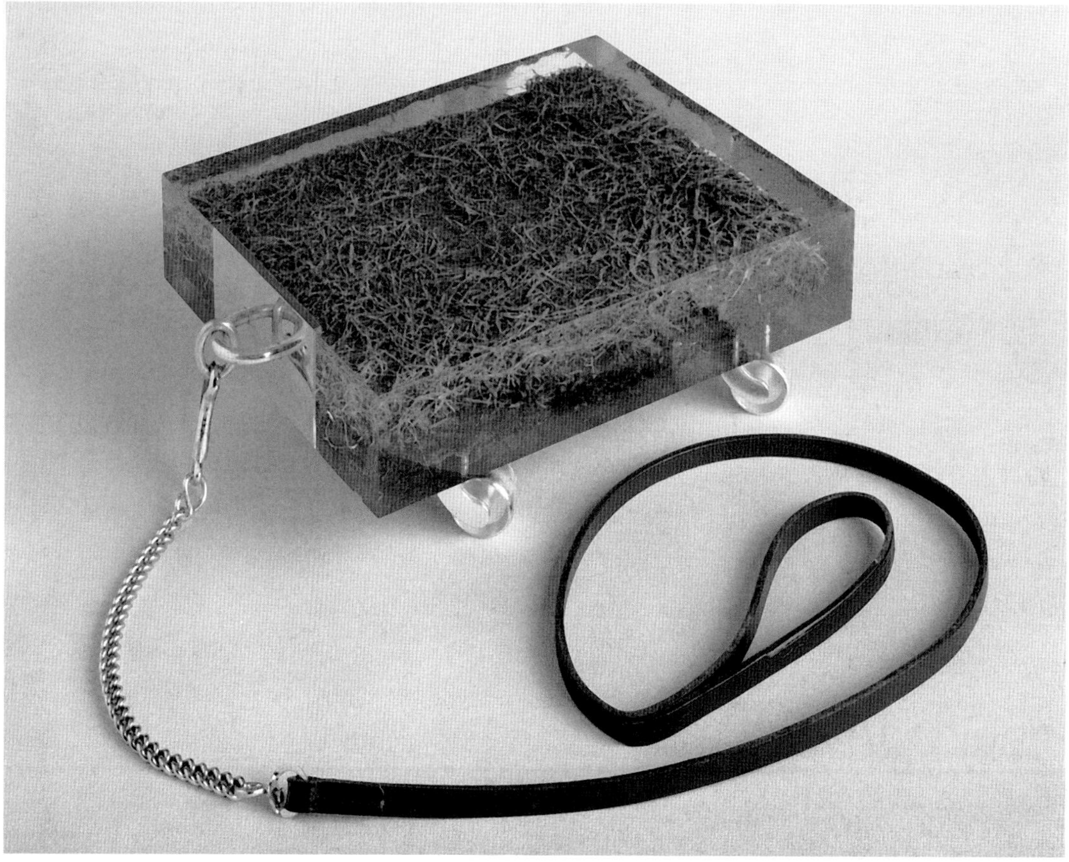

the potter Hans Coper or mute encounters with the sculptor Eduardo Paolozzi ('he didn't really talk to women') or mysterious glaze recipes provided by Joe Shipley. She submitted a spoof essay for the Department of General Studies on a multi-celled organism, Spirogyra, viewed as a work of art. There followed a heated correspondence with the Department's head, Christopher Cornford. She succeeded in temporarily making the mandatory long essay, 'the Discourse', optional. She sent up serious design concerns at her degree show in the summer of 1973 with her zip-up cup and saucer (8), explaining to the *Daily Mirror* that 'unzipped, the cup and saucer take up much less storage space'.[20] Also at the College she made her last work of 'art' – a mobile lawn on castors, set in a resin block (9). It was bought by the architect Peter Cook.

Though the atmosphere at the RCA was careerist, the ceramics course was helpfully unstructured. And McNicoll was taking on big commissions while a student, making a surreal 'Alice in Wonderland' teaset (10) for the painter Peter Blake and two elaborate dinner services, one cast from grass, leaves and lace (11) for the shoe designer Moya Bowler, and one for Zandra Rhodes that looked like an array of indented quilted cushions formed into vessels, decorated with transfers made from Rhodes's textile designs (12). A period at the Royal Staffordshire factory in Stoke-on-Trent arranged by the Head of Ceramics, David Queensberry, proved fruitful. She learnt a lot about mould-making and was given some obsolete moulds and transfers to take away. They surfaced in her 1974 show at the College, *China, My China*, in the form of two apparently classic teapots – except that one was a haunting Wedgwood blue through which cast birds appeared to be flying (13) and the other was three-spouted (14).

Behind the surreal humour, there were, however, fiercely held ideas about process and authorship that centred on an exclusive use of slip casting. It became a point of honour to make moulds from existing objects – from an actual cabbage leaf, not one modelled or carved, from actual cloth not an artistic rendering of cloth, or to use a pre-existing mould. This was part of a private debate about the idea of a ready-made, energised by a dislike of

10 **Alice in Wonderland Teaset** 1971

Slip cast earthenware

Silver, clear glaze and onglaze enamels

Private collection

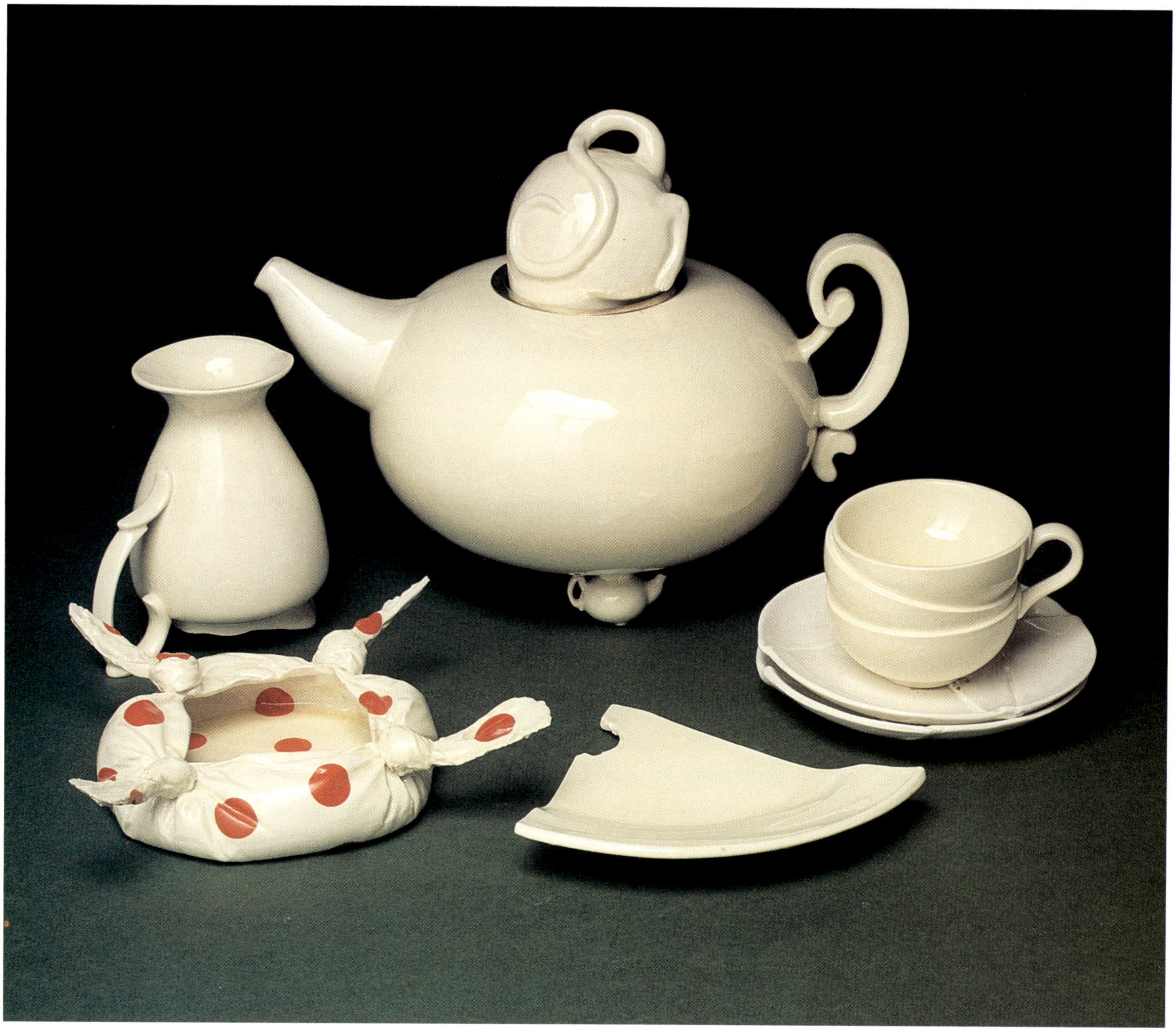

11 **Dinner Service for Moya Bowler** 1972

Slip cast earthenware

Using obsolete moulds from Royal Staffordshire and casting from life, clear glaze and onglaze enamels

Private collection

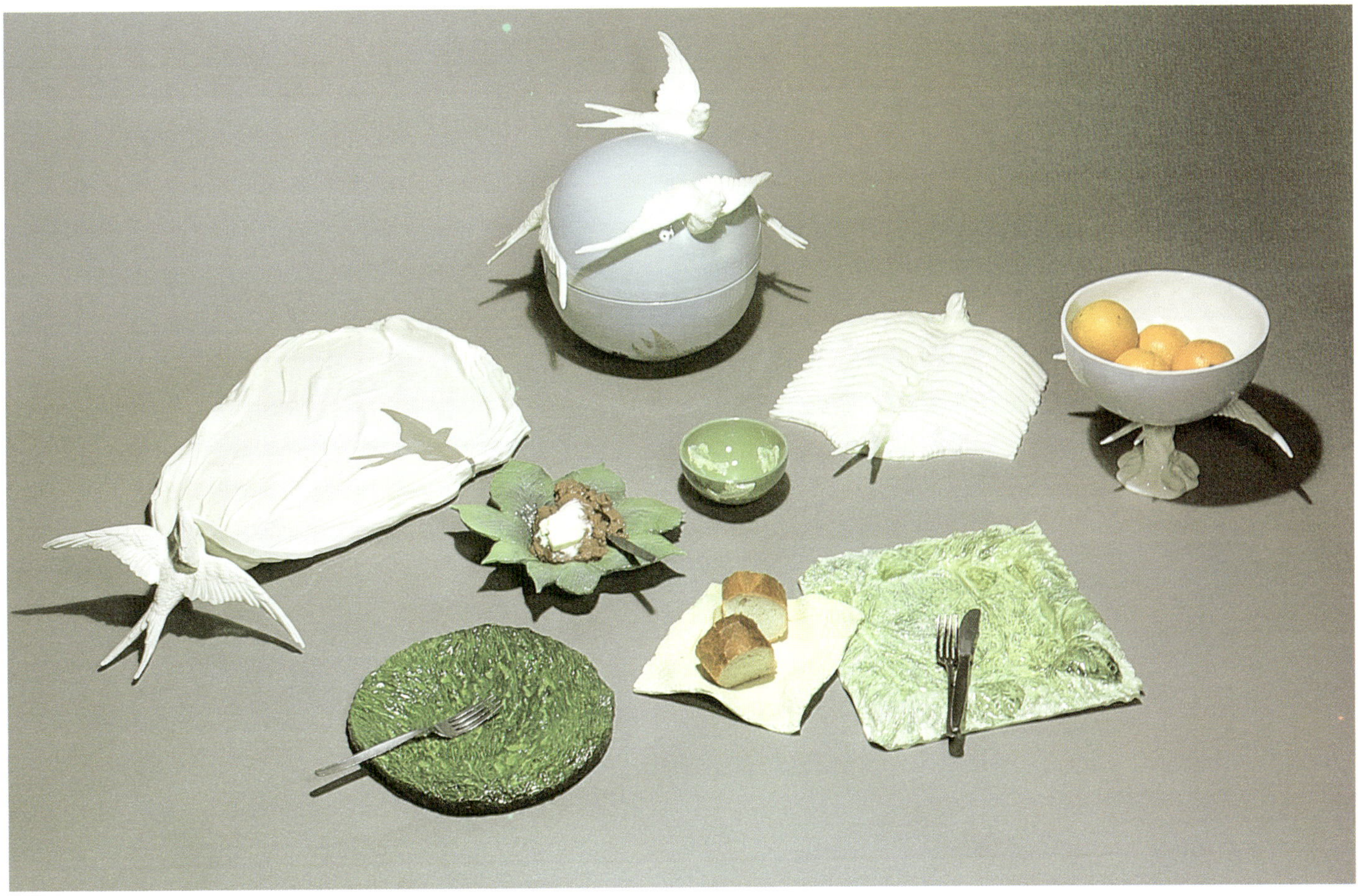

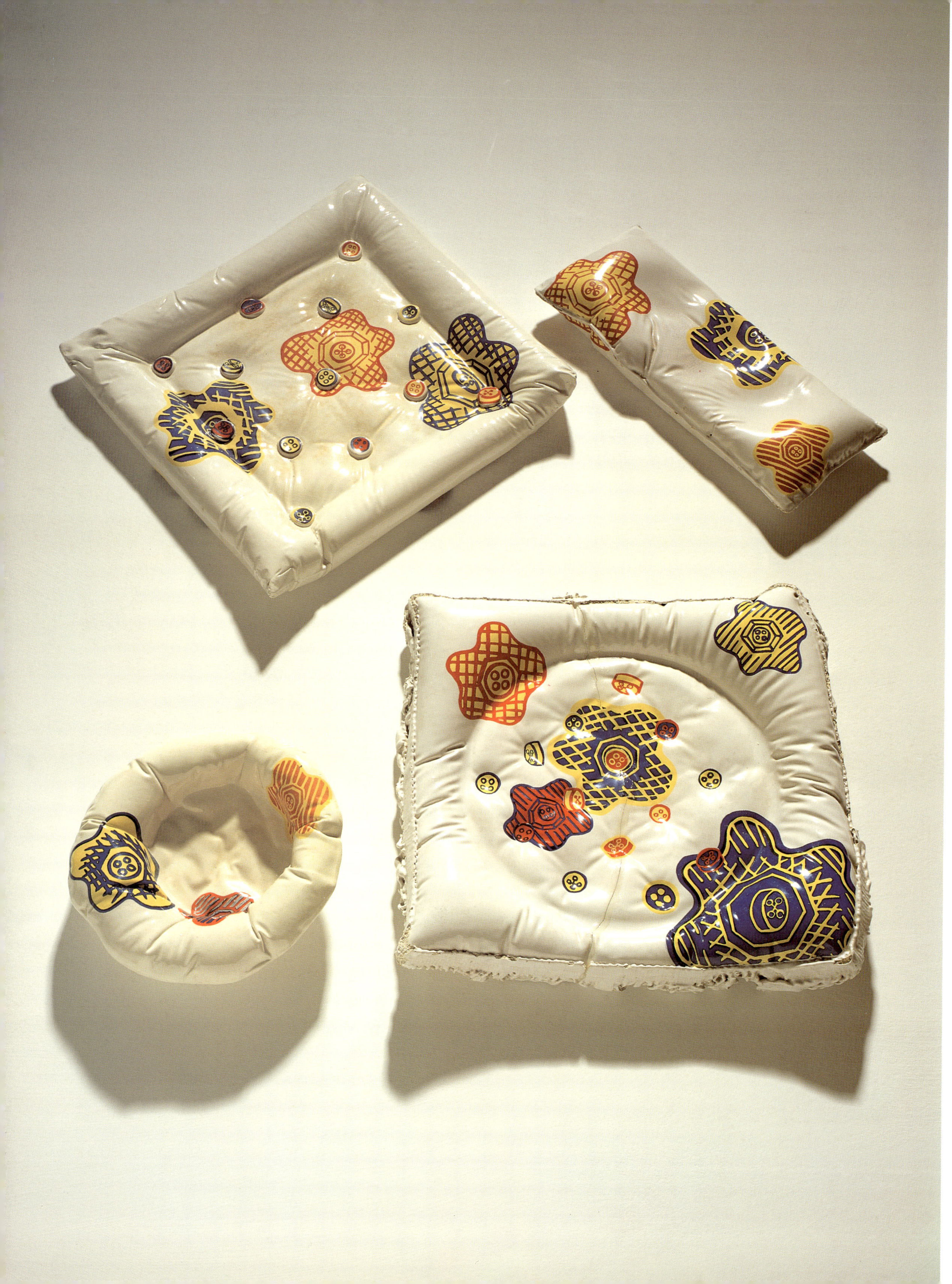

opposite
12 **Cushion Dinner Service for Zandra Rhodes**
1972
Slip cast earthenware
Moulds made from plaster-filled textile and braid dipped in slip, transfers made from Zandra Rhodes' Button Flower textile design
Collection: Zandra Rhodes

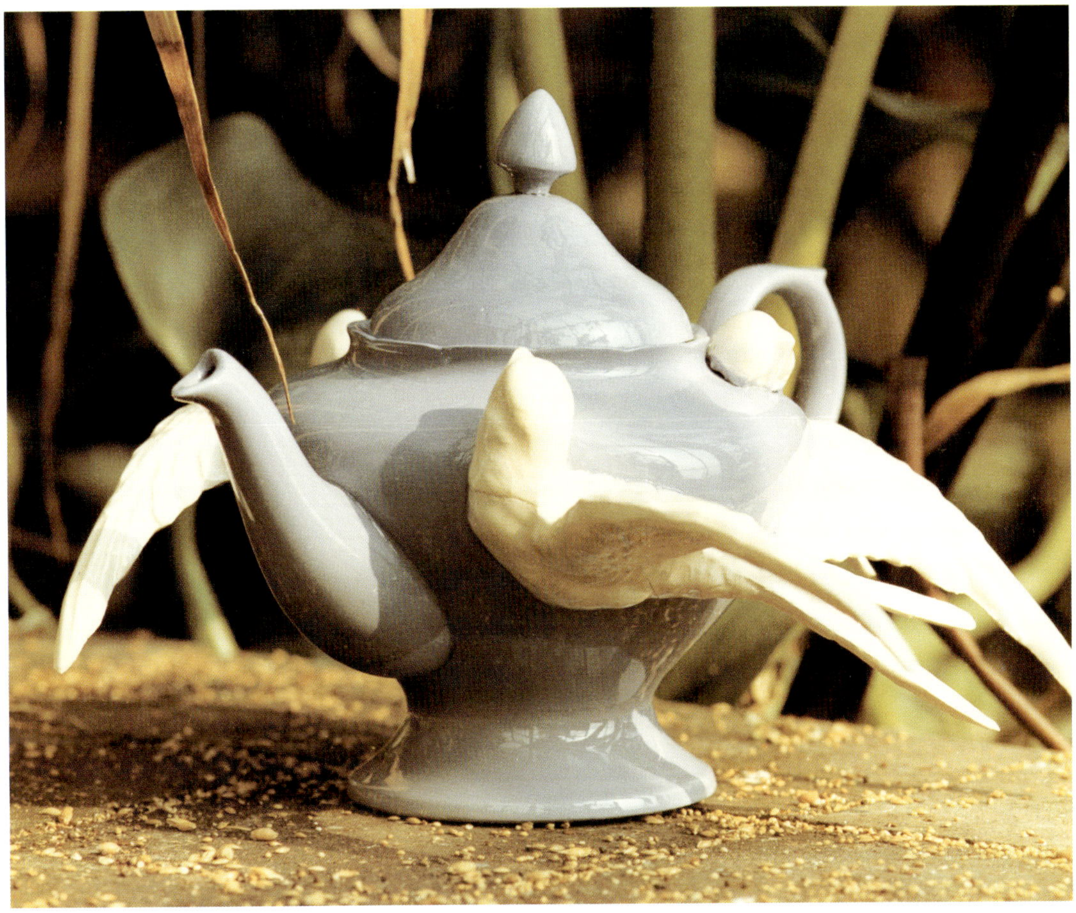

13 **Teapot with Birds** 1972
Slip cast earthenware
Using obsolete moulds from Royal Staffordshire, clear glaze and onglaze enamel
After Royal Staffordshire
H. 23 cm; 9 in
Photograph: Mick Dunn

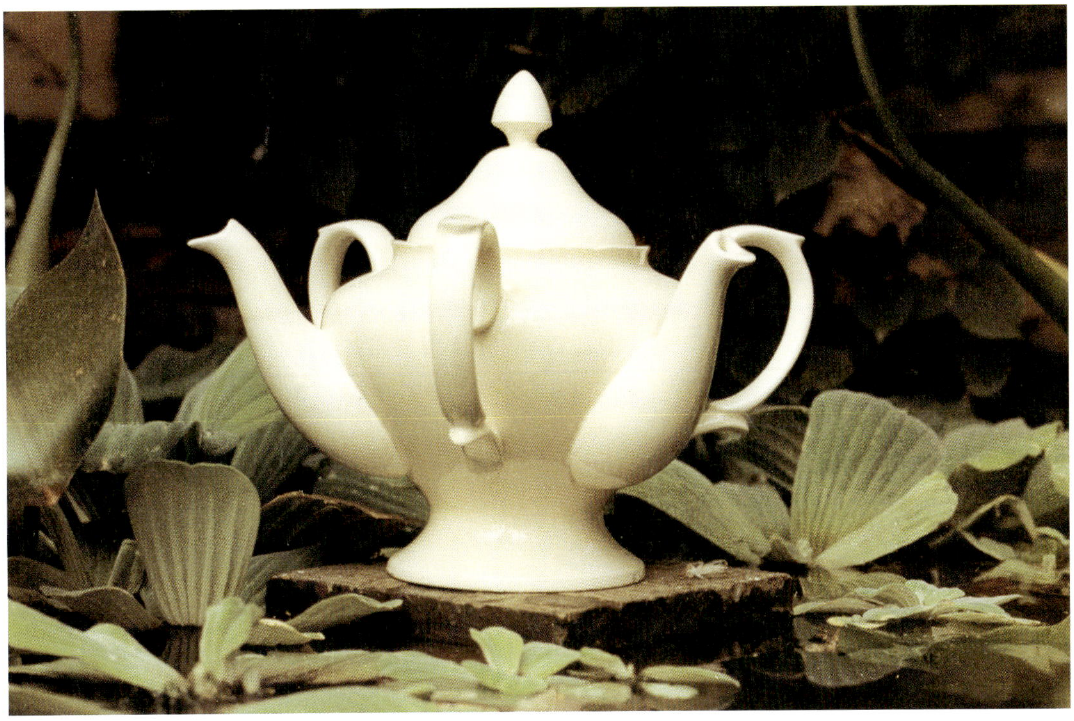

14 **Three-Spouted Teapot**
1972
Slip cast earthenware
Using obsolete moulds from Royal Staffordshire, clear glaze and onglaze enamel
After Royal Staffordshire
H. 23 cm; 9 in
Photograph: Mick Dunn

the world of studio pottery; it was also a ceramic take on what was going on in painting, and to an extent, sculpture. McNicoll sought a 'certain distance' from expressive making. By the time she left the RCA in 1973 she had decided to be a production potter, albeit of a particularly arcane kind.

In 1973, the year in which she graduated, the term 'production potter' usually referred to a maker of functional wares that were invariably hand-thrown and, with few exceptions, part of a wider, often counter-cultural and ruralist move towards craft activity based on reinvented and rediscovered traditions. Most art school trained potters at that date, however, turned their faces against this kind of spiritualised 'production' in favour of creating 'one-off' sculptural and painterly explorations of the vessel form and surface. McNicoll was out of step and out of sympathy with both camps. She was in fact ahead of her time, choosing to embark on a kind of batch production. It was an approach that was to become popular in the mid-1980s, particularly among young furniture designers who, in a period of industrial decline, found it almost impossible to get their designs manufactured. Using slip casting meant that McNicoll in effect became a small-scale industry of one.

'Surrealist crockery'

Vaisselle surréaliste

(Headline from an article on McNicoll in *L'Aurore*, 3 May 1976)

Moulds
There is no question of the convenience of this cheap, quick-setting, absorbent substance – plaster – in mould-making. Without it, casting, the most important process in mass-production, would be impossible. But it is debatable whether, from the point of view of beauty, plaster is to be welcomed, not so much because of any inherent evil in the material, as of the fatal facility with which it has been used to multiply florid forms.

(Bernard Leach, *A Potter's Book*, Faber & Faber, London, 1940, pp.93–4)

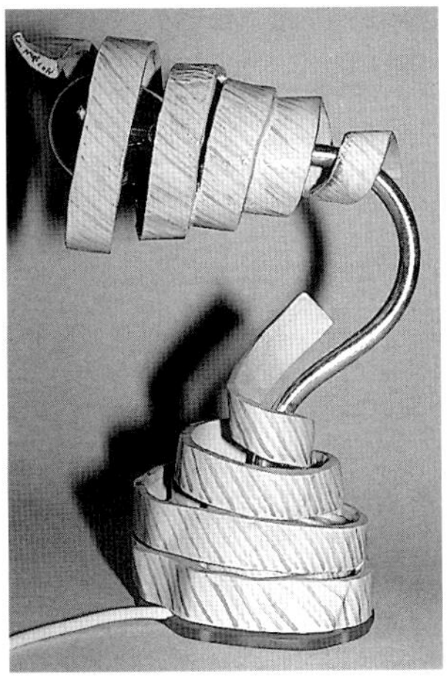

15 **Anglepoise** 1977
Mixed media
H. 28 cm; 11 in
Photograph: Robyn Beeche

McNicoll's work became extremely fashionable in the 1970s. From 1973 until 1976 she shared a studio with Alison Britton at 401½, the famous low-rent communal workshop in a Victorian warehouse in south London set up by the designer Michael Haynes,[21] subsequently moving in 1976 to a studio in Kensington Church Walk. There she had an employee, her old friend Colin Deekes. Both Britton and Deekes had studied ceramics with McNicoll at the RCA. Britton was to go on to become one of the most respected British ceramicists of the 1980s, a maker of cerebral one-offs that explored the possibilities of painting and sculpture. Deekes, on the other hand, chose to set aside his prodigious talent. His mordant pessimistic humour enlivened McNicoll's studio; he chose to assist.

A basic repertoire of punning, often collaged forms had been developed by McNicoll at the Royal College – a squashy teapot (16), a vase apparently made of folded paper, a nonsensical cup and saucer in which three cups became one. But these were followed by a stream of further inventions, such as a teapot partly made from a conventional mould and partly from a cabbage leaf mould (17), a little clock concealed in what looked like a folded hanky (18), a wrapping paper vase containing cast flowers, a cabbage lamp (19), a ceramic fan, an anglepoise (an iconic Modern Movement object) with a shade and base appearing to be unfurling (15), and a series of six origami plates suggesting paper that had either been folded or crumpled. What McNicoll was doing with supreme wit was marrying surrealist strategies with old ceramic tropes that stood for Englishness – the leaf plate, the pineapple tea caddy, the cottage teapot and so on. Perhaps that is why she was such a success in Paris where she showed from 1976 at Laurence Dumaine's Galerie Axis. Meanwhile in London her work was sold in shops and galleries that had a certain cult status, including Christopher Strangeways' eponymous shop, Nick Morris's Ablebest and, rather later, Brown's Living and then Tricia Guild's Designer's Guild.

16 **Squashy Teapot** 1972
Slip cast earthenware
Moulds made from plaster-filled
textile, metal handle
H. 16 x l. 24 x w. 15 cm;
6.25 x 9.50 x 6 in
Photograph: Robyn Beeche

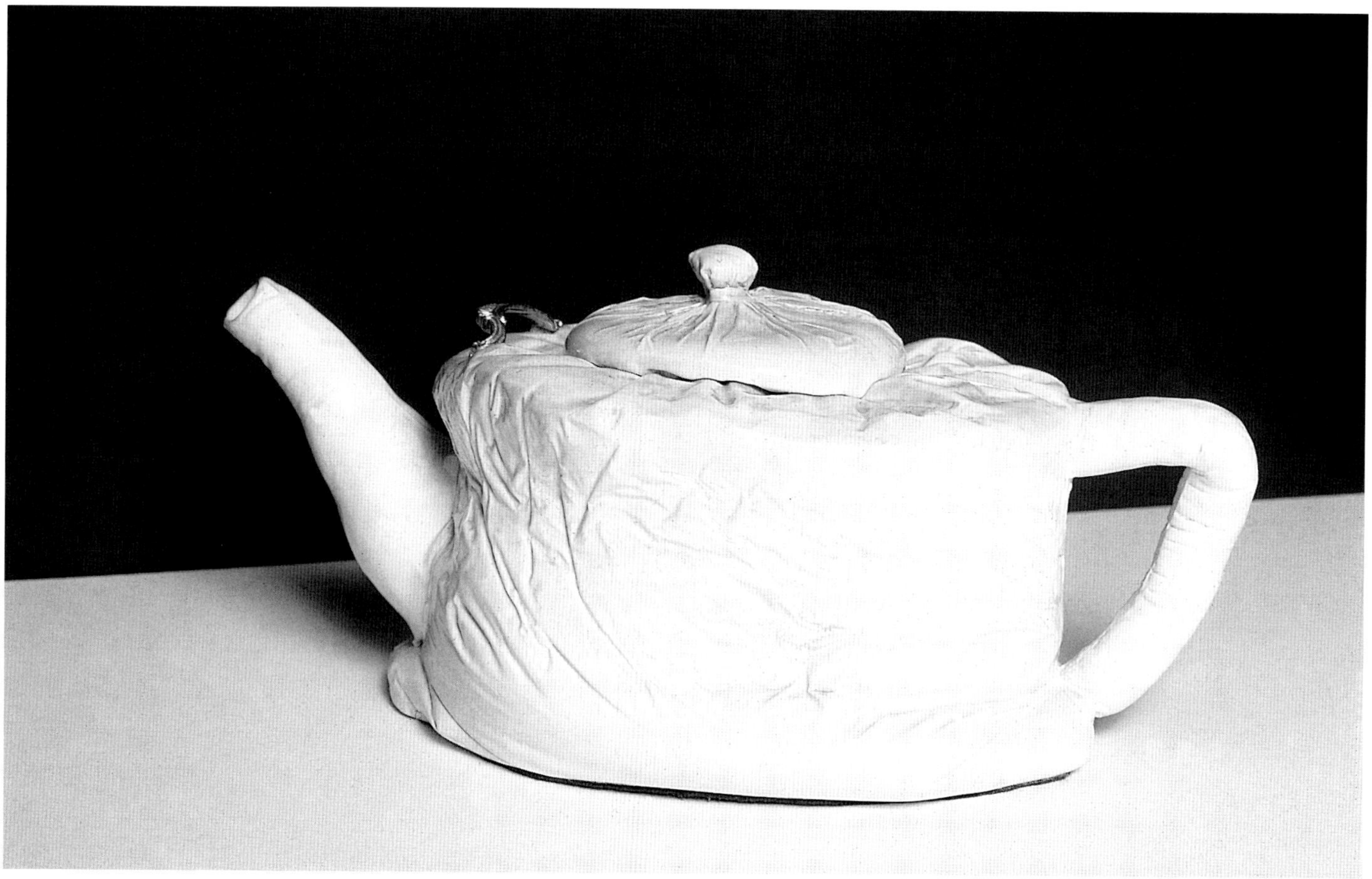

17 **Cabbage Leaf Teapot** 1974

Slip cast earthenware

Mould cast from collaged teapot and a cabbage leaf, clear glaze and onglaze enamel

H. 18 cm; 7 in

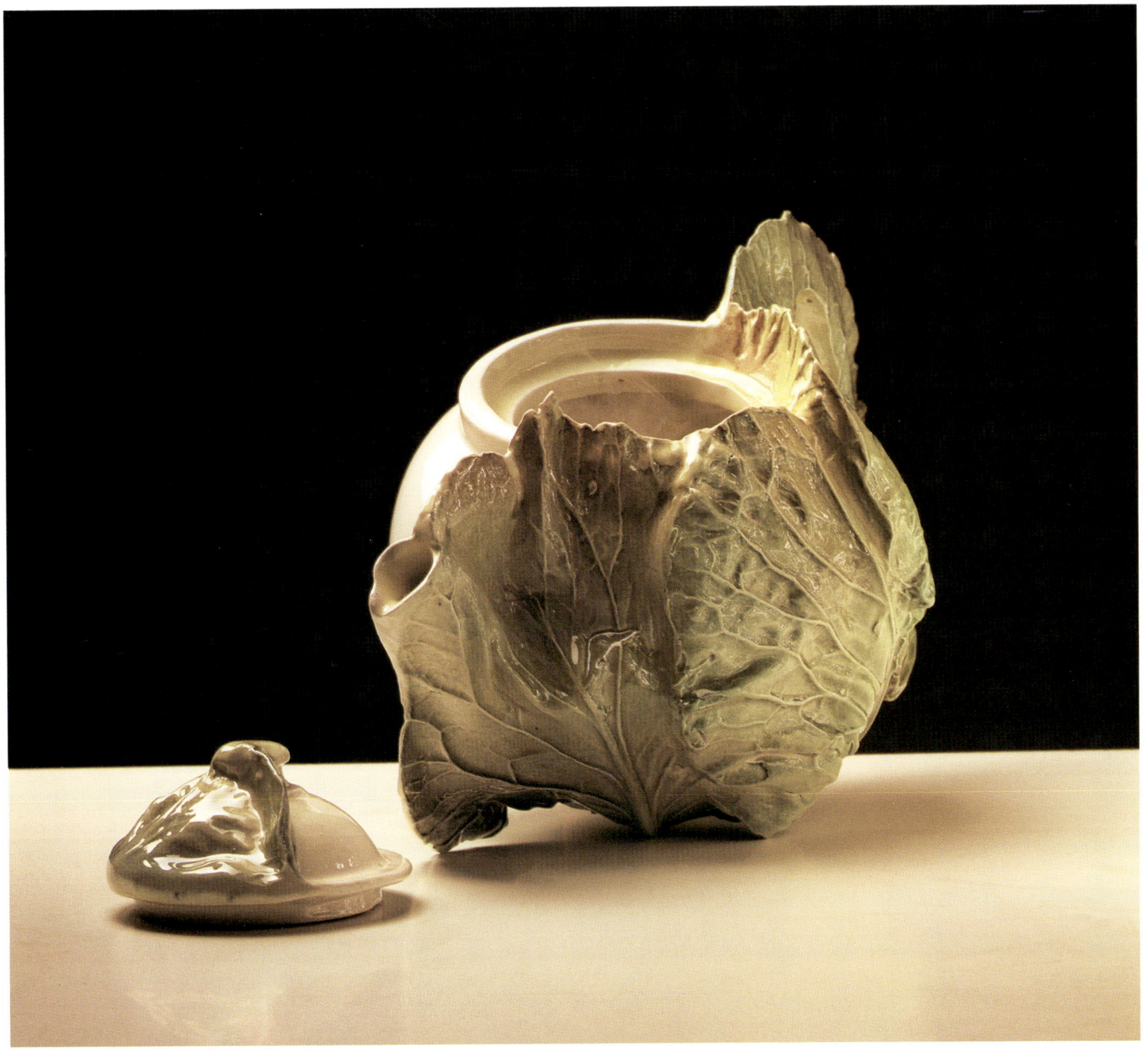

18 **Clock** 1973
Mixed media
18 x 18 x 12 cm; 7 x 7 x 4.75 in

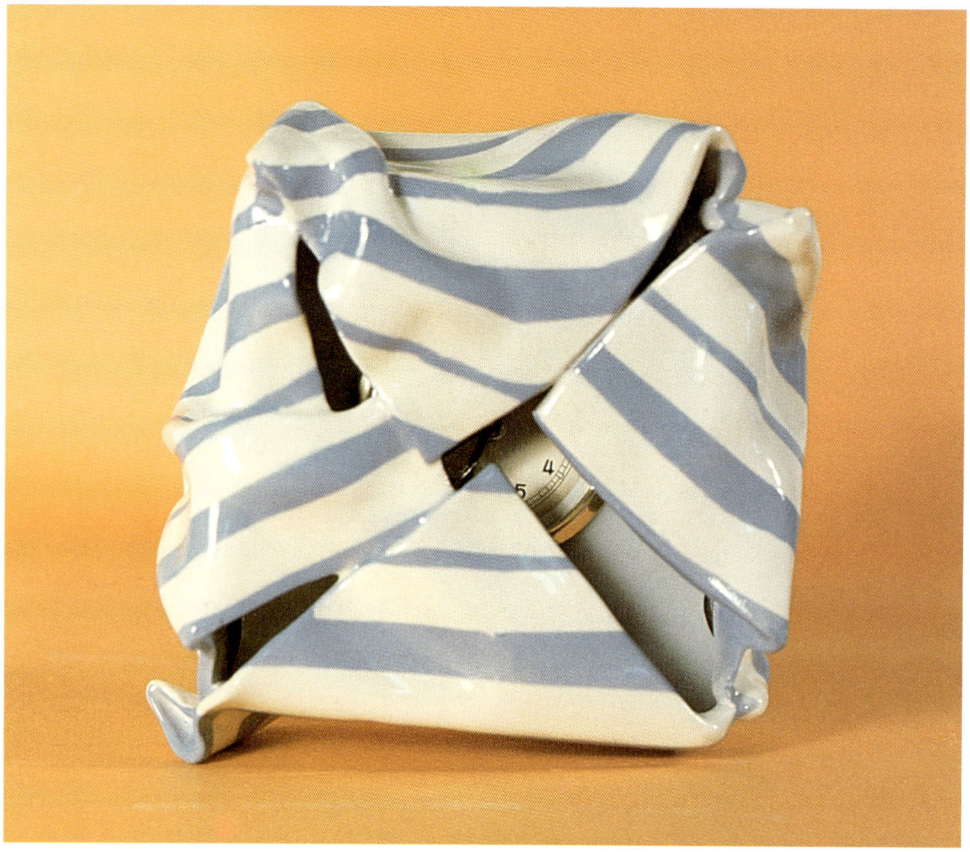

19 **Cabbage Light** 1976
Slip cast earthenware
Mould cast from cabbage, clear glaze with underglaze colour
H. 20, diam. 37 cm; 7.75 x 14.5 in
Photograph: Robyn Beeche

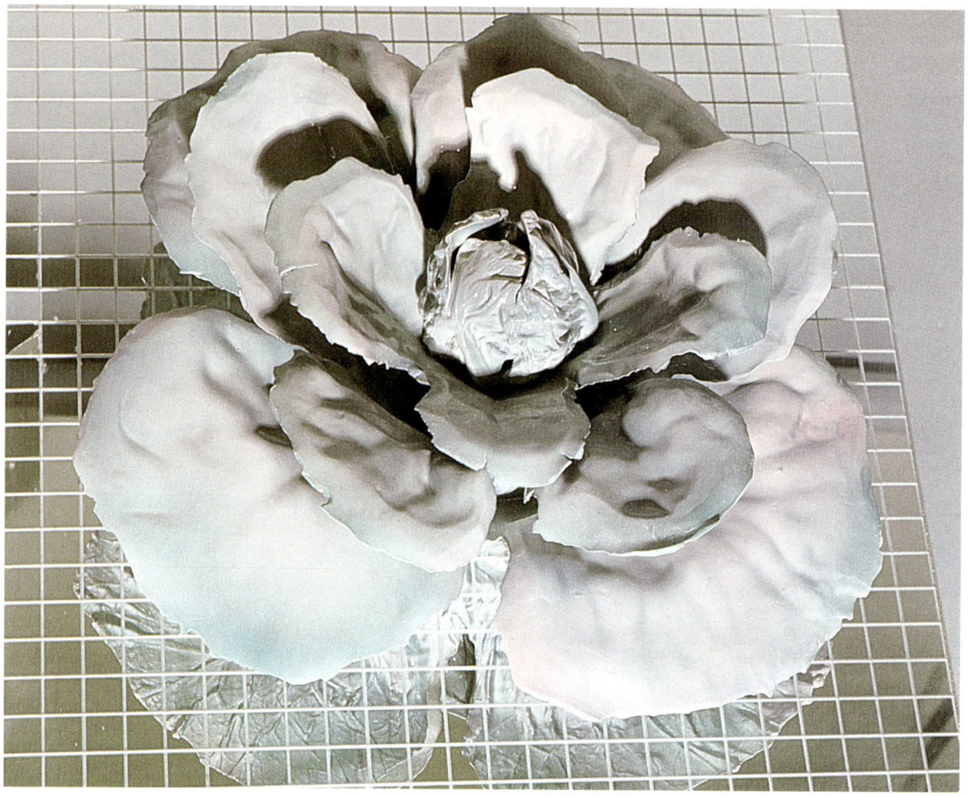

20 **Cup with Toes** 1972
Slip cast earthenware
Clear glaze and onglaze enamels
H. 16 cm; 6.25 in
Photograph: Mick Dunn

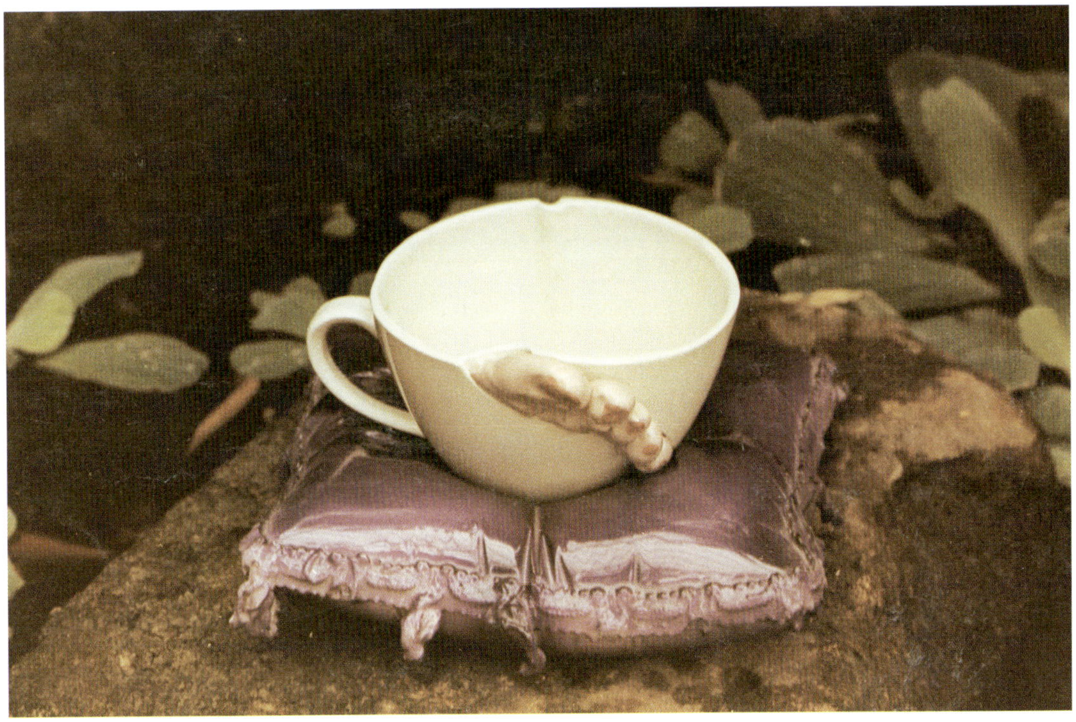

21 **Large Bolted Cup** 1972
One-off, silver, blown glass,
slip cast ceramic
H. 23, diam. 36 cm; 9 x 14.25 in
Photograph: Mick Dunn

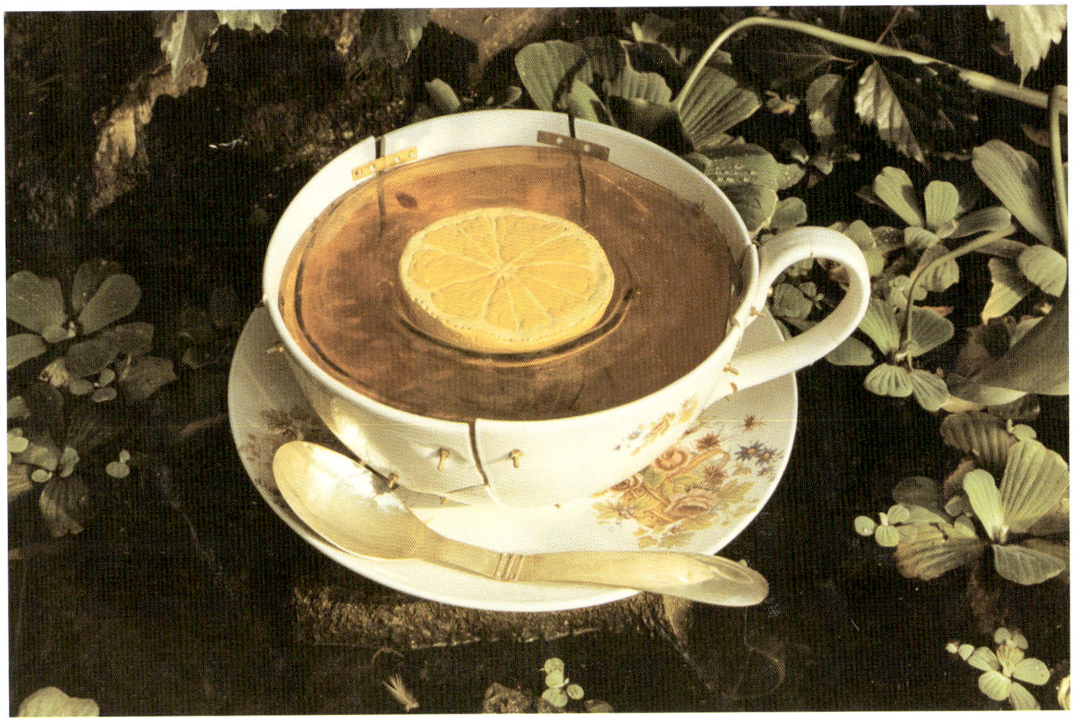

22 **Cabbage Leaf Plates** 1974
Slip cast earthenware
Mould cast from collaged plate and
a cabbage leaf, clear glaze and
onglaze enamel
Diam. 18 cm; 7 in
Photograph: Robyn Beeche

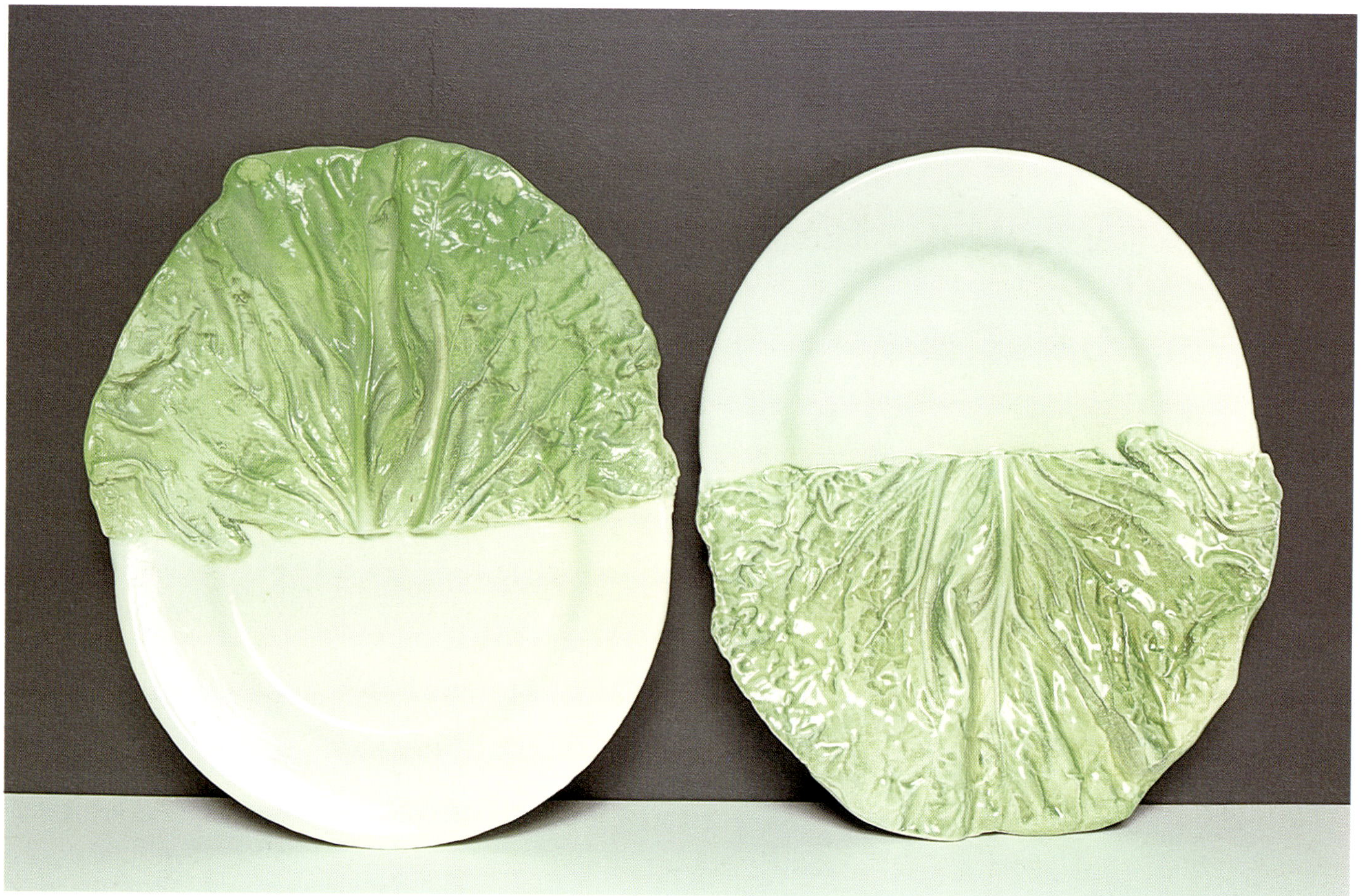

23 **Iris Lamp** 1975
Slip cast earthenware
Mould cast from flowers, clear glaze
with underglaze colour
H. 25 cm; 9.75 in
Photograph: Robyn Beeche

24 **Flower Lamp** 1976
Slip cast earthenware
Mould cast from aluminium foil,
flowers and leaves, clear glaze with
underglaze colour,
H. 25 cm; 9.75 in
Photograph: Robyn Beeche

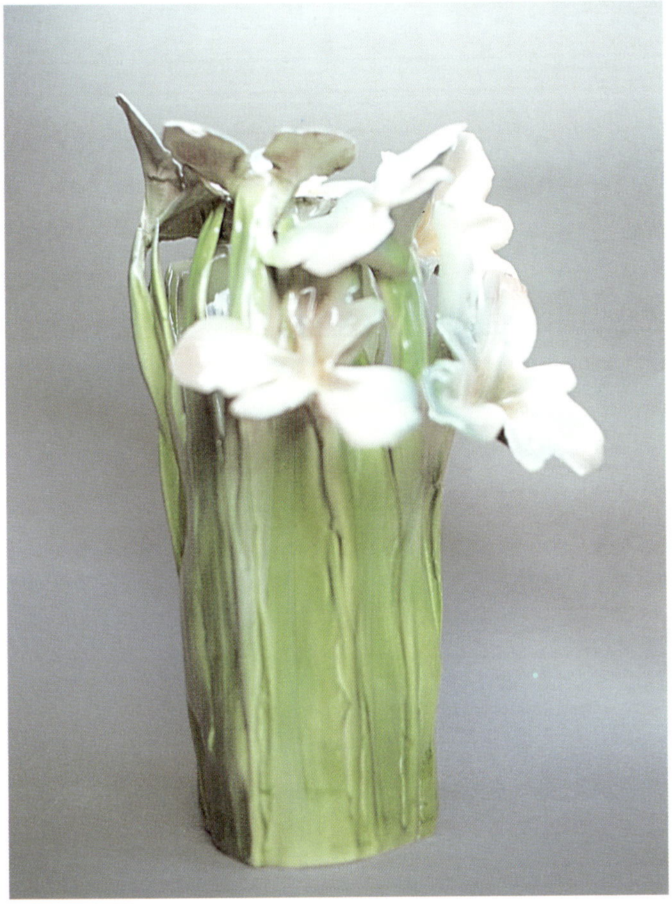

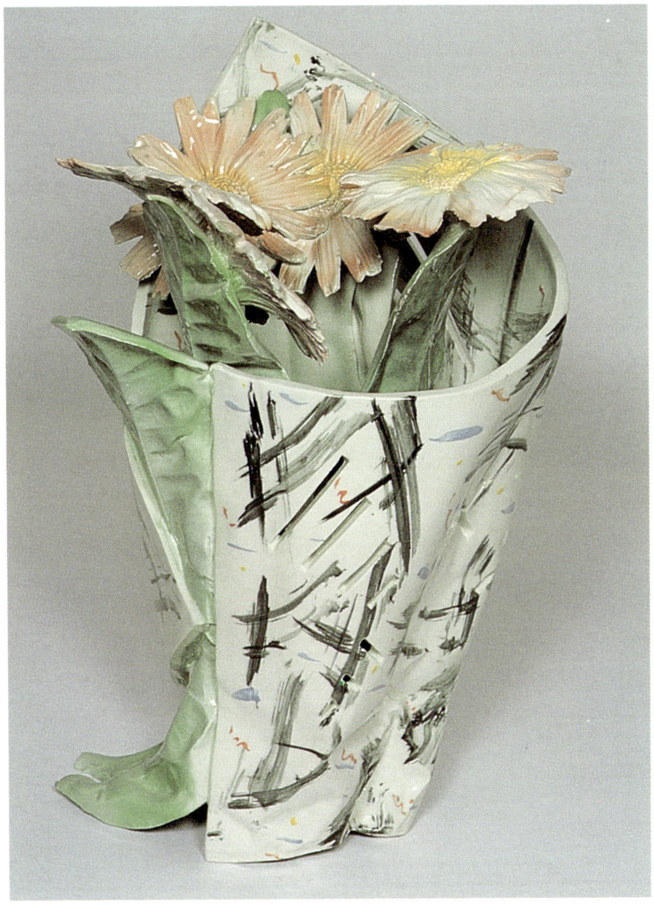

25 **Knot Vase**, 1976

Slip cast earthenware
Mould cast from aluminium foil and flower, clear glaze with underglaze colour
H. 15 x l. 25 x w. 15 cm;
6 x 9.75 x 5.75 in
Photograph: Robyn Beeche

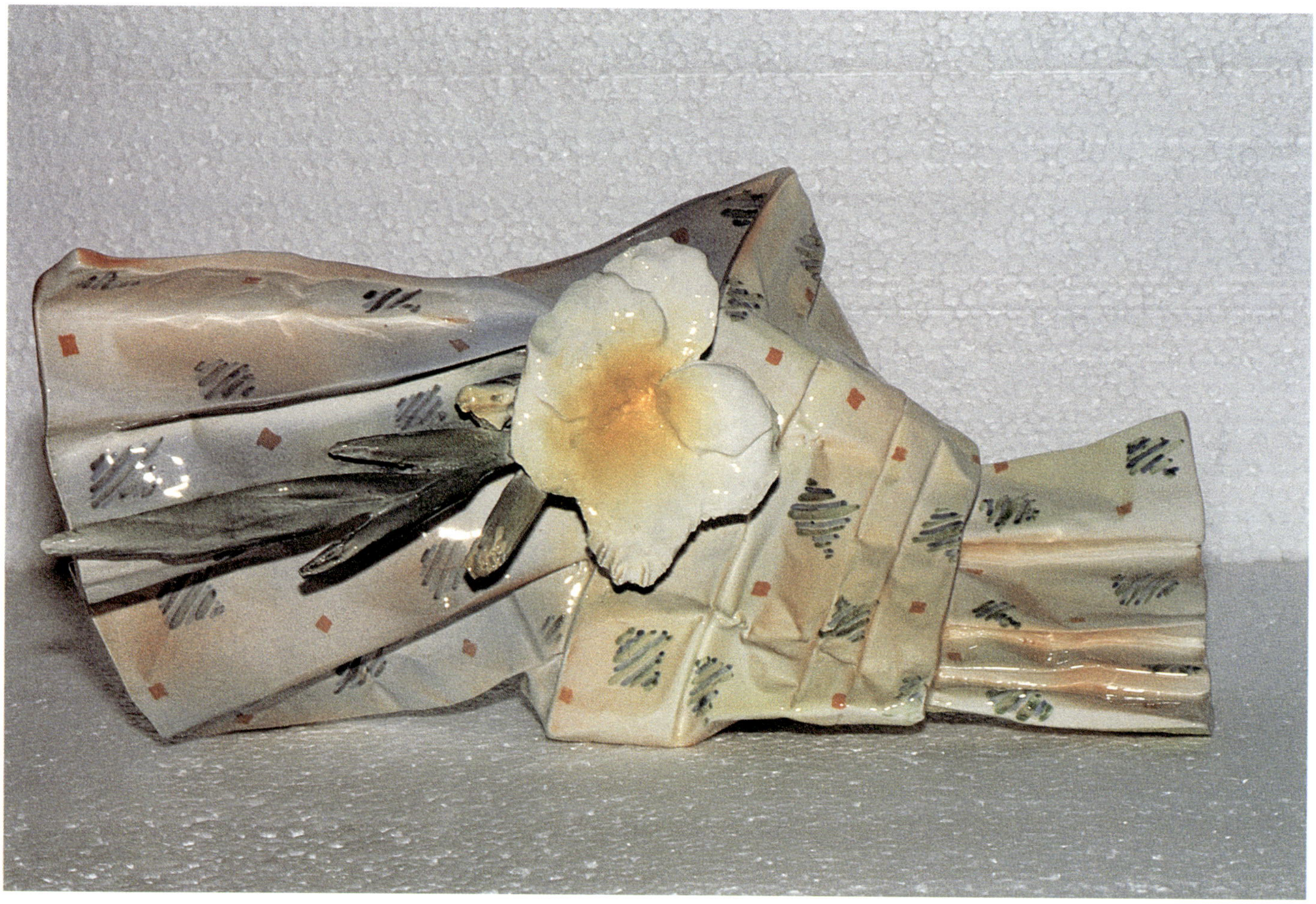

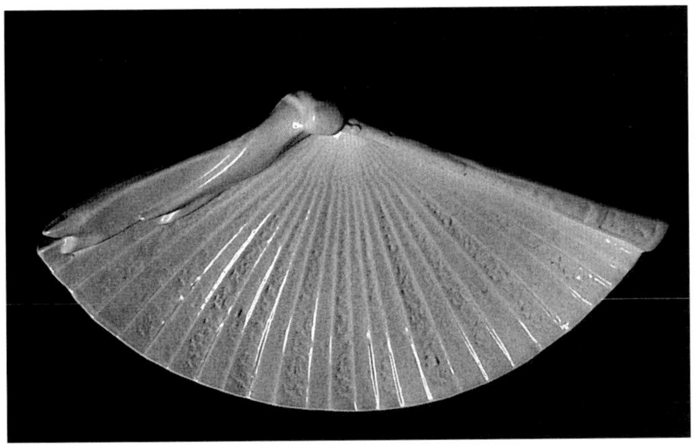

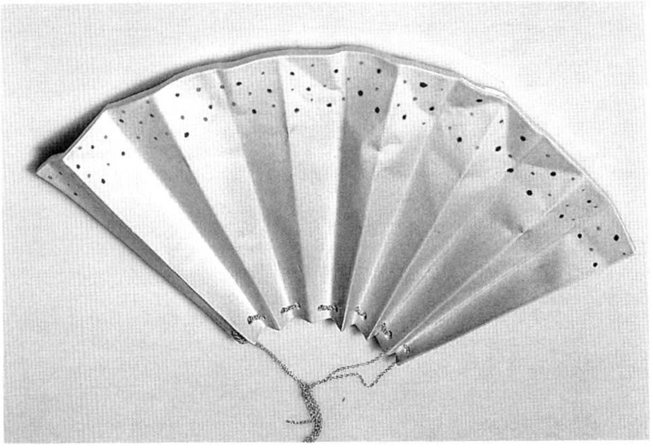

26 **Plates** 1970s

above left:
Slip cast earthenware
Paper fan plate
24 x 15 cm; 9.5 x 5.75 in

above right:
Slip cast earthenware
Fan plate
20 x 15 cm; 7.75 x 5.75 in

right:
Slip cast earthenware
Folded paper plates
24 x 17 cm; 9.5 x 6.5 in

below right:
Slip cast earthenware
Woven plate
22 x 22 cm; 8.5 x 8.5 in
Clear glaze with underglaze colour

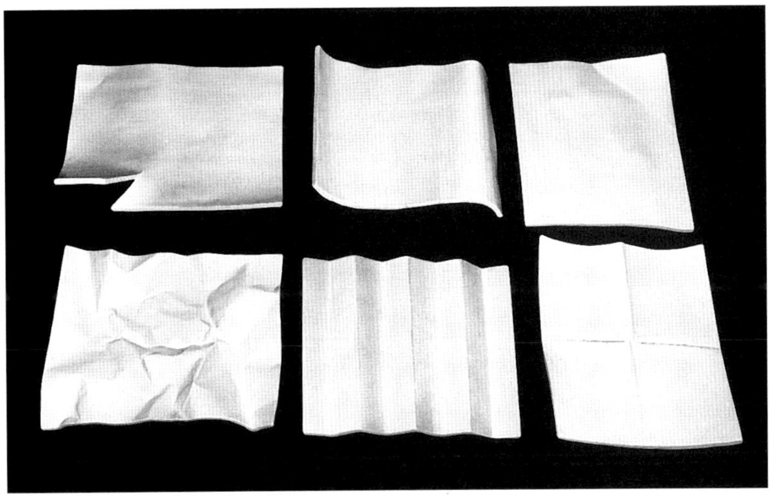

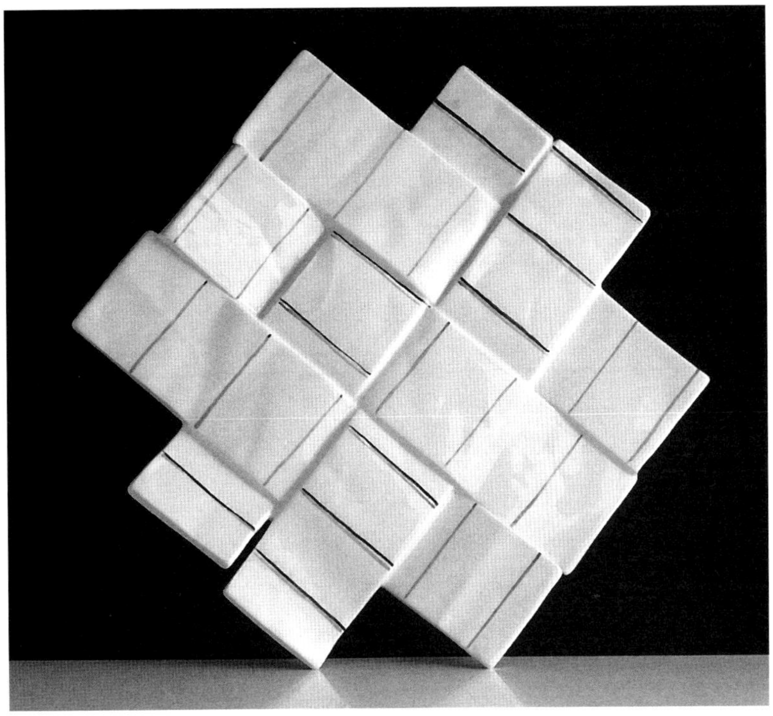

Reviewing McNicoll's work in 1974 the art critic William Feaver wrote enthusiastically of 'prototypes, which restore wit and expression to the field dominated by the well-meaning Council of Industrial Design.'[22] In fact, because of some residual modernist inhibition, McNicoll's earliest pieces, though strange in form, had either been undecorated or decorated in the simplest fashion. But in 1975, inspired by the major exhibition of Islamic rugs organised by David Sylvester at the Hayward Gallery in 1972, McNicoll made a series of heavily patterned 'carpet' bowls (27). Shown by Francis Kyle at the Thumb Gallery, these were perceptually more mysterious than her previous work. They were quite crude little objects that nonetheless managed to generate anxieties about representation. They operated as simulacra in which the idea of a battered carpet was engendered by a sheet of cast slip, hung to harden in a piece of cloth.

Other production pieces paid homage to, or sent up, the history of the twentieth-century avant-garde, particularly the 'dismembered planes'[23] of Cubism. Like another slightly younger potter, Andrew Lord, McNicoll catapulted these painterly investigations back into three dimensions with a series of faceted teapots and teacups. But other aspects of twentieth-century art were also for the taking. There was, of course, collage, which validated her preference for casting and constructing using oddly twinned existing objects. A heavily decorated jug with corrugated sides pierced by a quill pen suggested surrealist experiments with automatic writing. And McNicoll's increasingly free and confident use of pattern recalled the rococo aspects of early School of Paris painting.

In February 1975 McNicoll exhibited in The Women's Free Arts Alliance show *Sweet Sixteen and Never Been Shown* held near Chalk Farm. This was a result of her friendship with New Yorker Joanna Walton, a co-founder of the Alliance and formerly a member of Living Theatre.[24] The developing Woman's Art Movement in the visual arts might have been a natural home, but while the friendship with Walton was important, McNicoll's involvement remained informal. At this point there was no overt political dimension to McNicoll's work

27 **Carpet Bowl** 1975

Sheet of cast slip, clear glaze with underglaze colour and coloured slips, safety pin

24 x 20 x 12 cm; 9.5 x 7.75 x 4.75 in

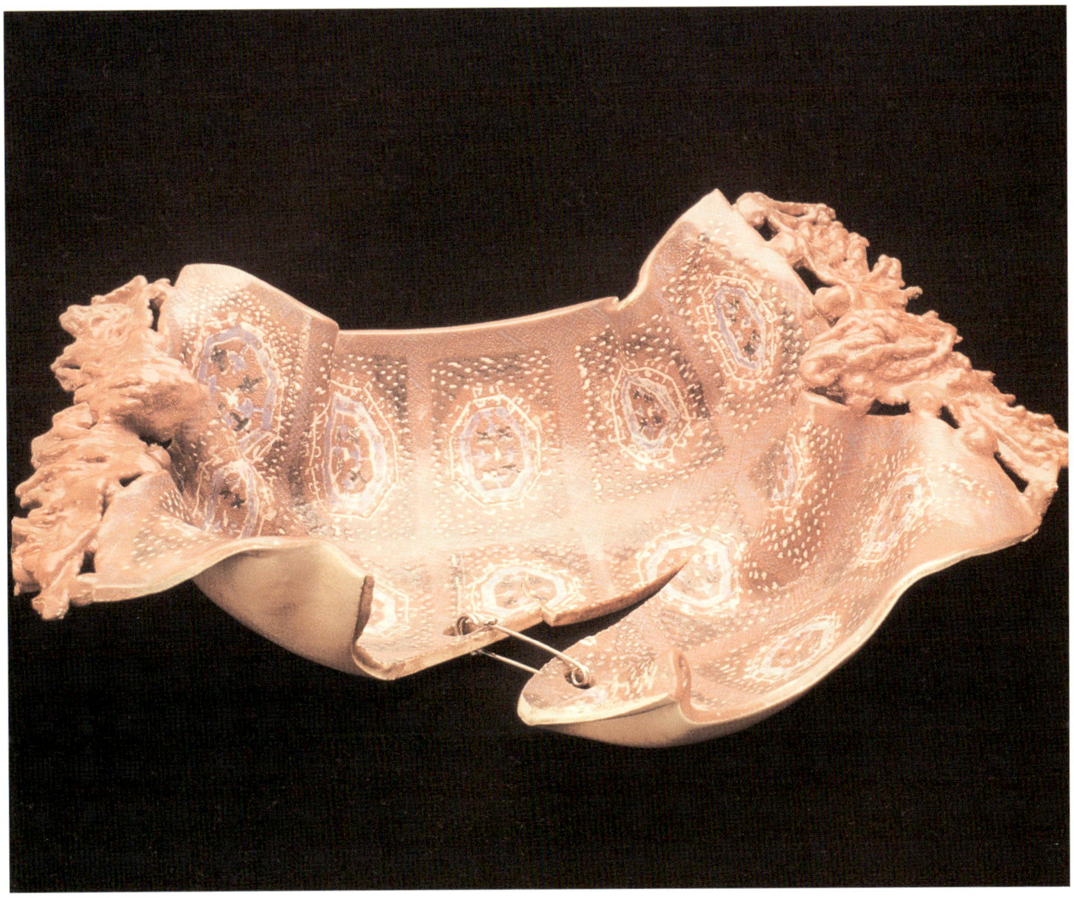

28 **Corrugated Cup and Saucer** 1976

Slip cast earthenware

Mould made from aluminium foil and plaster, clear glaze with underglaze colour,

H. 12 cm; 4.75 in

Photograph: Robyn Beeche

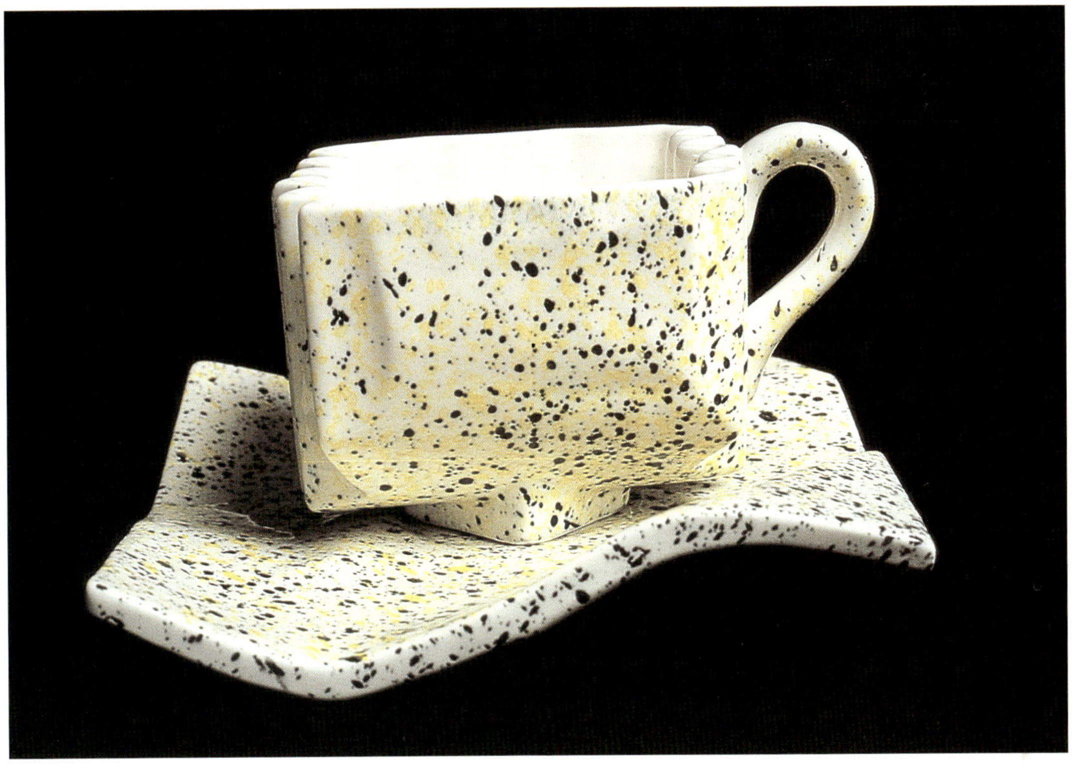

29 **Concertina Jug** 1977
Slip cast earthenware
Mould made from aluminium foil and a
feather, clear glaze with underglaze colour
H. 20 cm; 7.75 in
Photograph: Robyn Beeche

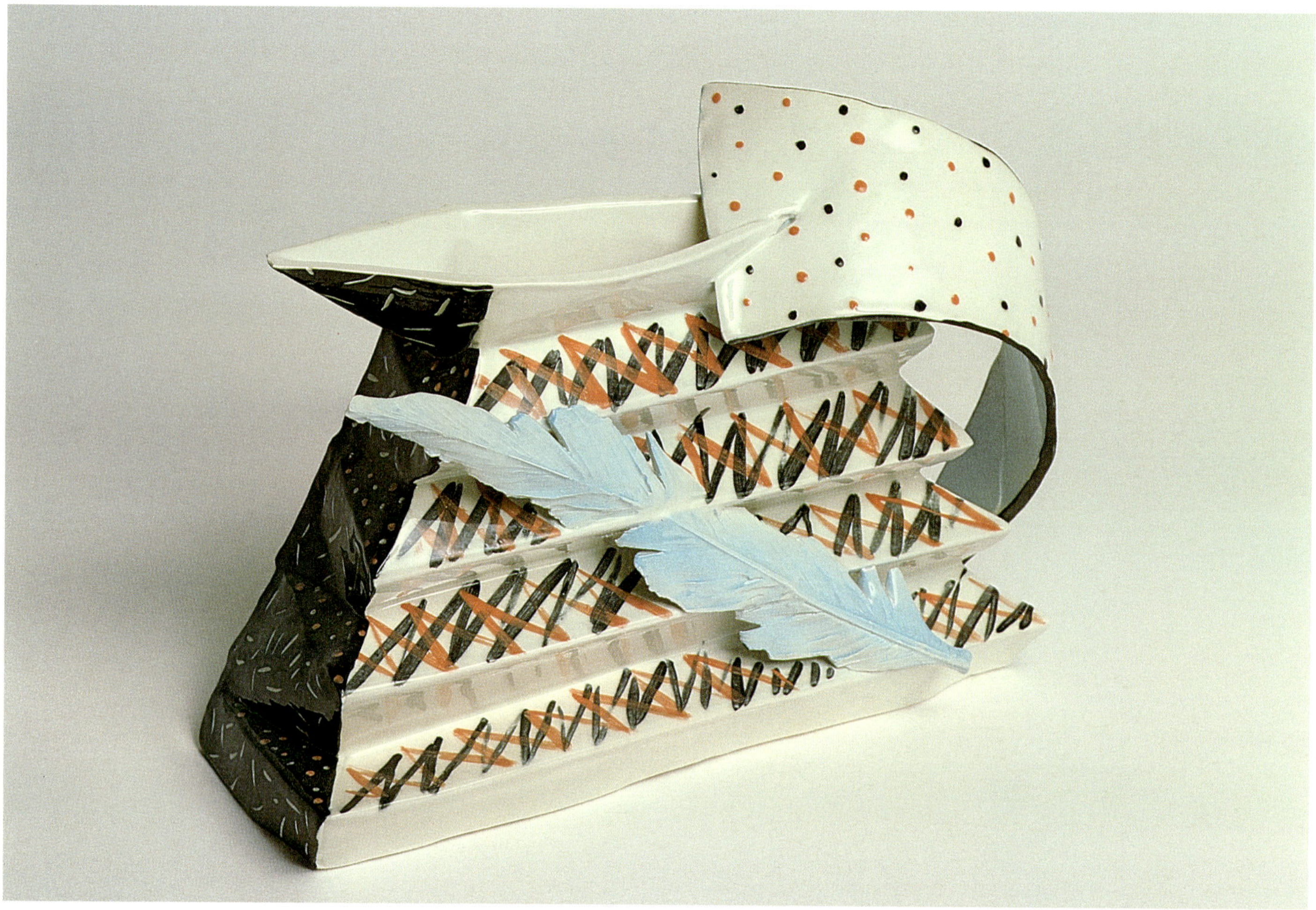

30 **Cube teapot, Cup and Plate** 1978

Slip cast earthenware

Mould made from plaster and foil, clear glaze

with underglaze colour and coloured slips

Teapot h. 20 cm; 7.75 in

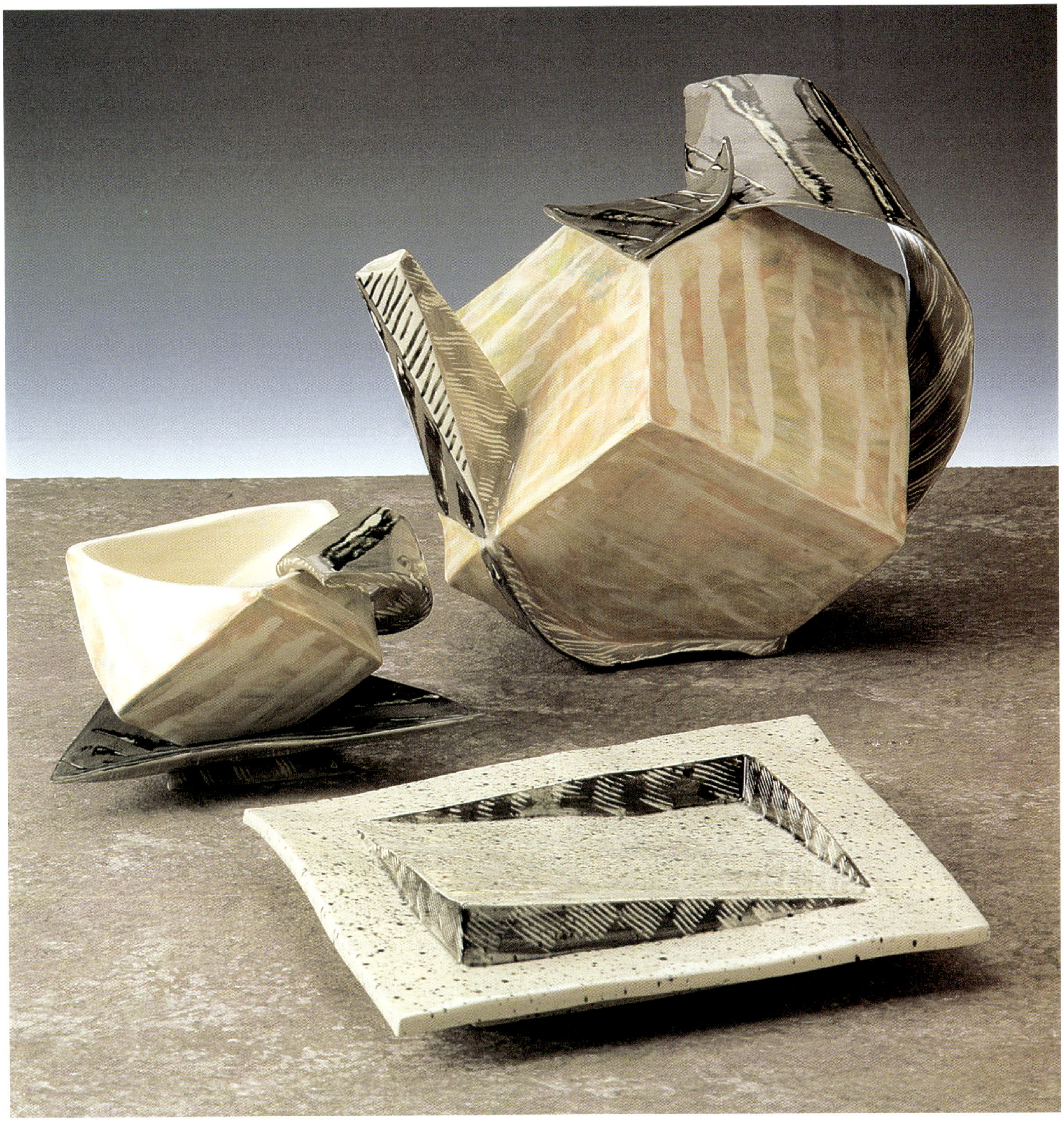

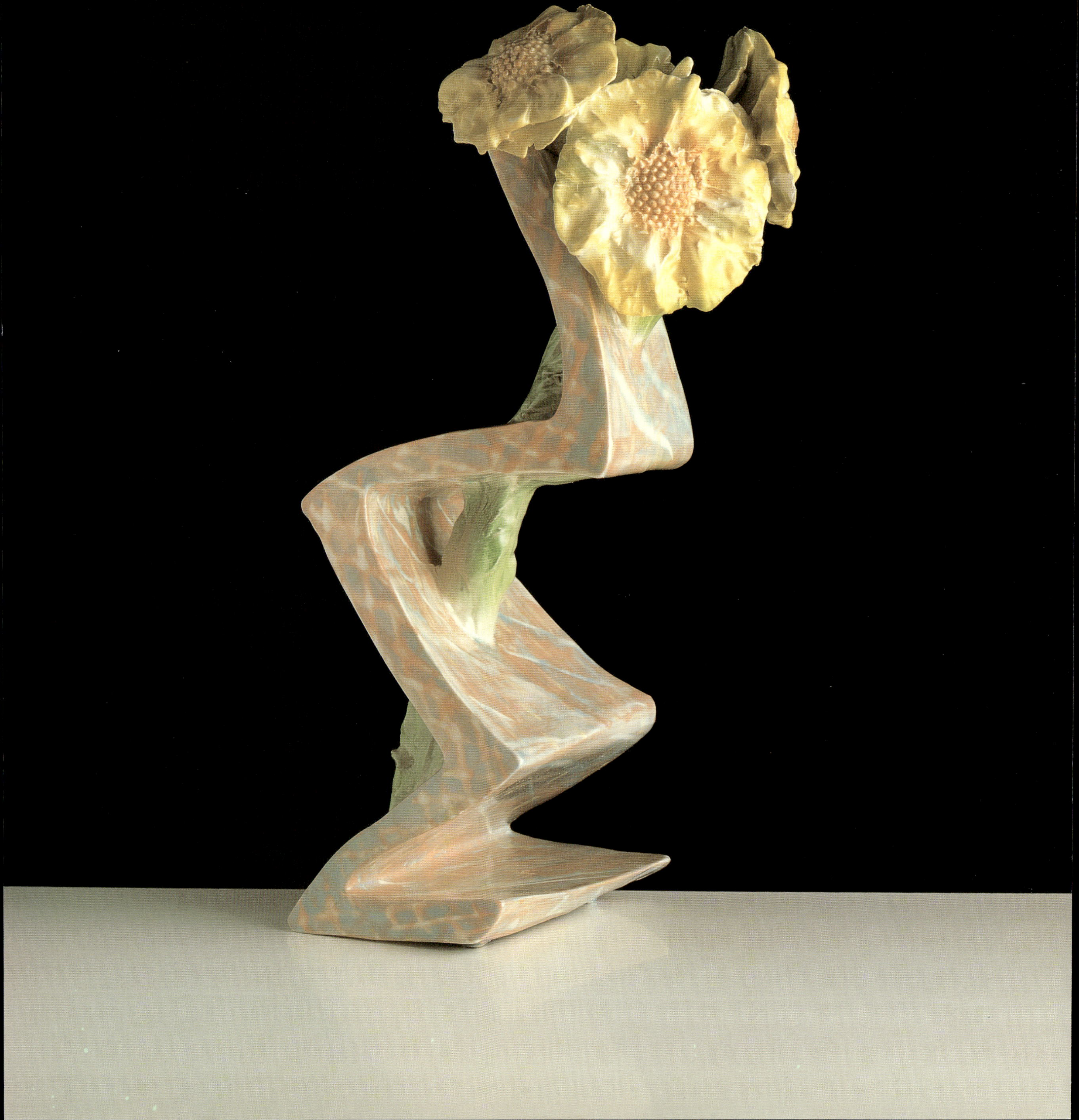

opposite

31 **Zig Zag Candlestick** 1978

Slip cast earthenware
Mould made from aluminium foil
and flowers, clear glaze with
underglaze colour and coloured slips
H. 22 cm; 8.5 in

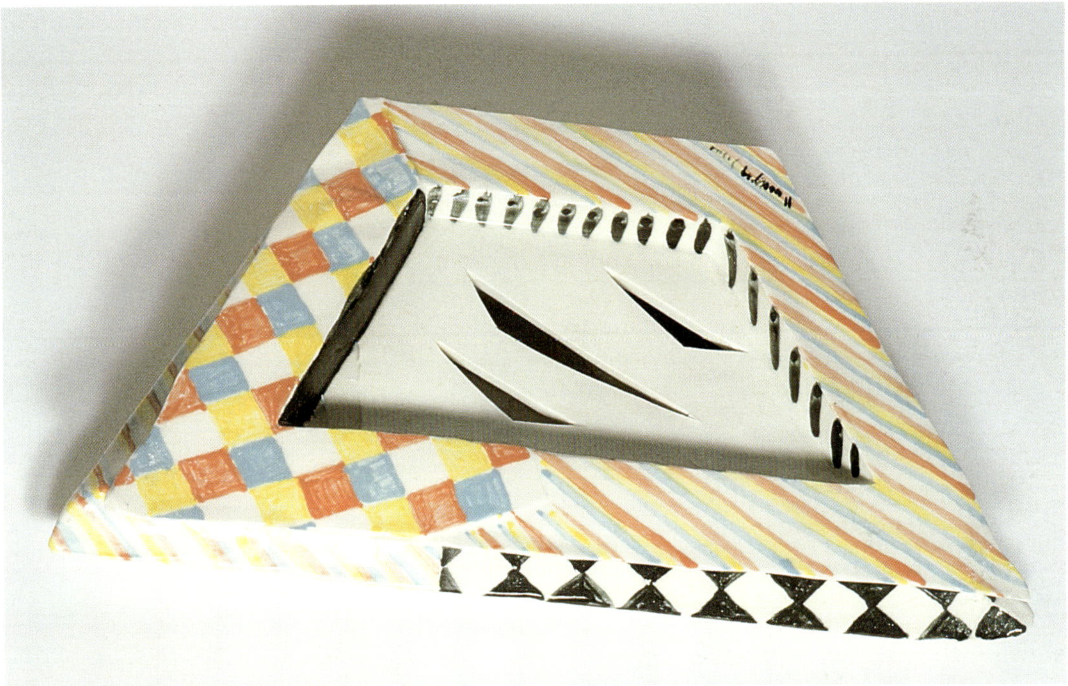

32 **Soap Dish** 1977

Slip cast earthenware
Based on an Oribe dish, clear glaze with
underglaze colour and coloured slips
28 x 15 x 4 cm; 11 x 5.75 x 1.5 in

and she was so successful that she hardly needed a defended space in which to explore her potential. On the other hand her creative practice was, and continues to be, braided with activities stereotypically associated with women – such as dressmaking for example – and with the domestic arena.

Craft and design

Letter to Carol McNicoll from J. E. Strangeways, Rising Hawk, Stoke-on-Trent, 9 October 1984

Unfortunately I have been unable to maintain Rising Hawk sales during this period other than nominally. Therefore the royalties accrued have not been as good as expected. Also, due to the insolvency of Merrysilver Ltd and the period of readjustment afterwards, records have not been kept as well as they might have been.

Up until her exhibition at the Francis Kyle Gallery in 1980, McNicoll had stayed firmly outside the craft world as defined by the government-funded Crafts Council. This was to change. Much of the craft validated by the Crafts Council since its formation in 1971 had been characterised by the conspicuous consumption of time, by what has been characterised as 'chronomanuality'.[25] McNicoll, on the other hand, was using a process associated with the ceramics industry, and at the start of the 1980s she entered into a series of agreements to mass produce some of her simpler designs such as the wrapping paper vases, first with Rising Hawk Pottery in collaboration with Christopher Strangeways, and subsequently with Galerie Axis.

These reproductions of her designs were fairly crudely done and devoid of decoration but, in 1985, she entered into an agreement with Next Interiors. Designs by herself and Janice Tchalenko were produced in Stoke-on-Trent to very high standards, including the involvement of a team trained to use McNicoll's complex sgraffito decorating techniques.[26] They were hugely successful.

33 Alison Britton's selection for *The Maker's Eye*

Carol McNicoll plate in foreground on the right

Photograph: David Ward, 1981

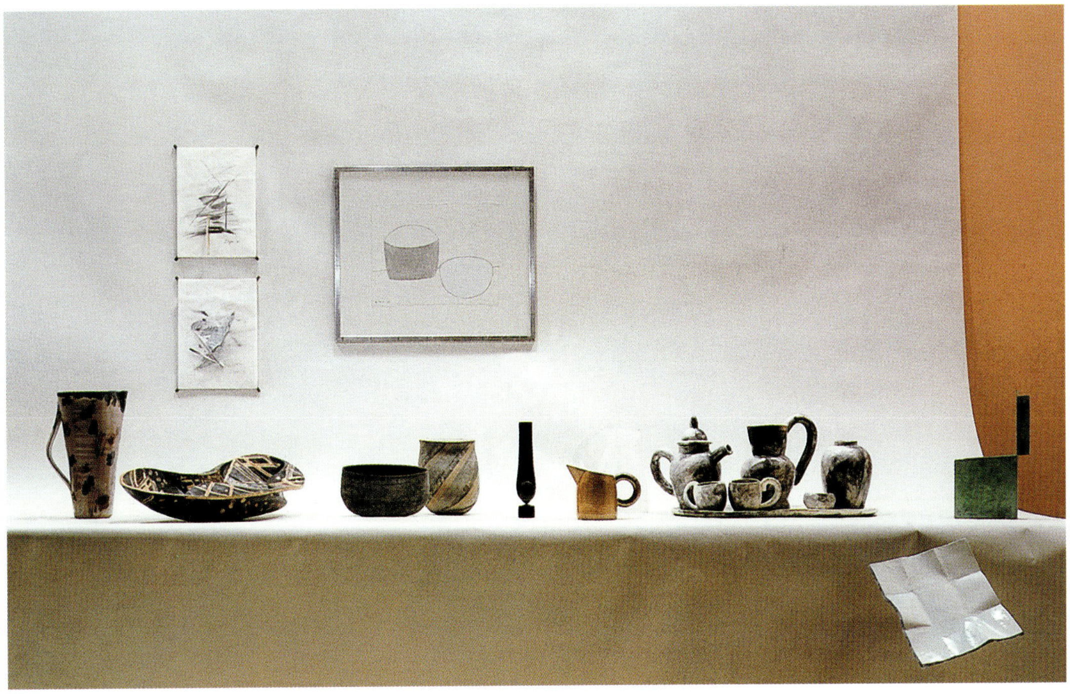

34 Production ware designed by Carol McNicoll:

(from left to right) Tea cup, tea pot, wrapped paper vases for Axis, two vases for Next Interiors, crumpled teapot and plate for Axis, plate for Next Interiors

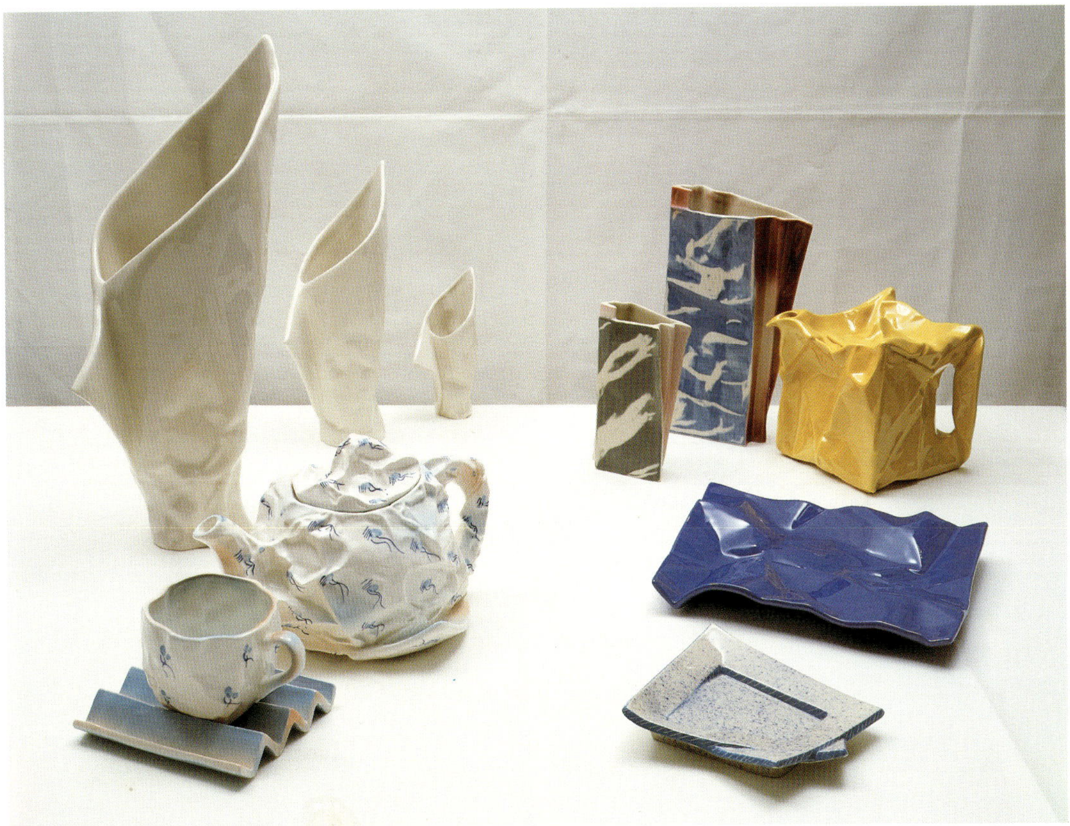

35 Installation shot of part of Carol McNicoll's 1980 show at the Francis Kyle Gallery

opposite

36 **Unravelling Jug** 1980

Slip cast earthenware

Clear glaze, coloured slips and underglaze colour

H. 23 cm; 9 in

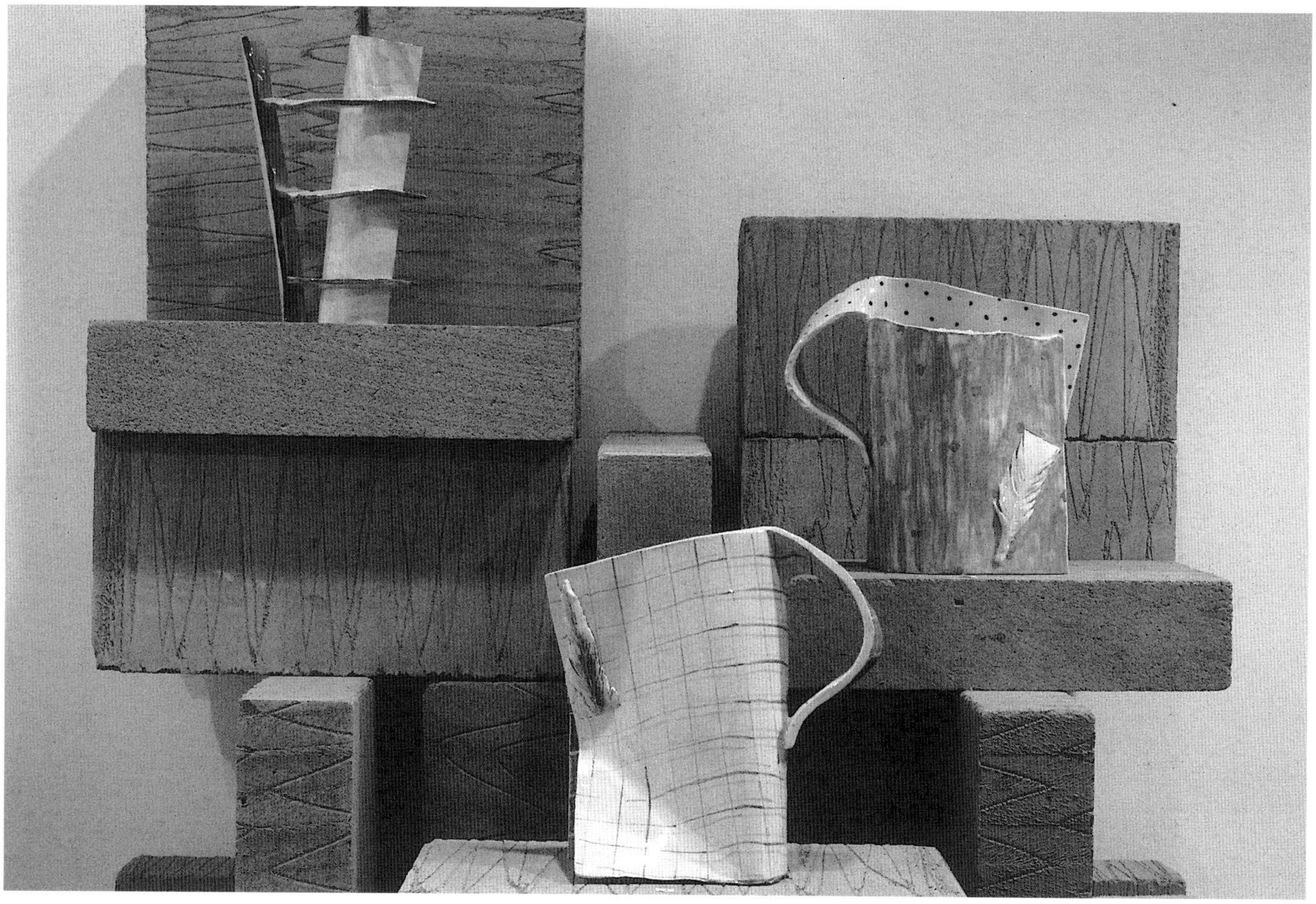

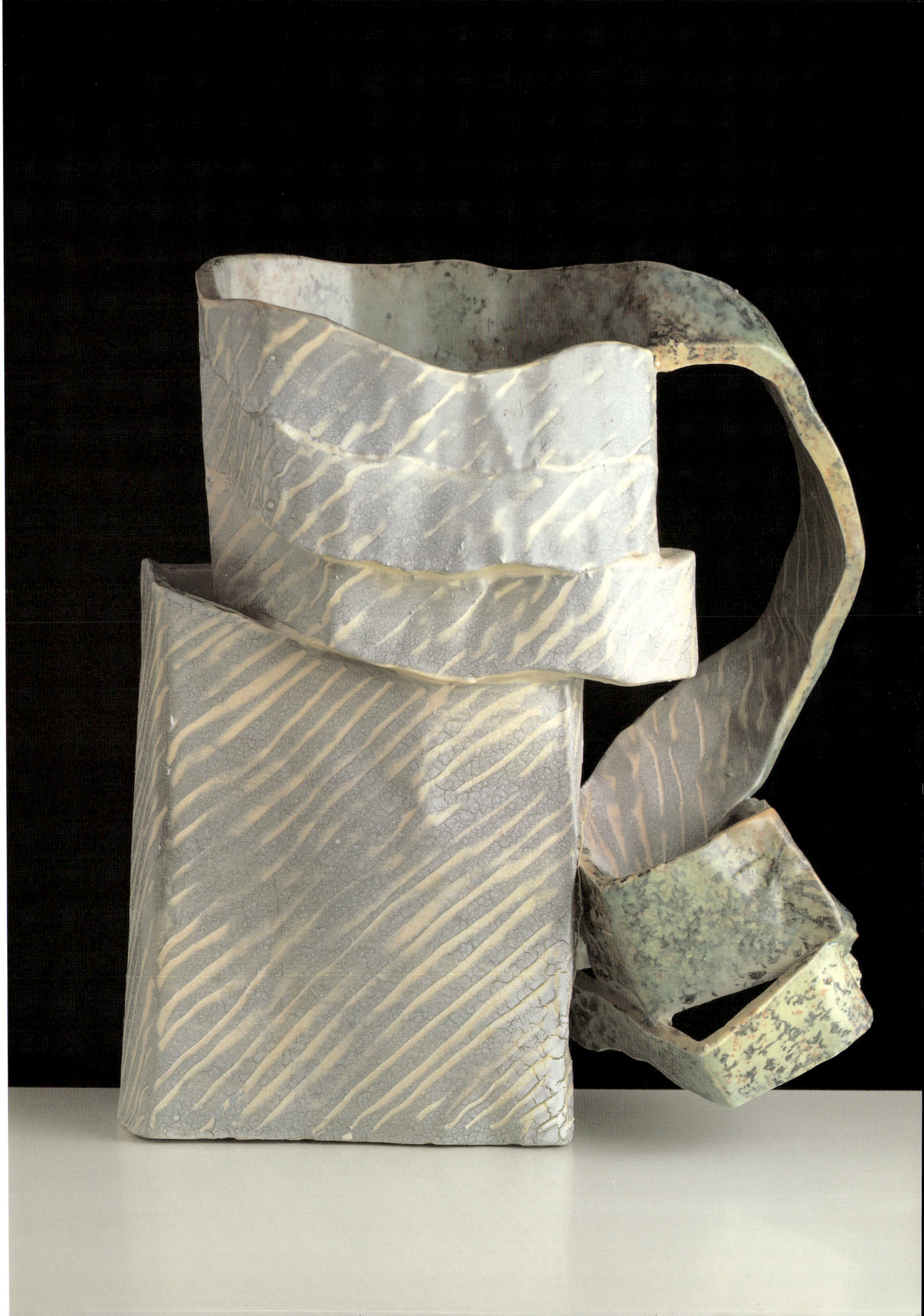

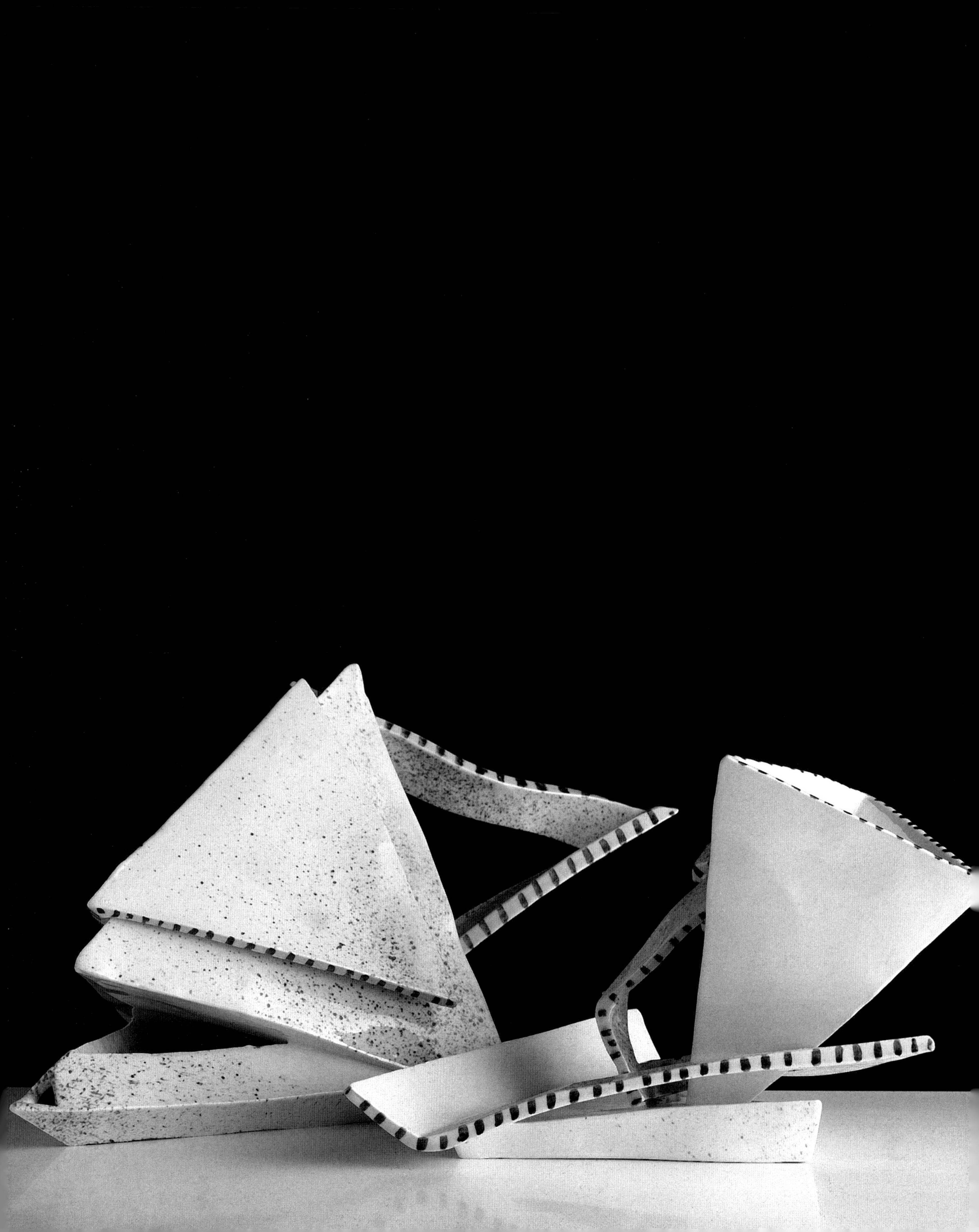

opposite

37 **Teapot and Cup and Saucer**
1980

Slip cast earthenware
Clear glaze, coloured slips and underglaze colour
Teapot h. 18 cm; 7 in

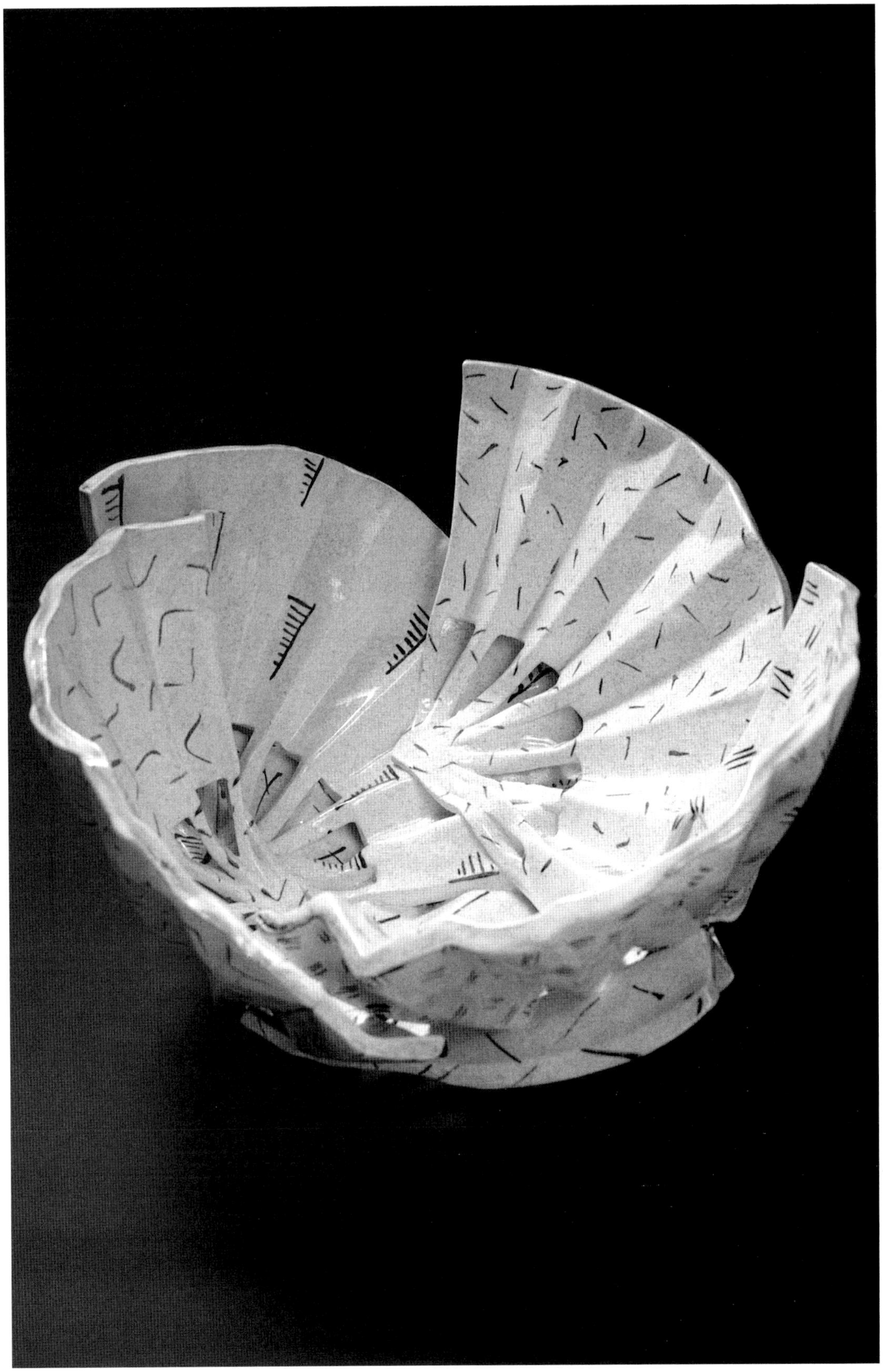

38 **Fan Bowl** 1980

One-off, slip cast and assembled, clear glaze with underglaze colour, purchased by the Crafts Council from the Francis Kyle Gallery

39 **Teaset for Piers Gough** 1983
Slip cast earthenware
Clear glaze, coloured slips
Teapot h. (including handle)
23 cm; 9 in
Collection: Piers Gough
Photograph: David Cripps

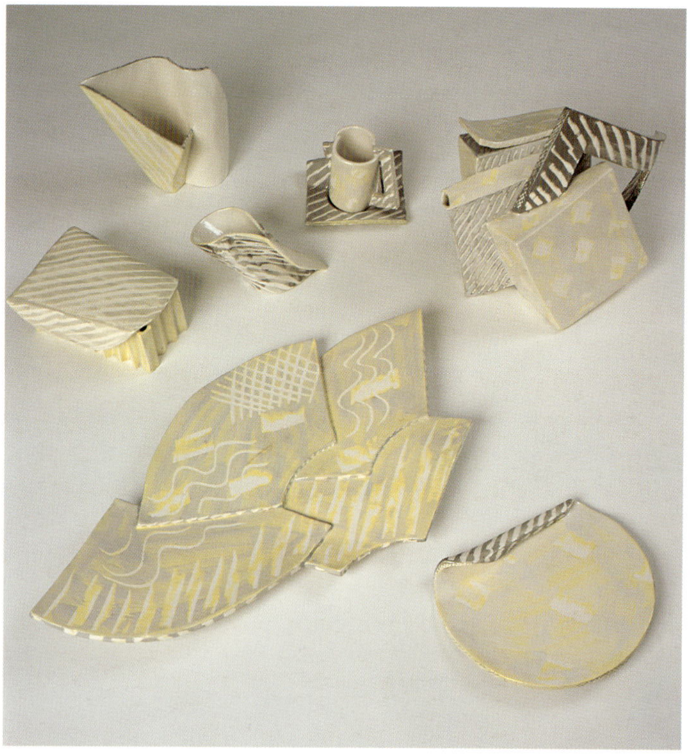

opposite
41 **Large Woven Dish** 1988
One-off, slip cast, fired cloth dipped in slip and assembled, clear glaze, coloured slips and underglaze colour
42 x 28 cm; 16.5 x 11 in
Collection: Ed Wolf
Photograph: David Cripps

40 **Moving Dish** 1982
One-off, slip cast, fired cloth dipped in slip, porcelain squares, assembled, clear glaze, coloured slips and underglaze colour, made at the Keramisch Werkcentrum, Heusden, Holland
H. 5 x 29 cm square;
2 x 11.5 in square
Collection: Crafts Council

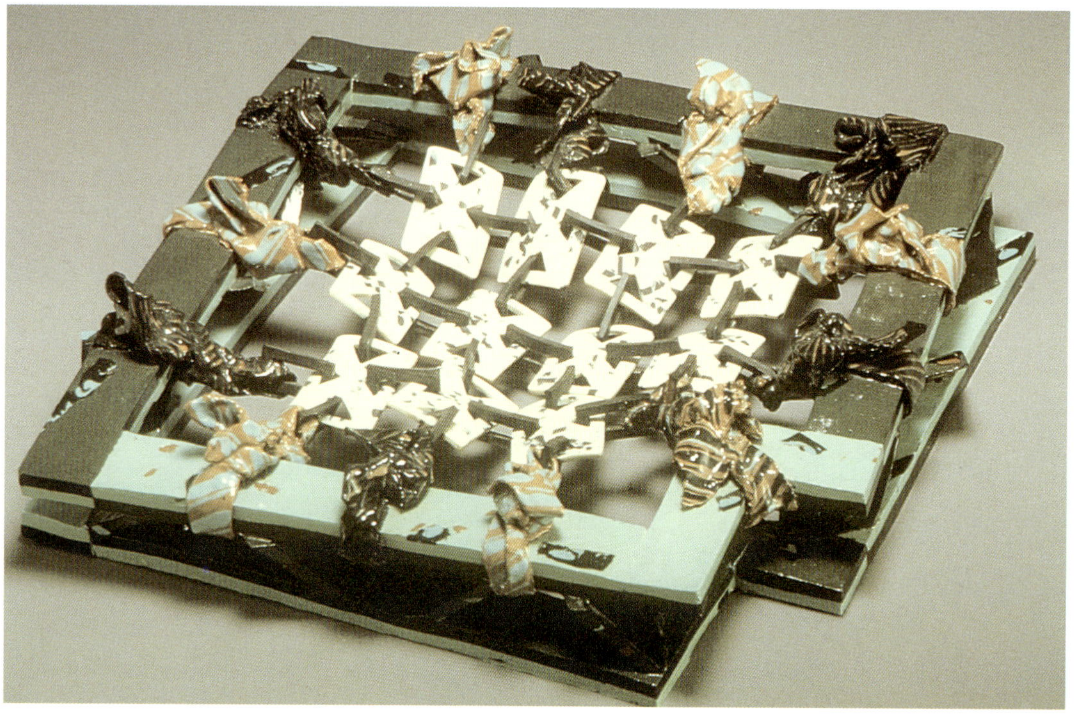

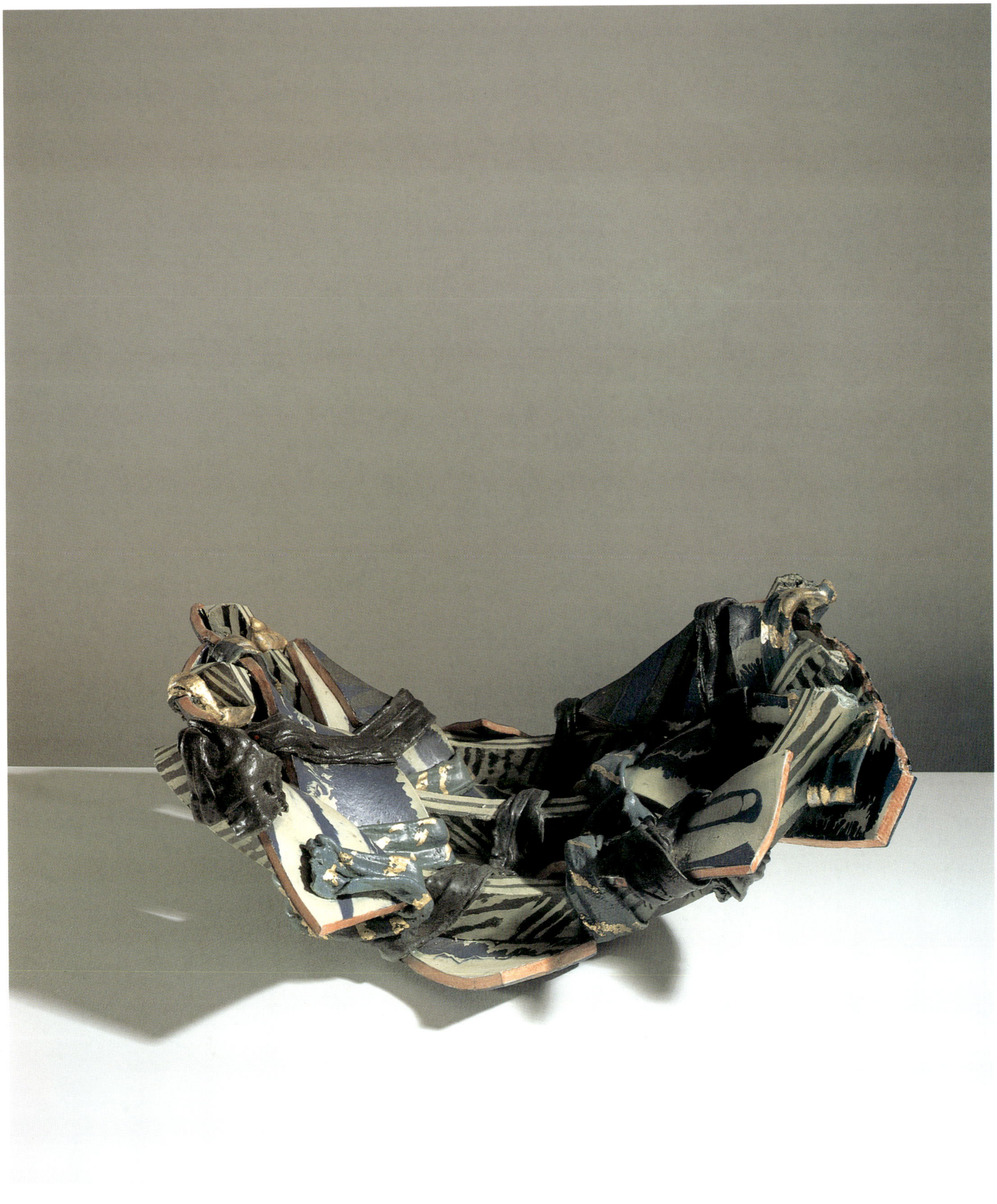

In retrospect McNicoll realises that at that time she misunderstood the nature of design. She was too much of an artist to produce a stream of ideas that could be realised at low cost. The Next experiment was not to be repeated.

During the 1980s, alongside her production work, she embarked on a series of bowls that were elaborate assemblages (see 40–52). The moulds were based on strange bedfellows – foil, clay, tree branches or fabric. These were slip cast and then assembled like constructed sculpture. At times the complexity of these pieces appears visually overpowering. Rods of clay and cast branches were woven into bowl forms using cloth dipped in slip. Slabs of layered, coloured, slip cast clay were cut up to create hard-edged constructions from which hung 'knitted' slip-impregnated cloth or linked rings or small rectangular plates, creating a chain-mail effect. Most ceramic art is strong on silence and stillness, but several of these 'knitted' pieces chinked musically and moved.

However, the finest 'one-offs' of the 1980s were the simplest in conception, like the 1980 *Form* (53), now in the Victoria and Albert Museum, in which a slab of clay was cut and folded to create a distinctly architectural tower holding an angled cylinder. Then there was a splendid series of bowls created by horizontally stacking the same cast curved elements (52). McNicoll's solo show at the Crafts Council in 1985 included some of the best of these 'architectural' pieces. The disingenuously entitled *Plate* (54) was constructed from a flat square cut in a square spiral that was twisted and supported by little columns to create a bowl. In both *Form* and *Plate* the decoration goes its own way, creating a tension between construction and surface through camouflage tactics. Tension is created in other ways, for McNicoll made her 'surface' decoration by cutting and scraping into clay sheets to reveal layers of differently coloured slip – as well as using coloured slips on the surface and occasionally refiring with enamel decoration.

42 **Fruit Dish** 1983

One-off, slip cast, fired cloth dipped in slip and assembled, clear glaze, coloured slips and underglaze colour
31 x 23 x 20 cm; 12.25 x 9 x 7.75 in
Photograph: David Cripps

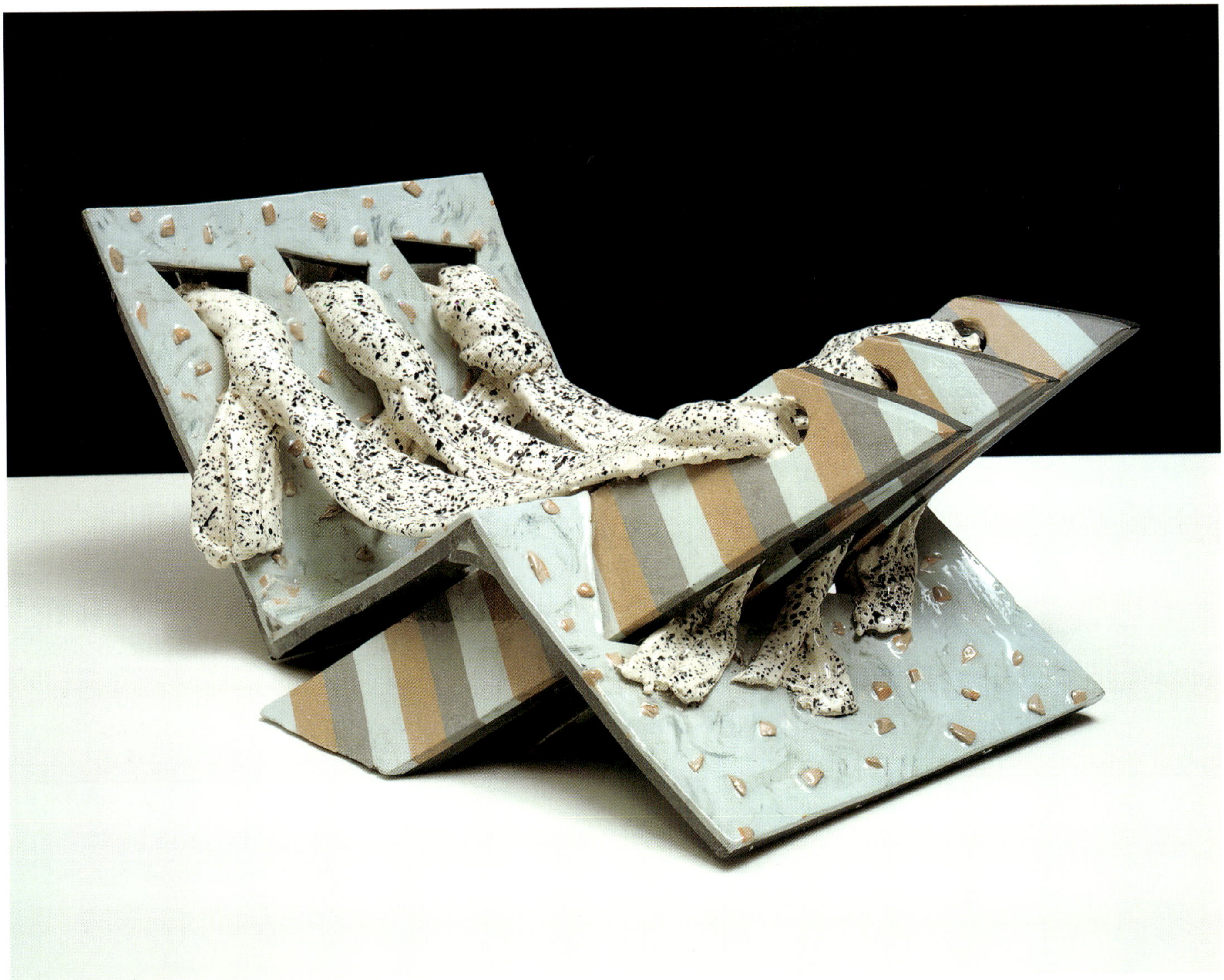

43 **Knitted Bowl** 1985
One-off, slip cast, fired cloth dipped in slip and assembled, clear glaze, coloured slips and underglaze colour
H. 22, diam. 26 cm; 8.5 x 10.25 in
Collection: Crafts Council

opposite
44 **Fruit Bowl** 1985
One-off, slip cast, fired cloth dipped in slip and assembled, clear glaze, coloured slips and underglaze colour,
H. 23, diam. 35 cm; 9 x 13.75 in
Collection: the Artist
Photograph: David Ward

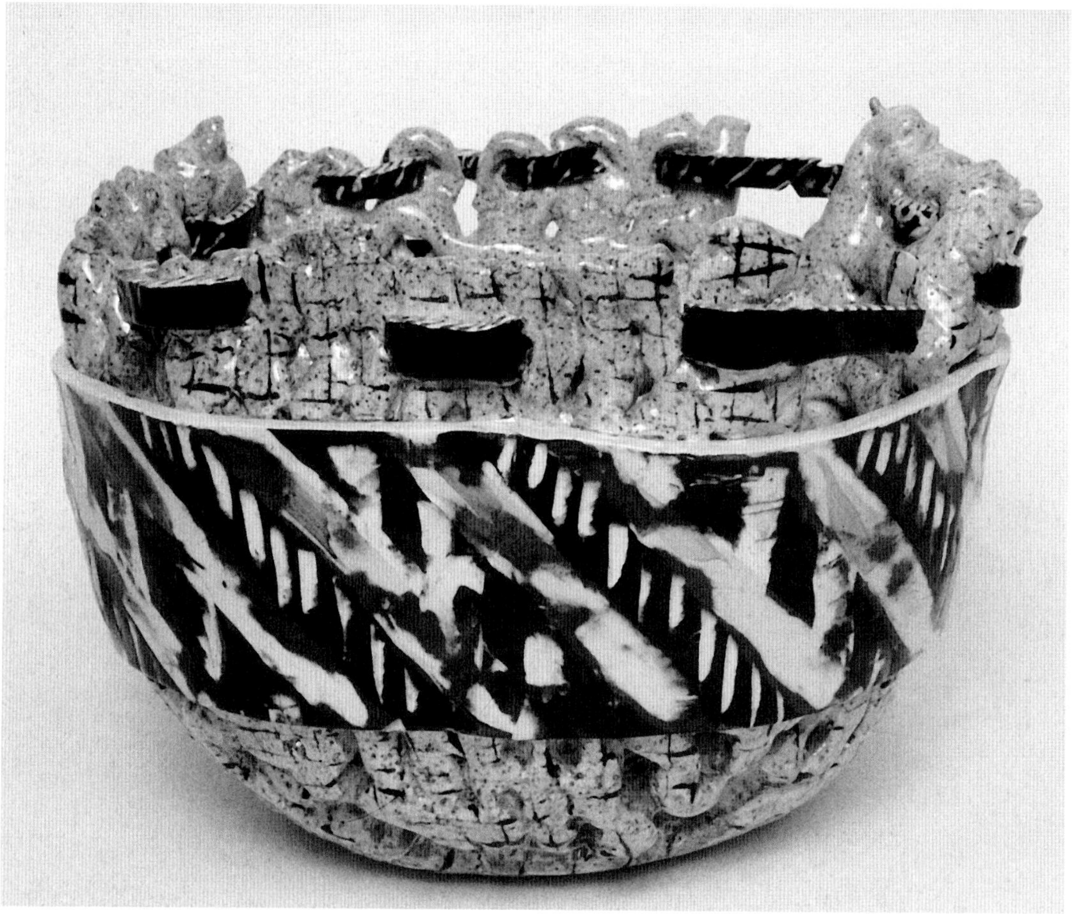

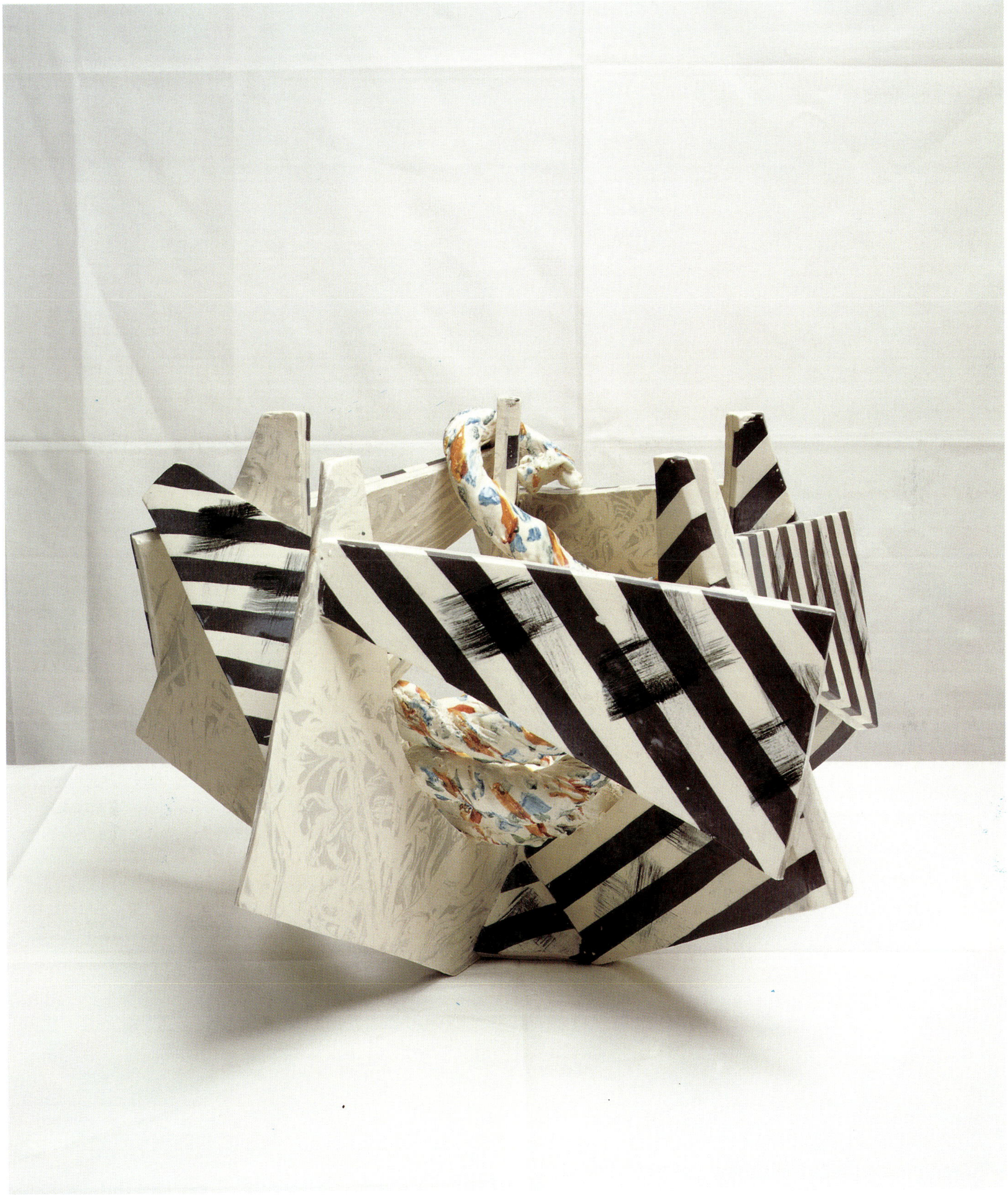

53

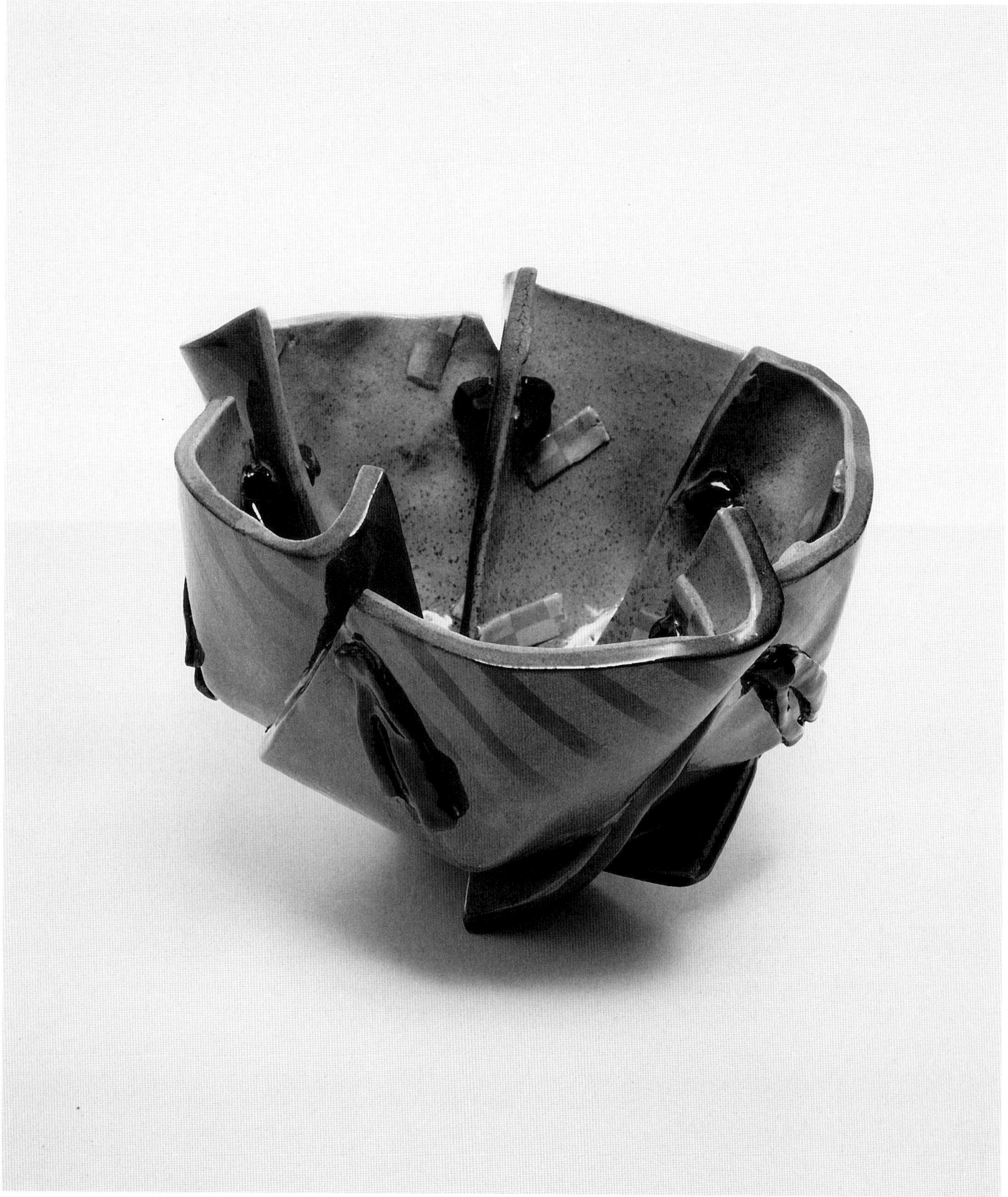

46 **Twig Fruit Bowl** 1983
One-off, slip cast branches, fired cloth dipped in slip and assembled, clear glaze, coloured slips and underglaze colour
H. 23, diam. 26 cm; 9 x 10.25 in
Photograph: Robyn Beeche

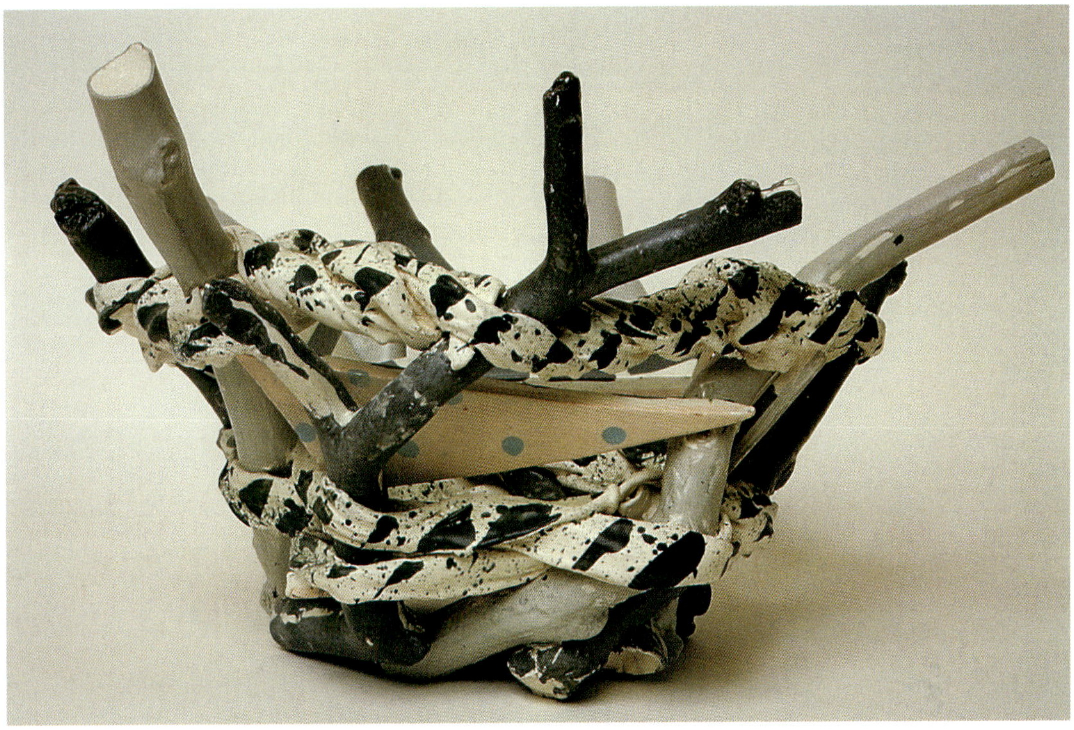

47 **Pretzel Dish** 1984
One-off, slip cast and assembled, clear glaze, coloured slips and underglaze colour
Diam. 32 cm; 12.5 in
Collection: the Artist
Photograph: David Cripps

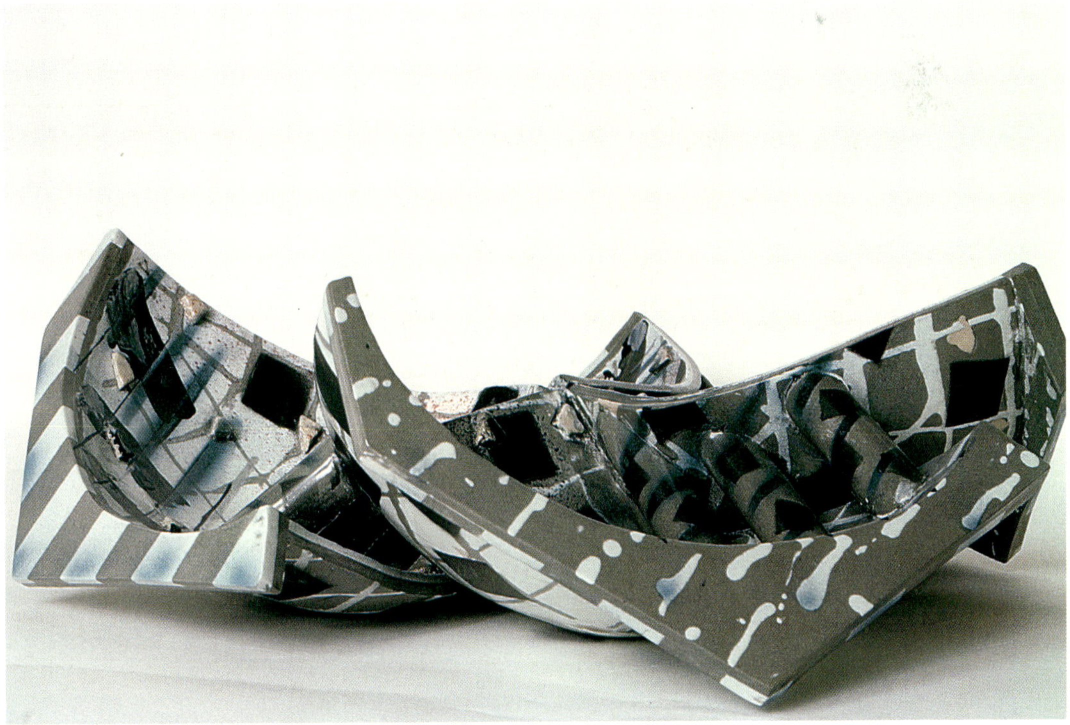

opposite
45 **Grey Fruit Bowl** 1985
One-off, slip cast, fired cloth dipped in slip and assembled, clear glaze, coloured slips and underglaze colour
H. 18, diam. 18 cm; 7 x 7 in

48 **Fruit Bowl** 1985
One-off, slip cast and assembled, clear glaze, coloured slips and underglaze colour
26 x 17 x 18 cm; 10.25 x 6.5 x 7 in
Collection: Cleveland Craft Centre

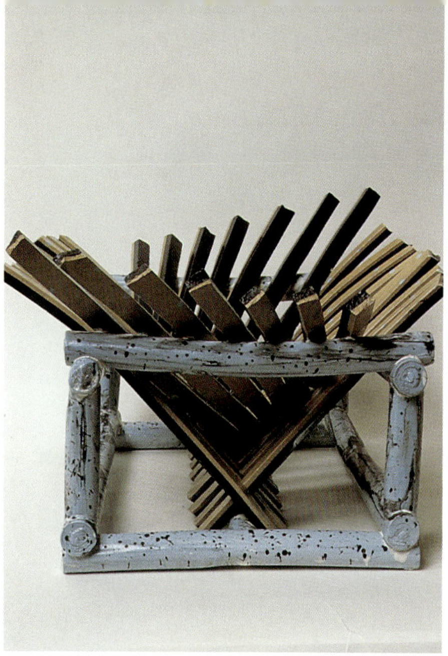

49 **Fruit Bowl** 1988
One-off, slip cast and assembled, clear glaze, coloured slips and underglaze colour
H. 23 cm; 9 in
Collection: Ed Wolf

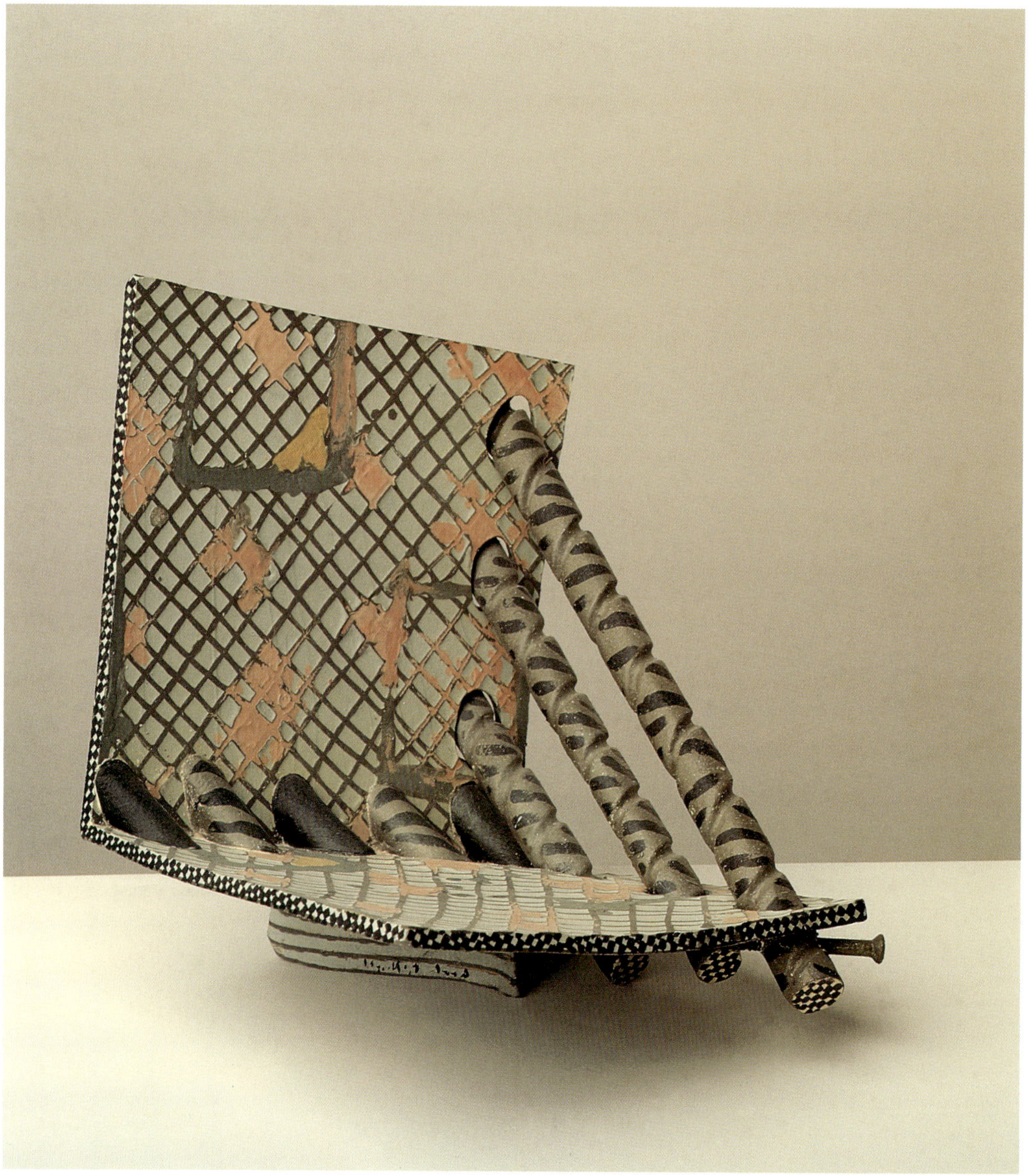

50 **Lucca Fruit Bowl** 1988

One-off, slip cast and assembled, clear glaze,
coloured slips and underglaze colour
H. 30 cm; 11.75 in
Collection: Ed Wolf

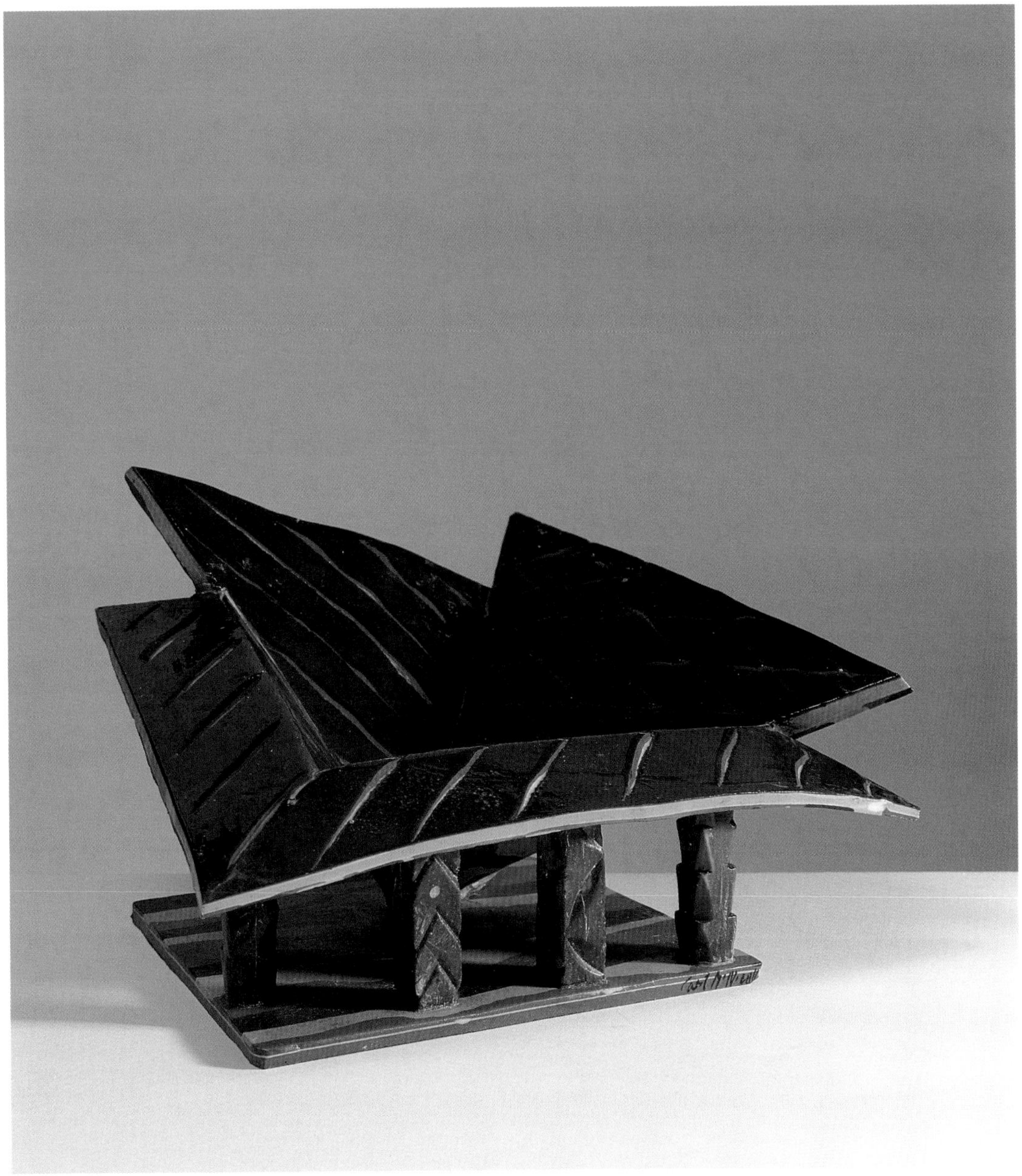

51 **Fruit Bowl** 1985
One-off, slip cast, fired cloth dipped in slip and assembled, clear glaze, coloured slips and underglaze colour
H. 16 x 26 cm square;
6.25 x 10.25 in
Collection: Susanna Heron

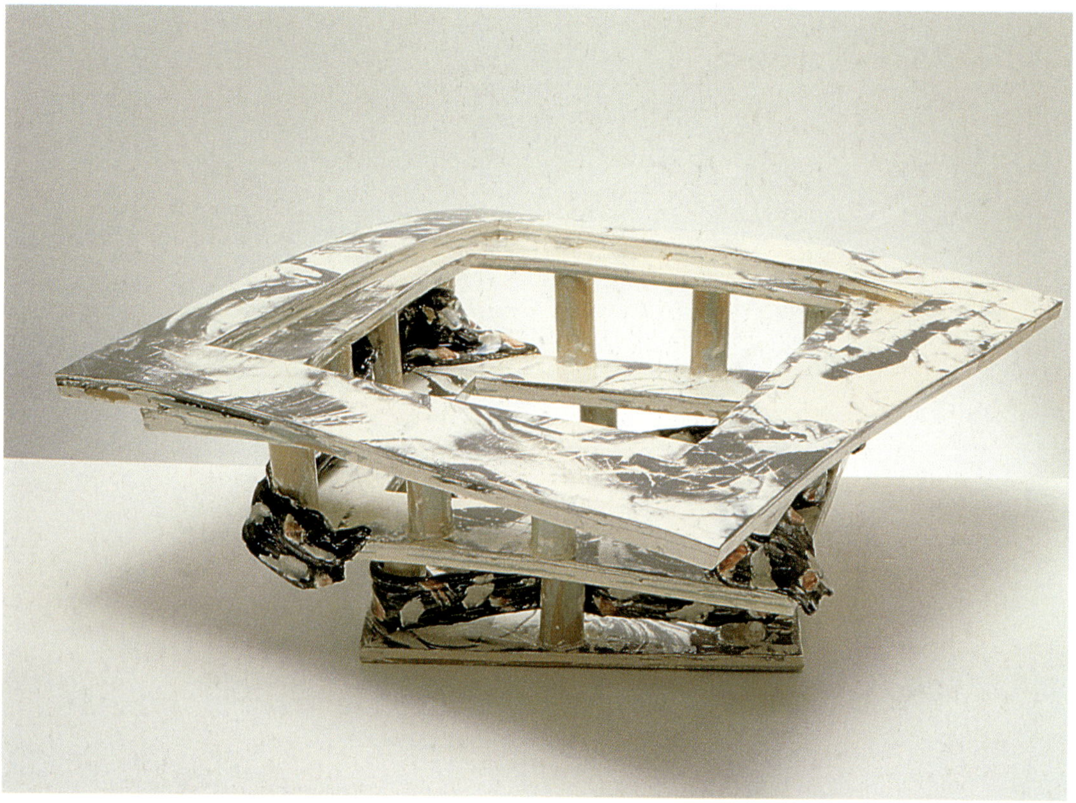

52 **Fruit Bowl** 1988
One-off, slip cast and assembled, clear glaze, coloured slips and underglaze colour
L. 48 cm; 18.75 in
Collection: The Shipley Art Gallery
Photograph: Stephen Brayne

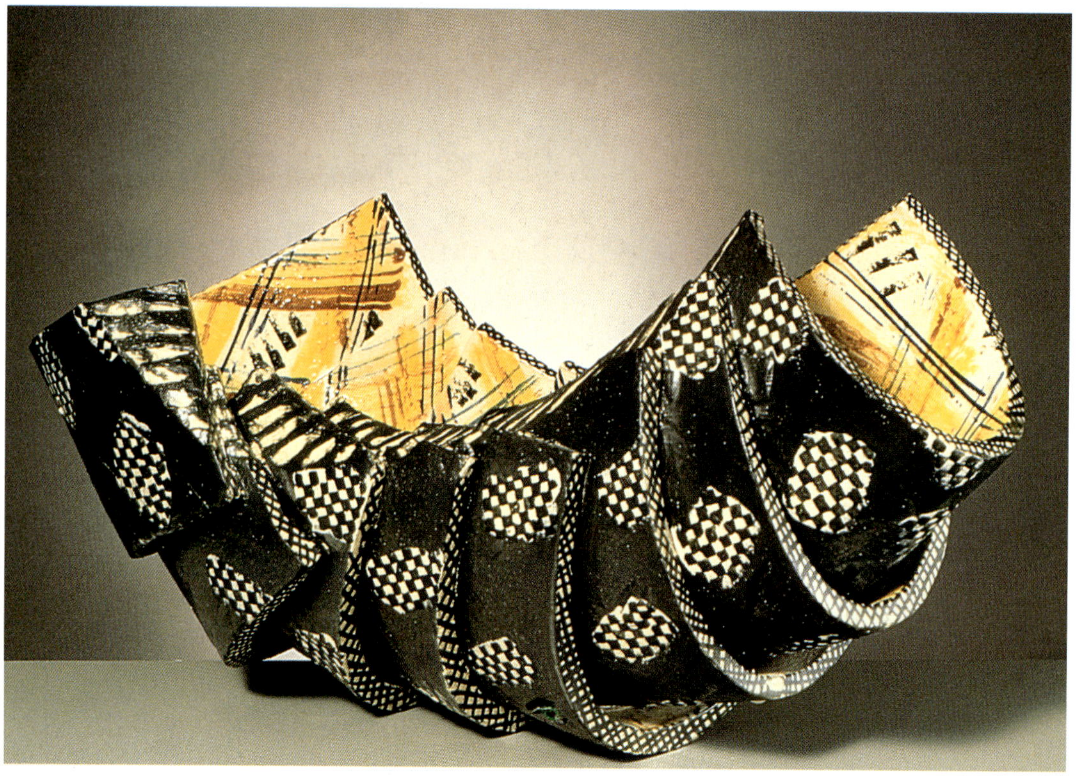

opposite
53 **Form** 1980
One-off, slip cast and assembled, clear glaze, coloured slips and underglaze colour
H. 40.2 x d. 28.5 cm;
15.75 x 11.25 in
Collection: Victoria and Albert Museum

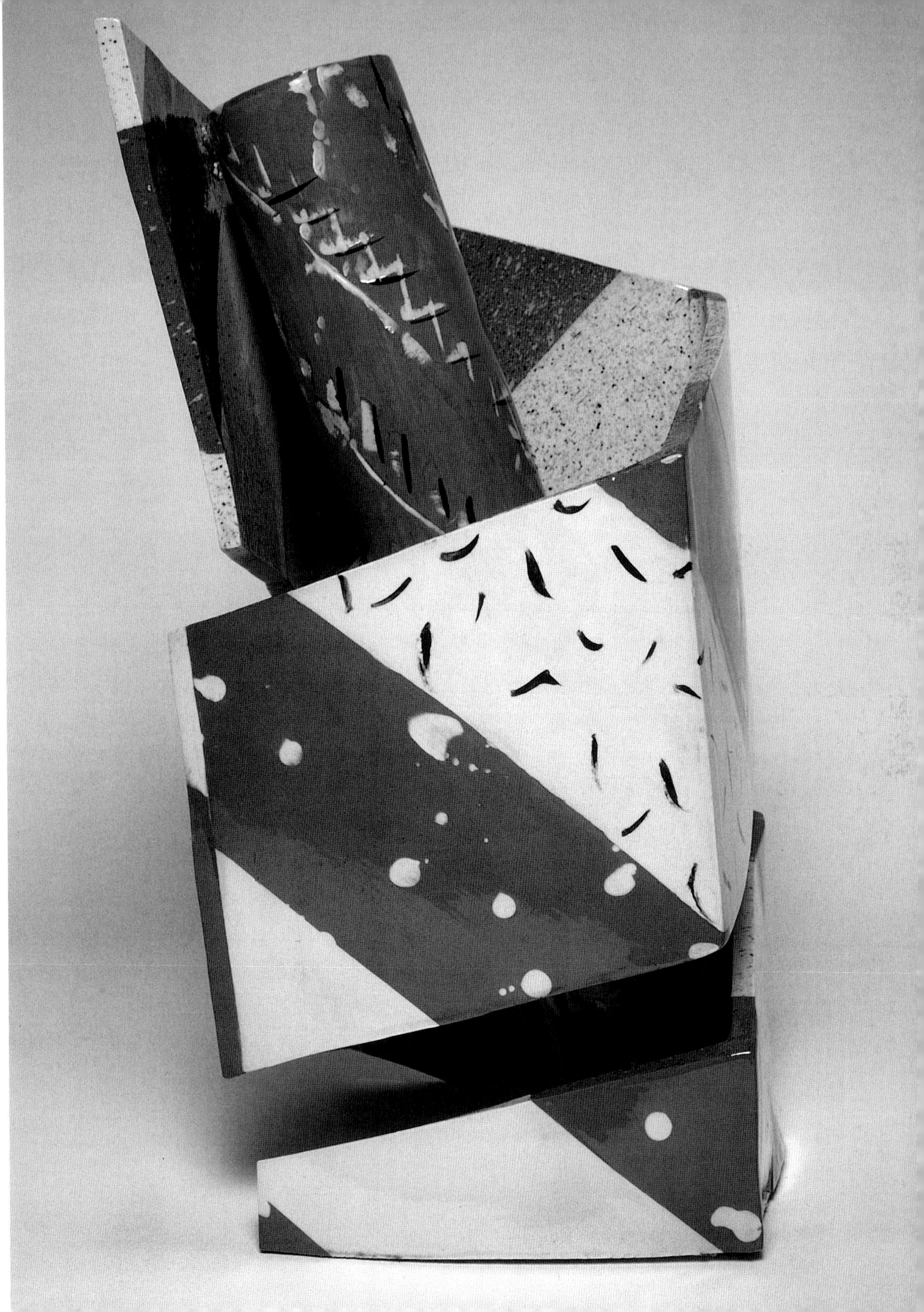

54 **Plate** 1985

One-off, slip cast and assembled, clear glaze, coloured slips and underglaze colour
Diam. 40 cm; 15.75 in
Collection: Ed Wolf
Photograph: David Ward

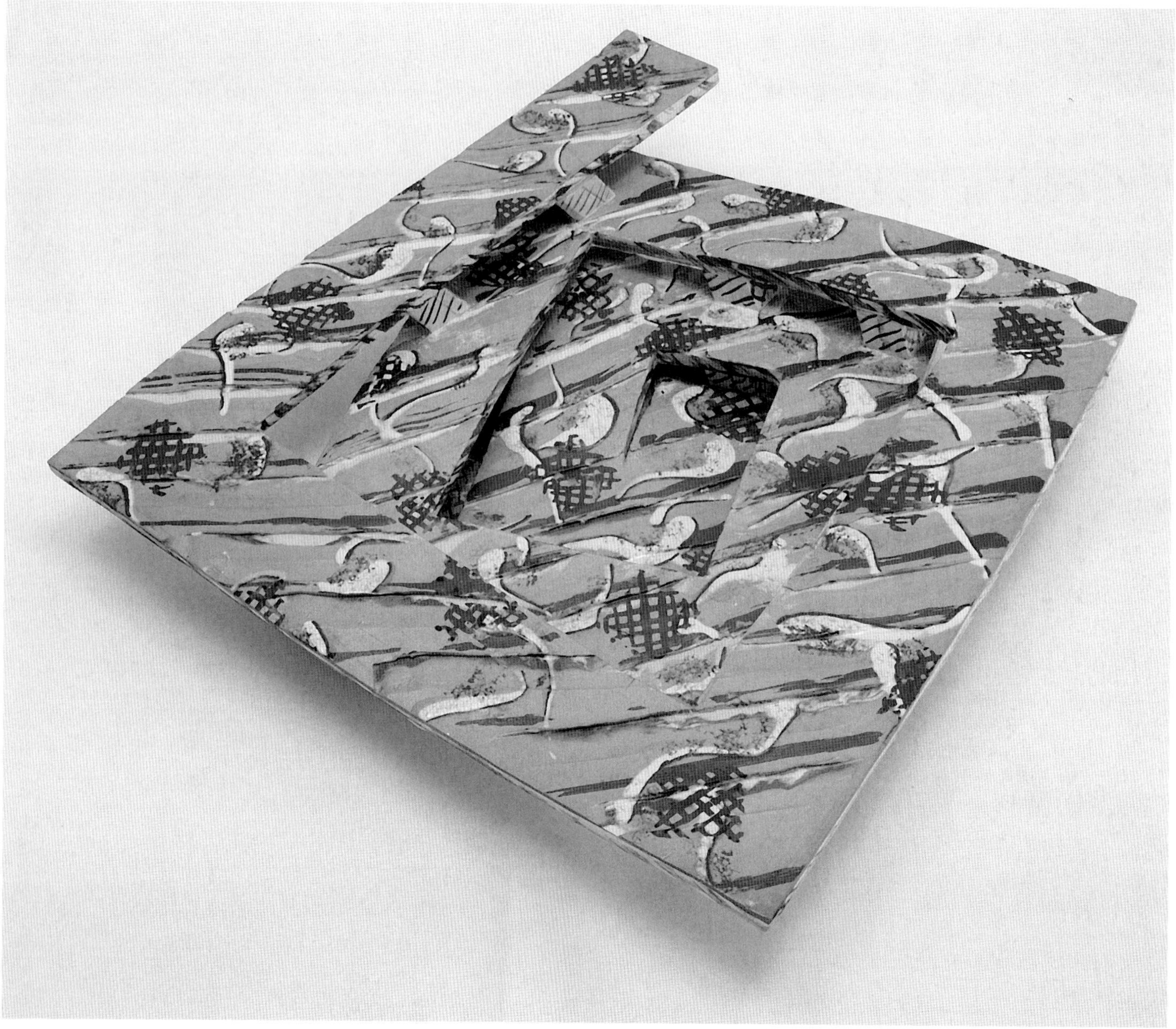

55 **Teapot and Teacup** 1980s

Slip cast earthenware
Clear glaze, coloured slips
23 x 15 cm; 9 x 5.75 in
Collection: Ed Wolf
Photograph: David Cripps

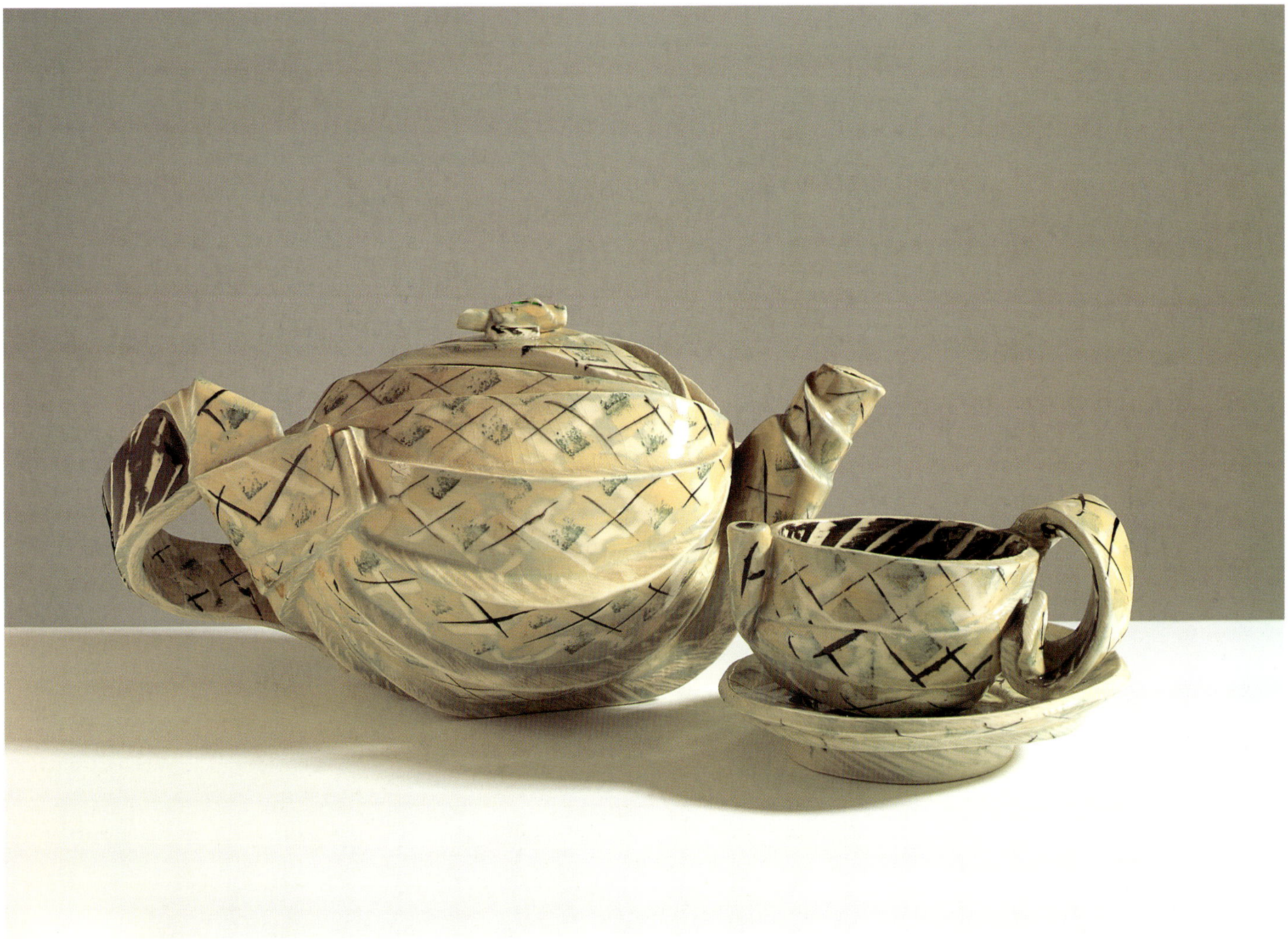

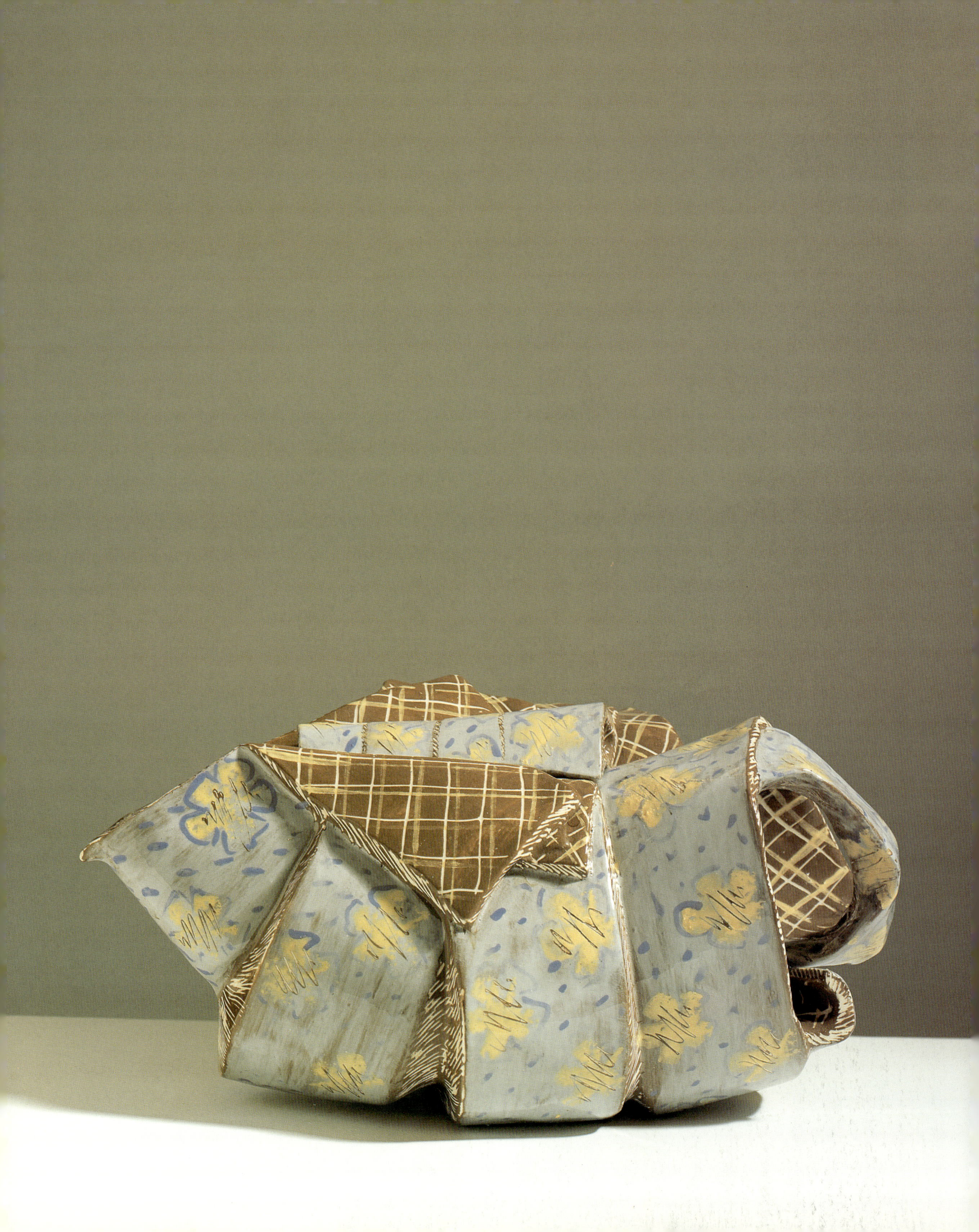

opposite

56 **Teapot** 1980s

Clear glaze, coloured slips

30 x 18 cm; 11.75 x 7 in

Collection: Ed Wolf

Photograph: David Cripps

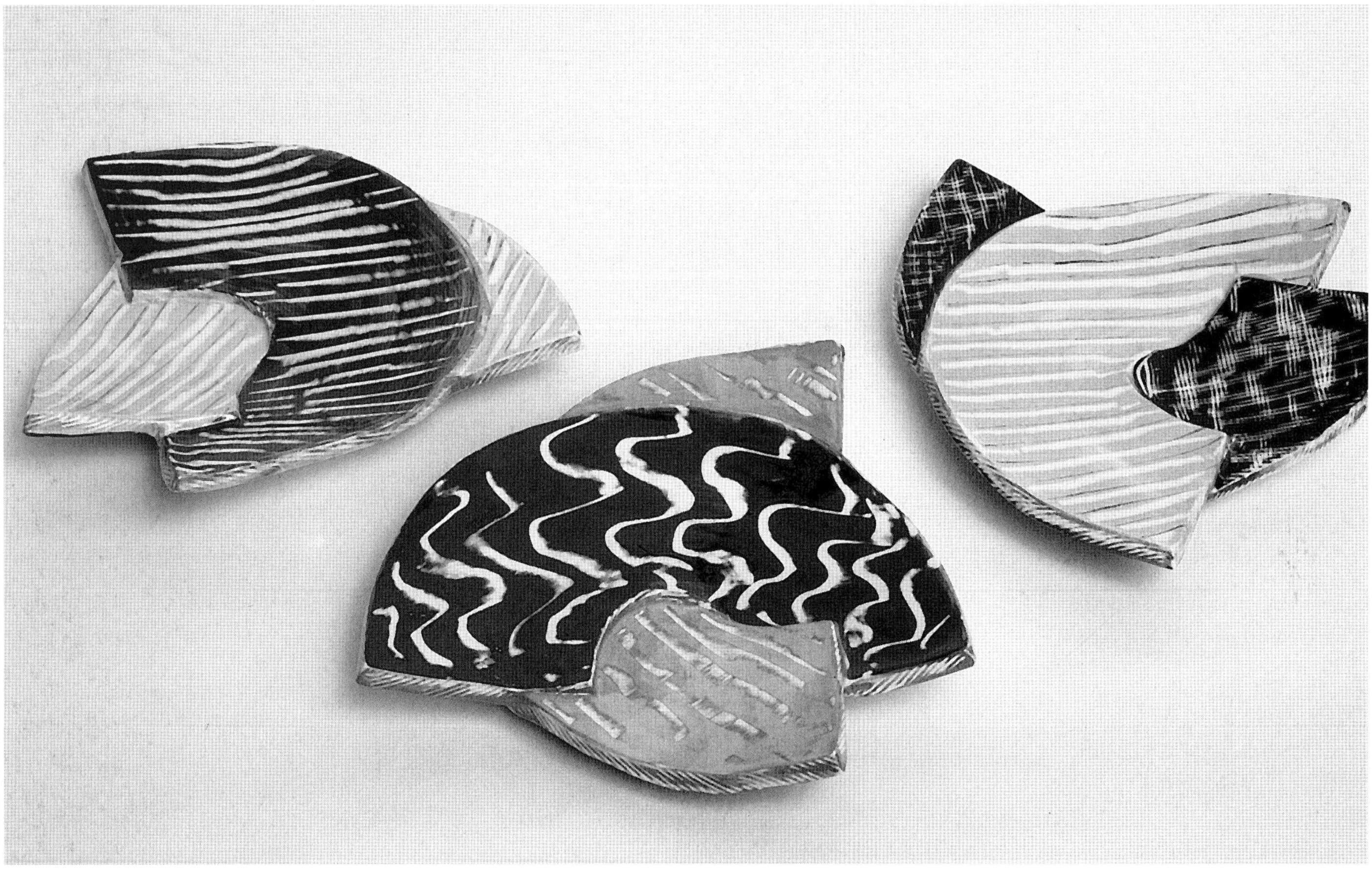

57 **Production Plates** 1980s

Clear glaze, coloured slips

Diam. 20 cm; 7.75 in

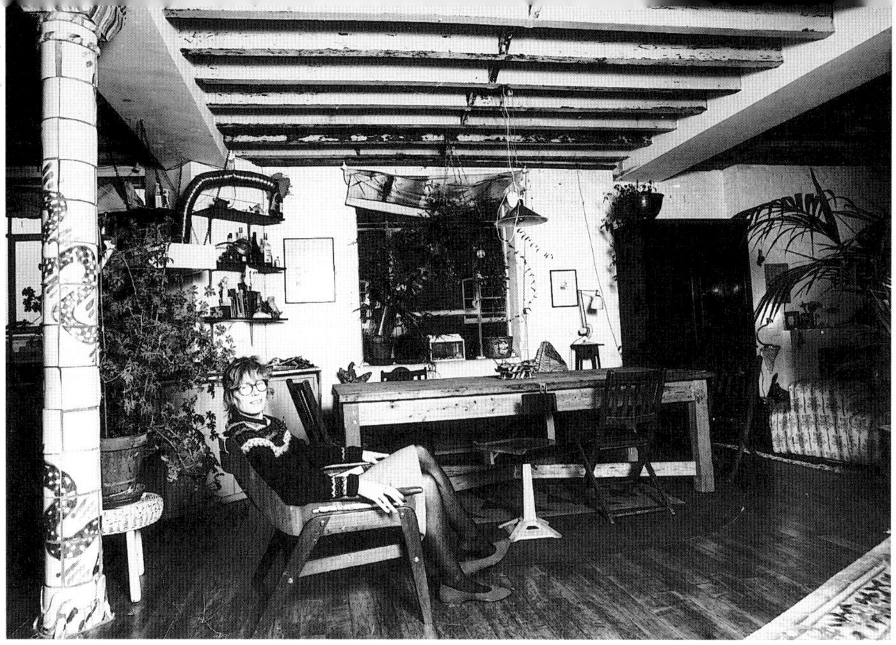

58 Interior of Carol McNicoll's flat designed by Piers Gough 1985
Photograph: Polly Eltes

The architectural feel of McNicoll's work in the 1980s was mirrored by her creation of a new studio and home at Apollo Works, a former piano factory in north London.[27] The original flat, completed in 1983 (58), was designed by the architect Piers Gough in exchange for a distinctly architectural teaset (39). The two interiors she created at Apollo Works – in 1983 and in 1995 – were in themselves works of art; a scaled-up extension of her pattern-making, collaging and salvaging activities (91). They remind us of the woman herself and her endlessly inventive spirit, in which the magus artist's tabula rasa is set aside in favour of playful experimentation with what already exists. As we shall see, this tendency to trawl, drift and wander through urban space was to come into its own in the late 1990s. But these predilections had always been apparent in her appearance – her clothes being an exquisite extension of herself.

Ornamentalism

Carol McNicoll returned from a trip to India recently with an altered, and much more negative, view of the English craft world.

(Alison Britton, *The Raw and the Cooked: New Work in Clay in Britain*, Museum Of Modern Art, Oxford, 1993)

At the end of 1990 McNicoll created ten richly decorated ceramic trophies for the ABSA/ Daily Telegraph Awards for Business and the Arts (59). These were presented to the lucky winners by the Duchess of York at the Royal National Theatre. It seemed an appropriate way to bid farewell to the enterprise culture of the 1980s. The trophies were fine examples of batch production and in 1991, after the first of three visits to India, McNicoll decided to abandon making unique objects and to return to serial production pieces.

In India she had seen a rich craft culture making remarkable objects for use that made her more complex individual pieces seem irrelevant. This was hardly a turn towards austerity, but the decision to make both production and function central had the odd effect of

59 **ABSA/Daily Telegraph Award for Business and the Arts** 1990

Slip cast earthenware
One of an edition of ten, clear glaze, coloured slips
45 x 33 x 15 cm;
17.75 x 12.75 x 5.75 in

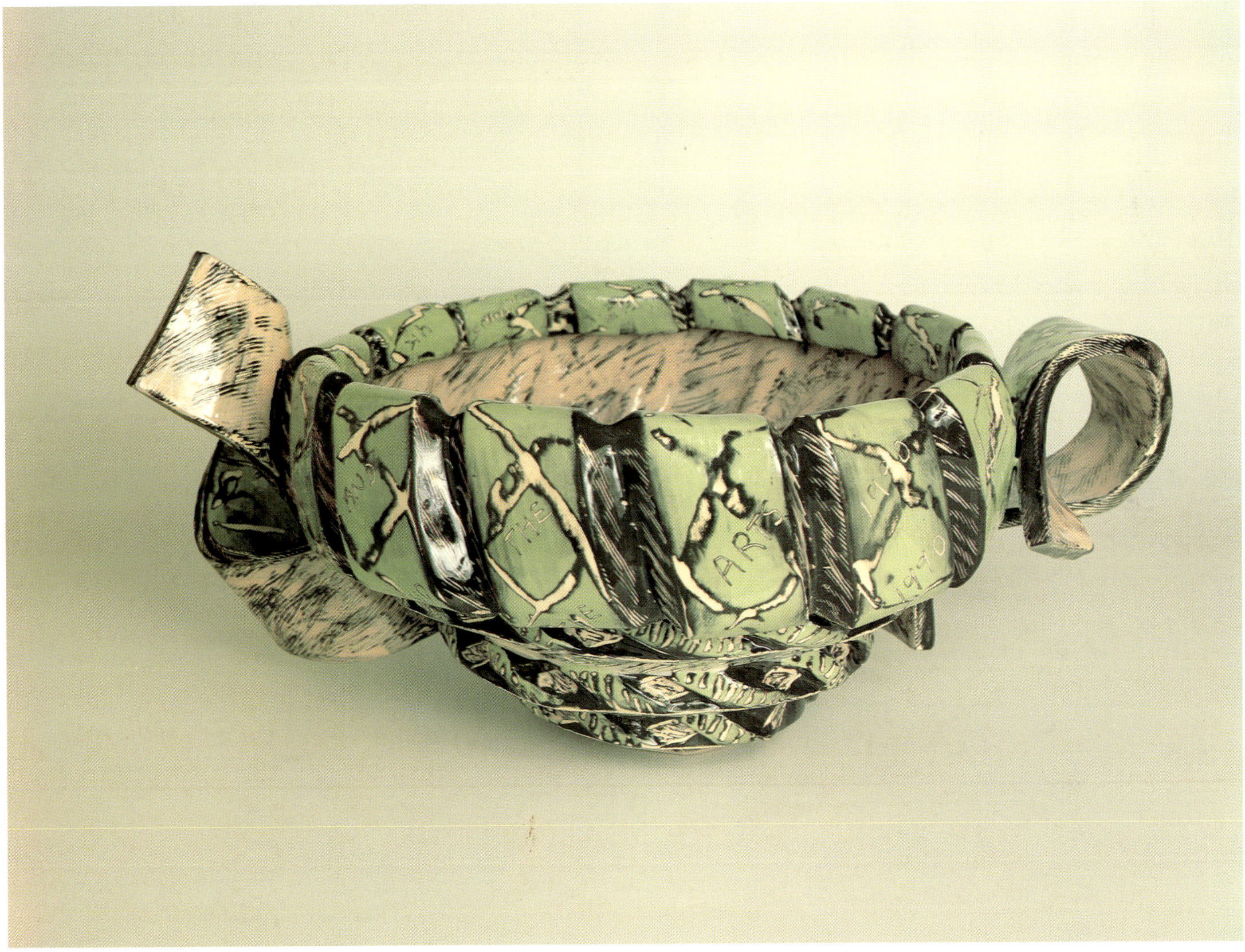

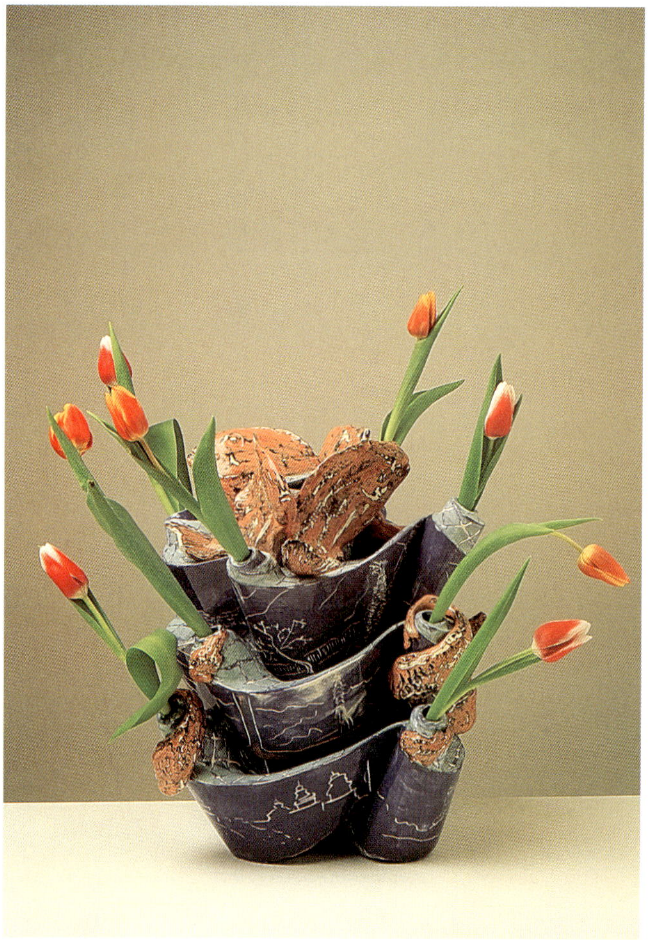

60 **Ladakh Tulip Pot** 1993
Slip cast earthenware
Clear glaze, coloured slips, sgraffito drawings
H. 25 cm; 9.75 in
Photograph: David Cripps

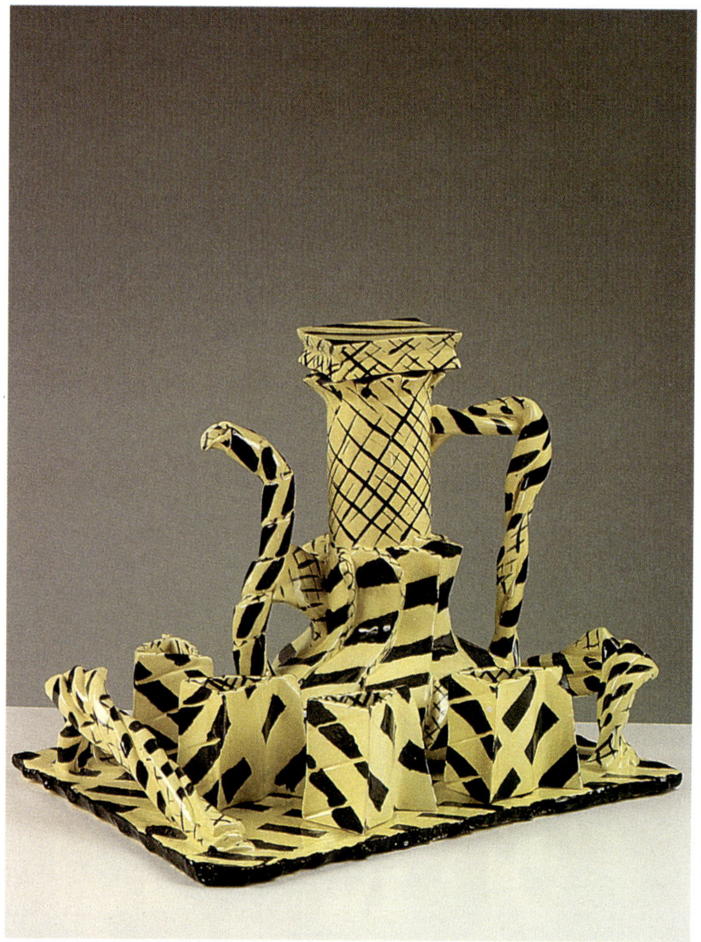

61 **Yellow Coffee Set with Tray** 1991
Slip cast earthenware
Clear glaze, coloured slips
H. of pot 29 cm; 11.5 in
Collection: Crafts Council
Photograph: David Cripps

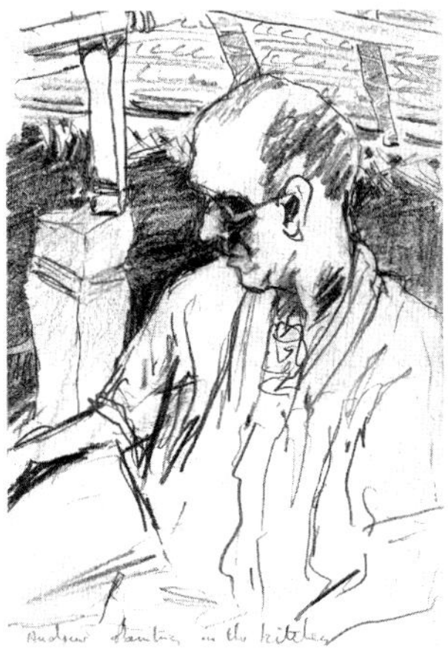

62 Page from Carol McNicoll's Sketch Book, 1994
Collection: the Artist

making her work look more focused and, perhaps surprisingly, more radical. After all, 'function' did not need to be quotidian. In 1993 she made a series of stacking tulip vases, inspired by seventeenth-century Delft potters' responses to Dutch tulip mania. Her yellow and black *Coffee Set* of 1991 on a ceramic tray (61: the tall coffee pot was based on a Middle Eastern metal vessel), set an absolute standard of bold form at a time when both the industry and the world of studio pottery had decided that coffee sets were commercially redundant. In effect she was ranging though the history of domestic forms, keeping the self-expression that had developed in the 1980s in check by studying historical responses to human needs.

Nevertheless, a new ornamental richness was developing. Parts of the tulip vases were cast from marbled coloured slip. There were also passages of sgraffito landscape scraped through a deep blue ground. Until the early 1990s her surface decoration had always taken the form of abstract pattern – for which she had a real, unselfconscious genius. But on her visit to India she began to draw. By 1994 the idea of making pattern with representational motifs developed, inspired by memories of two exhibitions seen exactly a decade earlier – the MOMA show, *Art into Production: Soviet Textiles, Fashion and Ceramics* (which included a range of inter-war textiles printed with repeat propagandist images of biplanes and Red Army soldiers harvesting cotton) and the Arts Council's *Raoul Dufy*, which had devoted a generous section to the painter's textile designs. Drawing became a passion and once a week she and the potter and painter Ewen Henderson drew from a model. She had transfers made out of her drawings. Some were disciplined into pattern, and others, like the images on the vases *Jacqui on the Beach* and *Trip to India* of 1998 (63 and 64) were presented as straightforward pictorial designs to be studied and admired.

Drawing appears to have affected her work in other ways too. She created a number of taut, complex functional designs. One was *Soft Jug* of 1996 (71), an apparent riposte to her *Unravelling Jug* of 1980 (36), in which an unyielding angular handle reaches round and compresses the pliable looking vessel. In the same year a series of tiny teacups combined

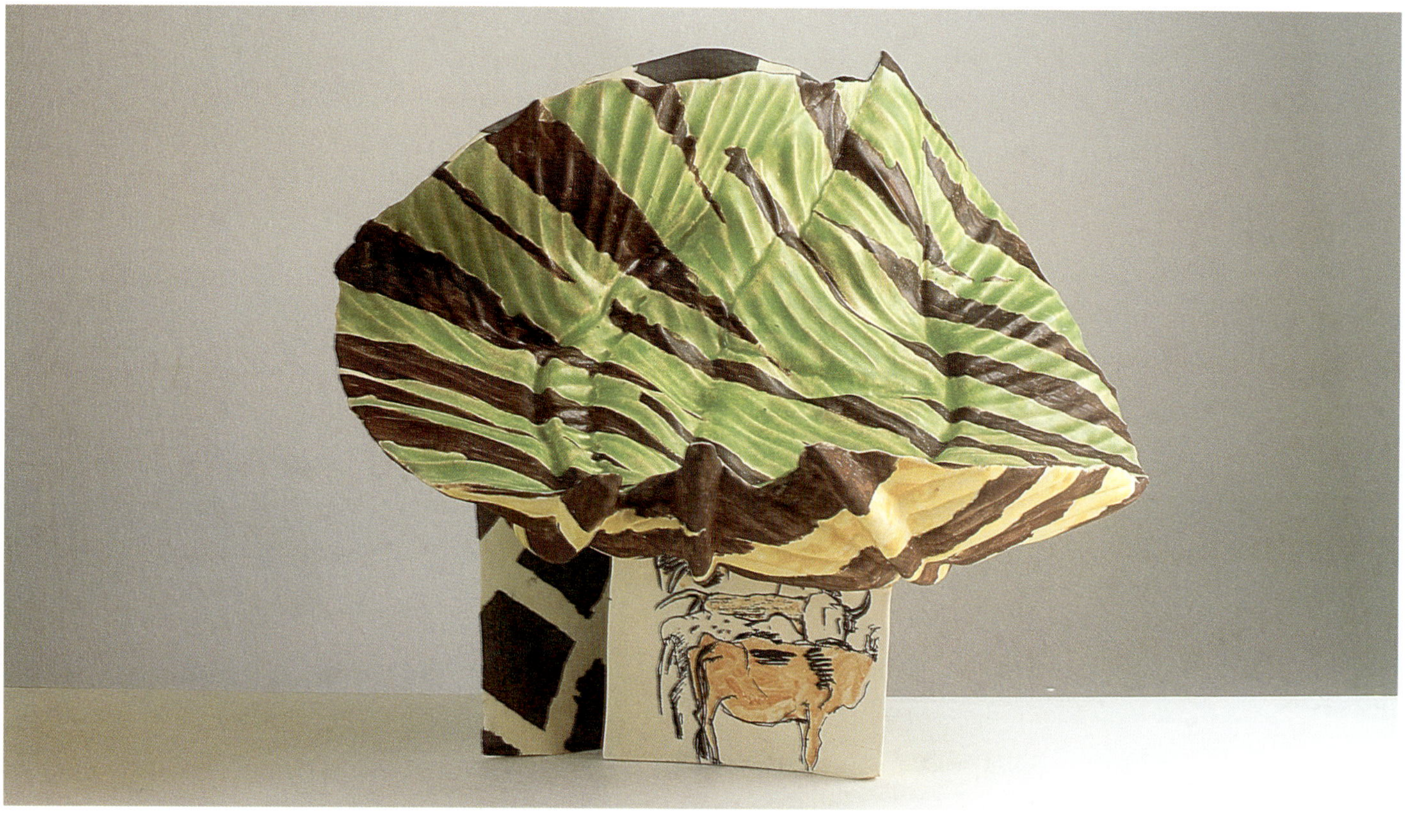

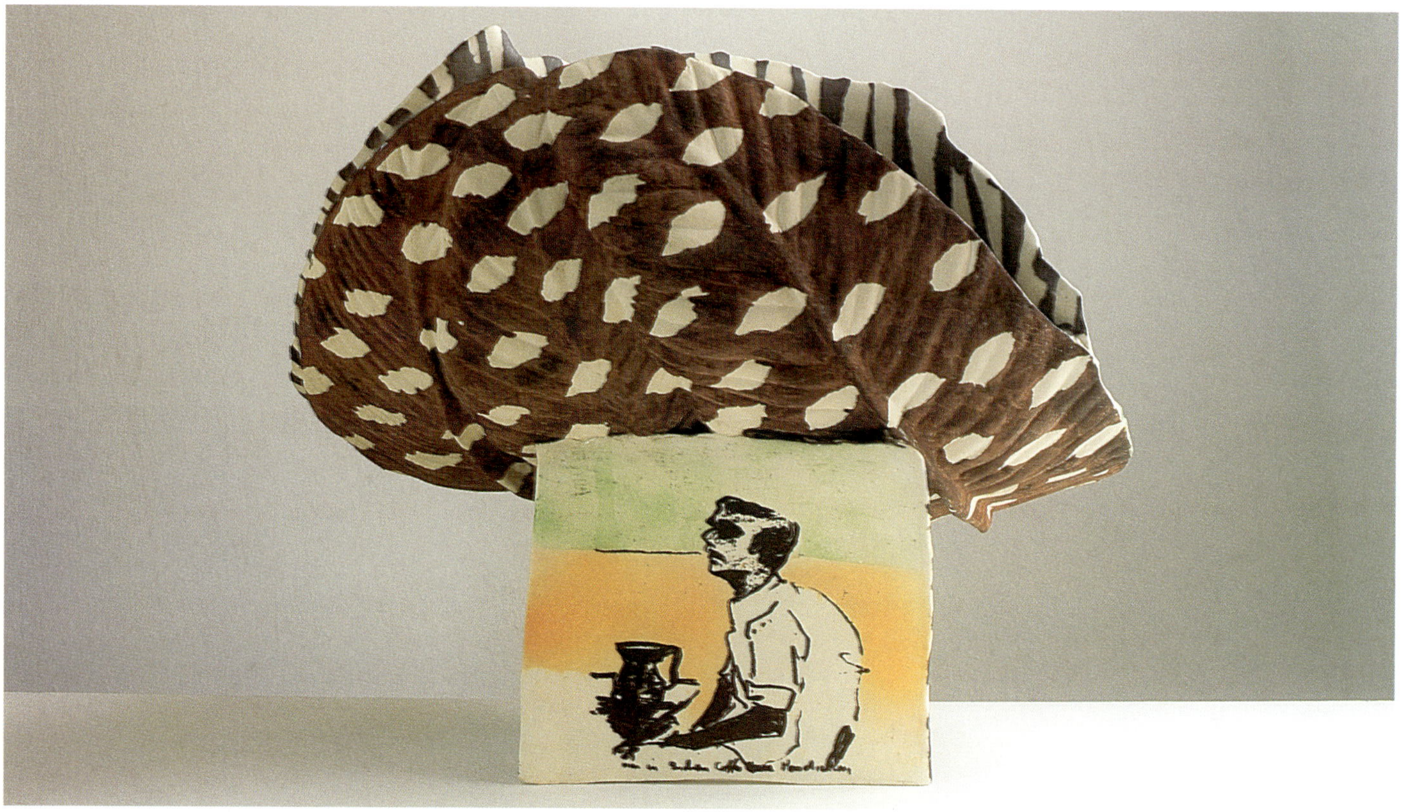

above
63 **Jacqui on the Beach** 1998
One-off, slip cast and assembled, stoneware glazes, transfers made from drawings by Carol McNicoll
H. 30 cm; 11.75 in
Collection: Mark Grainer
Photograph: David Cripps

below
64 **Trip to India** 1998
One-off, slip cast and assembled, stoneware glazes, transfers made from drawings by Carol McNicoll
H. 30 cm; 11.75 in
Photograph: David Cripps

boldly decorated slip cast earthenware with foliate unglazed red earthenware handles (65). These were shown to good effect beside porcelain domestic ware by Edmund de Waal in the 1996 show *Objects of Our Time.* The juxtaposition serves to remind us that the dominant ceramic aesthetic of the late 1990s centred on neo-orientalist, minimalist porcelain. This so-called 'new white' movement in ceramics had the effect of making much studio pottery look contextless and overblown, too anxiously striving to be art. But McNicoll was able to match this historicist call-to-order with a robust equivalent equally informed by the past. Thus, in collaboration with Steven Newell, she designed a series of glass jugs (66 and 67) in the language of central European Art Nouveau. Arguably it was the practice of drawing that gave her a new confidence in design and a sense of art historical continuity.

In addition, she was keenly aware of developments in other disciplines in the 1990s, particularly the odd interactions between material culture studies, anthropology and the fine art world. Her compulsive wanderings round flea markets and junk shops went hand in hand with her strongly nuanced sensibility concerning things and their odd trajectories from high social value to ambiguous status to the category of rubbish. The anthropological observation that 'objects create mediated relations'[28] was unconsciously intrinsic to her thinking. In 1998 she made a couple of teapots – *Tea for One* and *Tea for Two* (68 and 69) – incorporating found teacups to do duty both as teapot lids and as constituent parts of a tea service. A year later she was given a little turbaned figure – a shorthand depiction of a 'native' – that had probably once held a box of tea in a grocer's window. This stereotypical 'native' became the first of a series of 'resonant objects' to be cast in multiple to form part of a remarkable series of bowls and vases.

65 **Teapot with Terracotta Lid, Cups with Terracotta Handles** 1996
Slip cast earthenware
Unglazed press moulded terracotta, clear glaze coloured slips
Teapot 20 x 13 cm; 7.75 x 5 in
Photograph: David Cripps

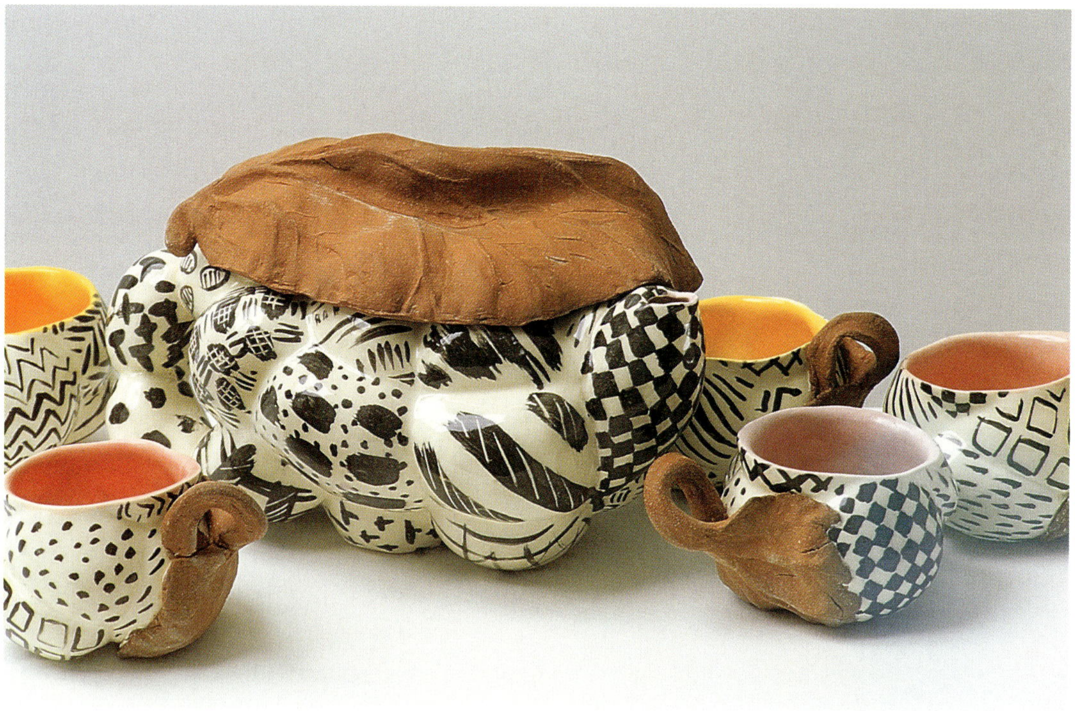

66 **Glass Jug** 1997
Glass blown into mould and free-blown, made in collaboration with Steven Newell
H. 35.5 cm; 14 in
Photograph: David Cripps

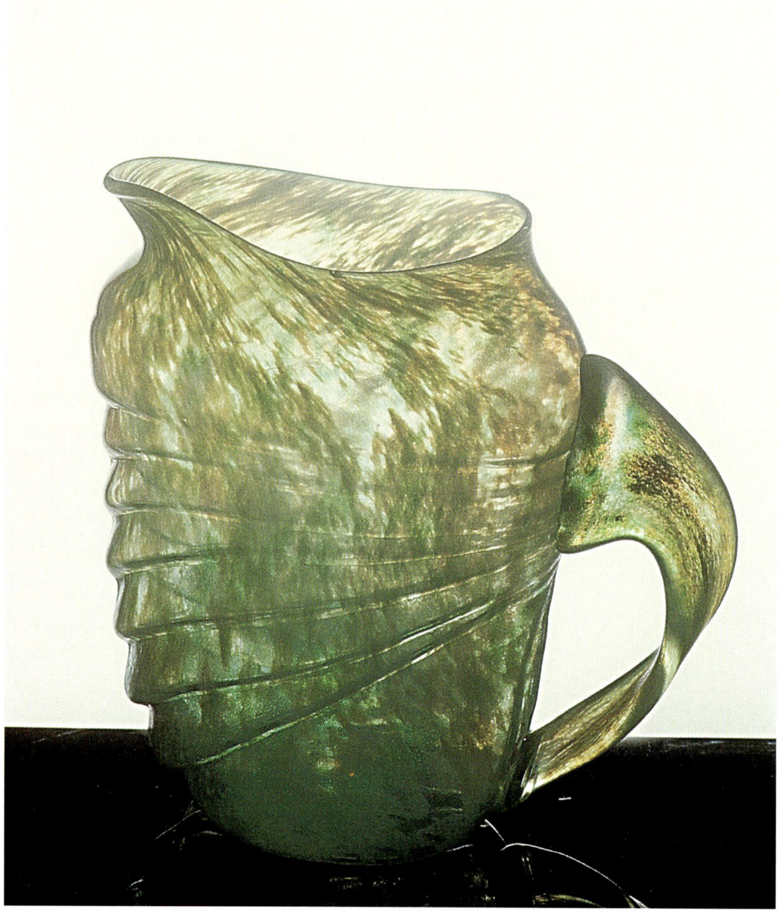

opposite
67 **Glass Jug** 1992
Glass blown into mould and free-blown, made in collaboration with Steven Newell
H. 35.5 cm; 14 in
Photograph: David Cripps

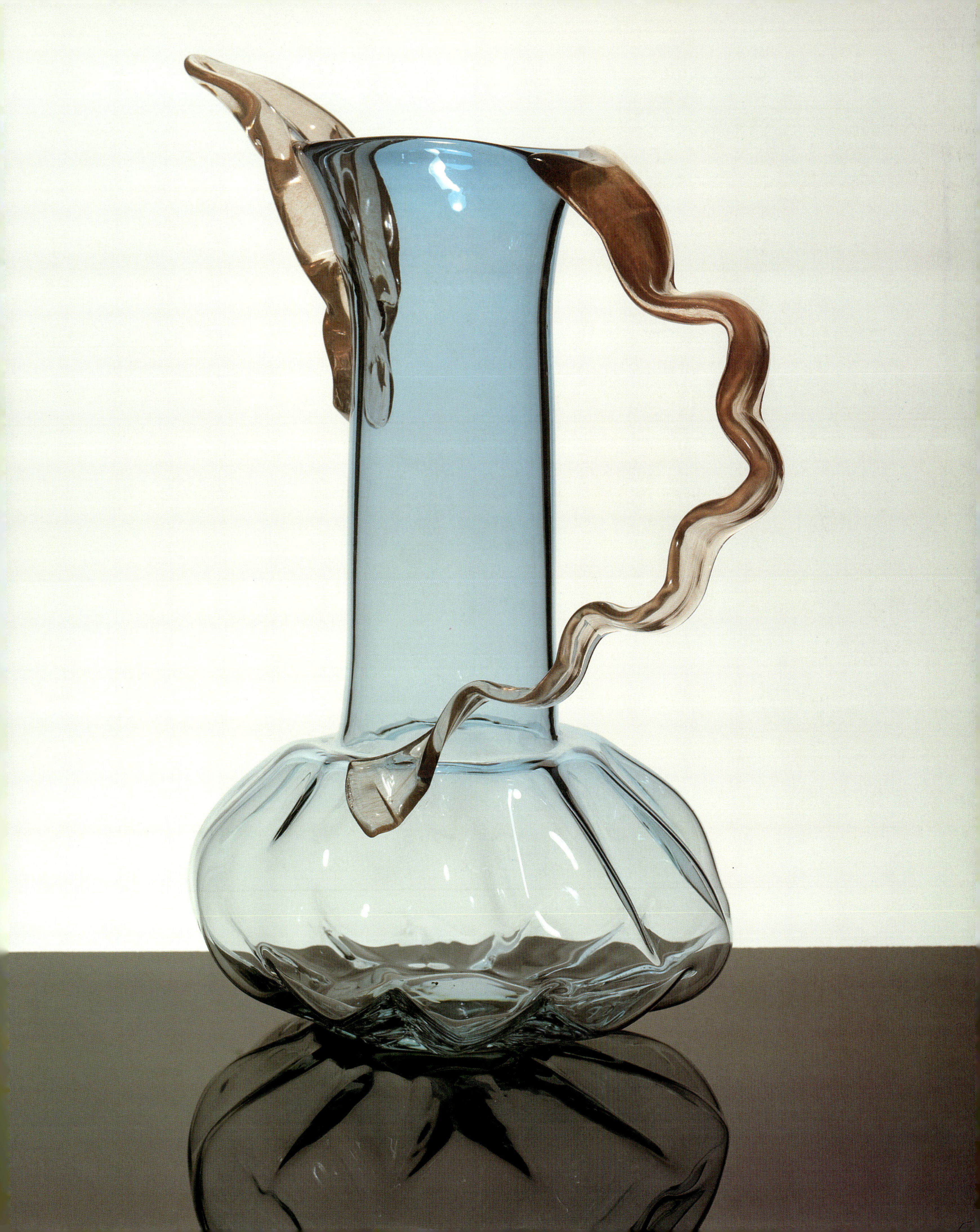

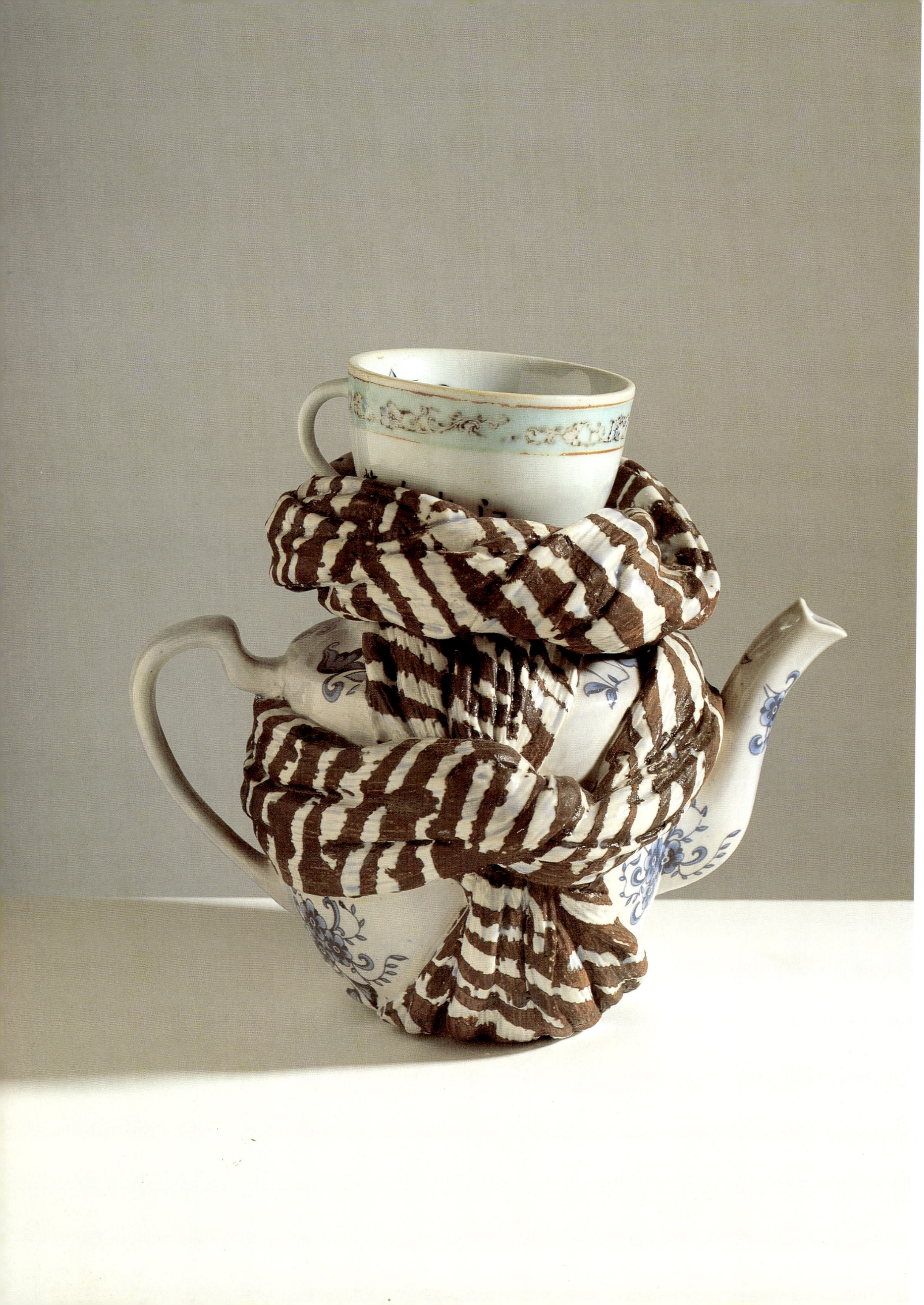

opposite

68 **Tea for One** 1998

Commercial teacup, slip cast, stoneware glaze, transfers, clear glaze

H. 22 cm; 8.5 in

Collection: Ed Wolf

Photograph: David Cripps

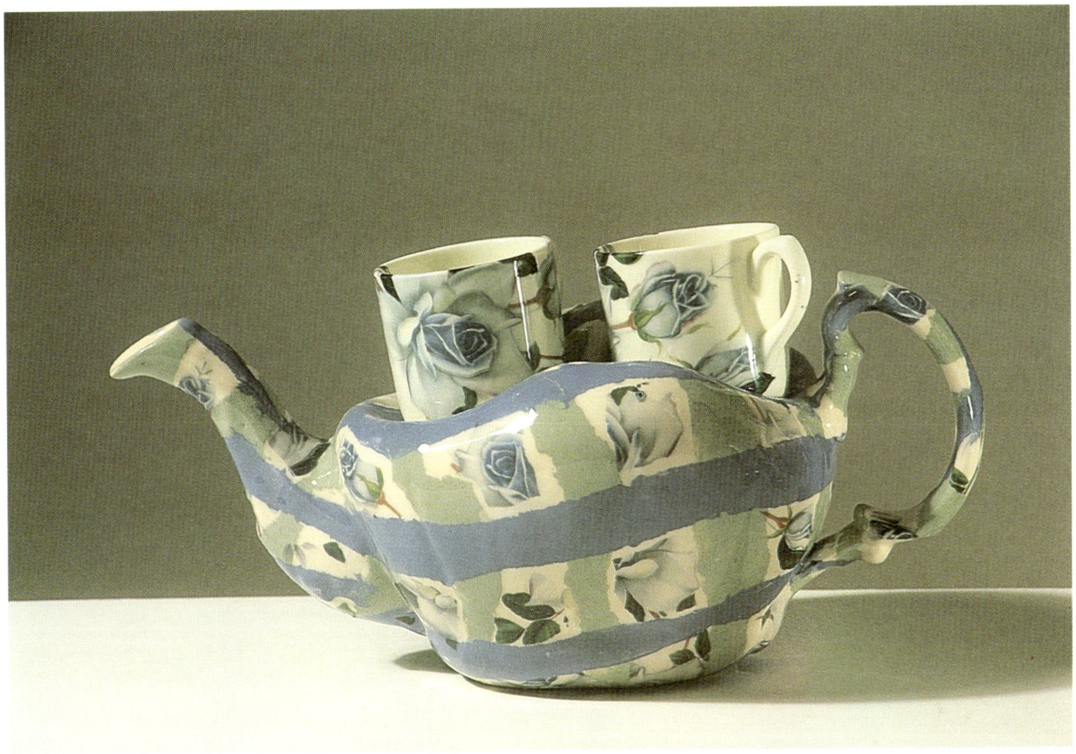

69 **Tea for Two** 1998

Commercial teacups, slip cast earthenware, coloured slips, transfers, clear glaze

H. 18 cm; 7 in

Photograph: David Cripps

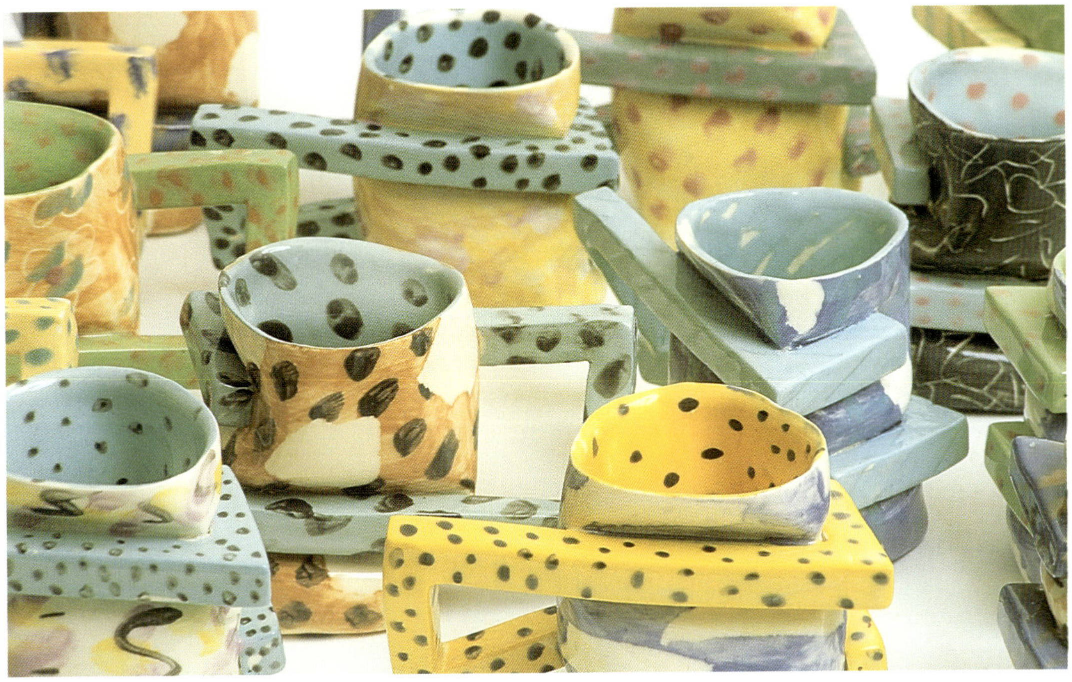

70 **Soft Mugs (Square Handled)** 1990s

Slip cast earthenware

Clear glaze, coloured slips

Photograph: David Cripps

71 **Two Soft Jugs (Square Handled)** 1990s
Slip cast earthenware
Clear glaze, coloured slips
H. 20.5 cm; 8 in
Photograph: David Cripps

Knick-knacks

In an age of information technology, making things by hand is a supremely anachronistic occupation. The first world has relegated the unglamorous and unprofitable activity of production to the third world, reserving the cleaner and more lucrative manipulation of information for itself. The capacity for making things has always seemed to me to be a defining human characteristic. I now realise that its expression is a great luxury which is only available to the very poor, the very rich or the very foolish. I count myself as one of the very foolish, still believing it is possible to make a living as a potter, while the rest of the first world is engaged in e-commerce. The home, a context the cutting edge of the art world abandoned around 1945, is the context I find the most intriguing.

(Carol McNicoll statement in *British Ceramics*, exh.cat., Rhodos/Keramikmuseet Grimmerhus, Denmark, 2000)

In 1999 the then Tate Gallery launched a touring exhibition entitled *At Home with Art*. Nine sculptors had been invited to conceive a work that could be mass produced for the home. These were to be made available at the DIY store Homebase. It was a well-intentioned project but arguably misconceived, not least because it seemed that few of the invited artists saw the home as a challenging site for creative practice. An air of embarrassment hung about the whole venture. Perhaps the project's organiser, Colin Painter, had simply picked the wrong collaborators. Certainly, by the late 1990s significant numbers of artists began to create art through processes associated with craft and design and displayed a marked interest in domestic objects and in consumption as a dominant representational paradigm. The resulting work could involve adapting existing materials or copying and replicating existing objects. Much of this work was concerned with process, with procedures for making art in difficult times, art for a full world.[29] Much of it interrogated our assumptions about 'home'.

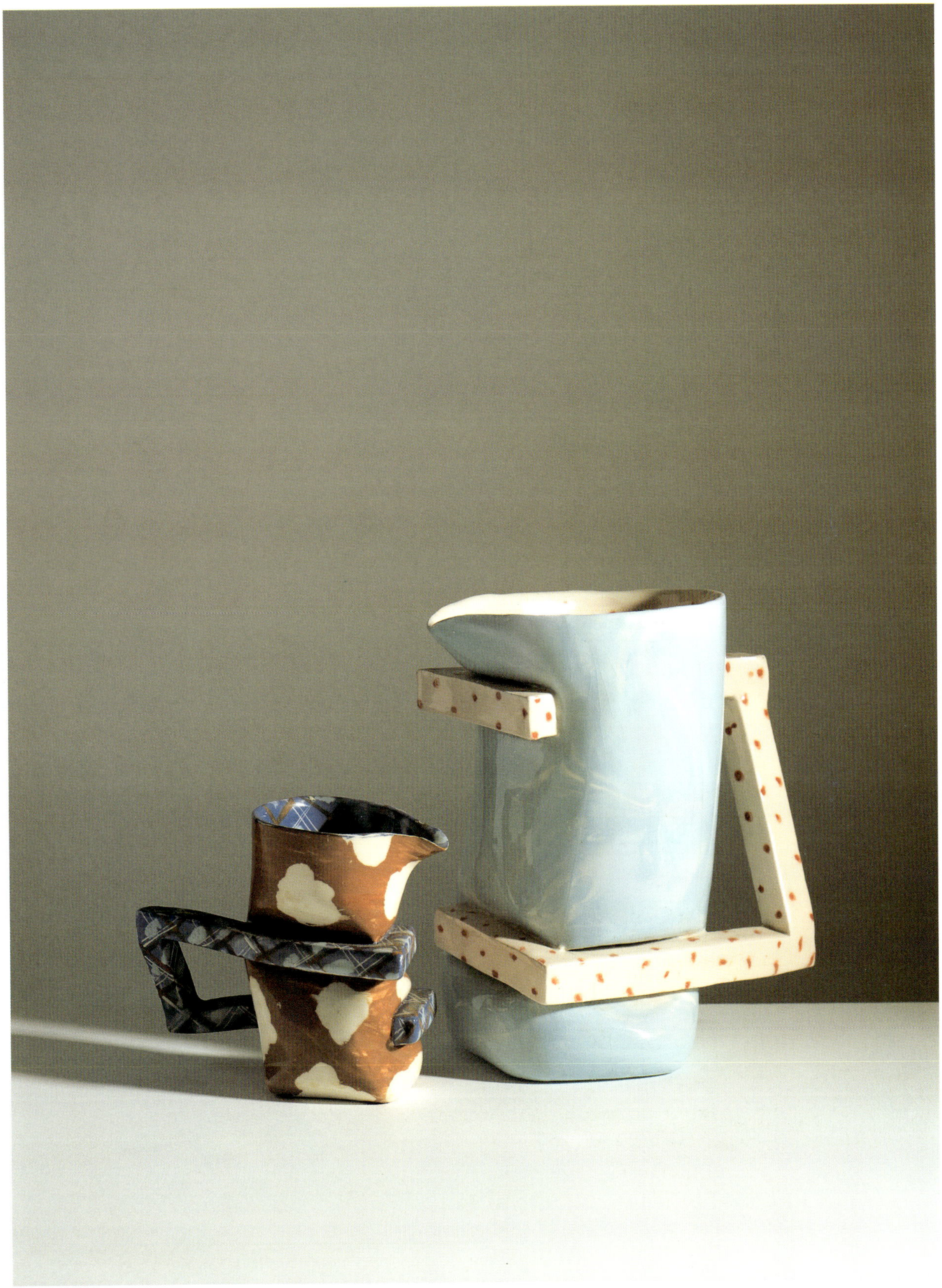

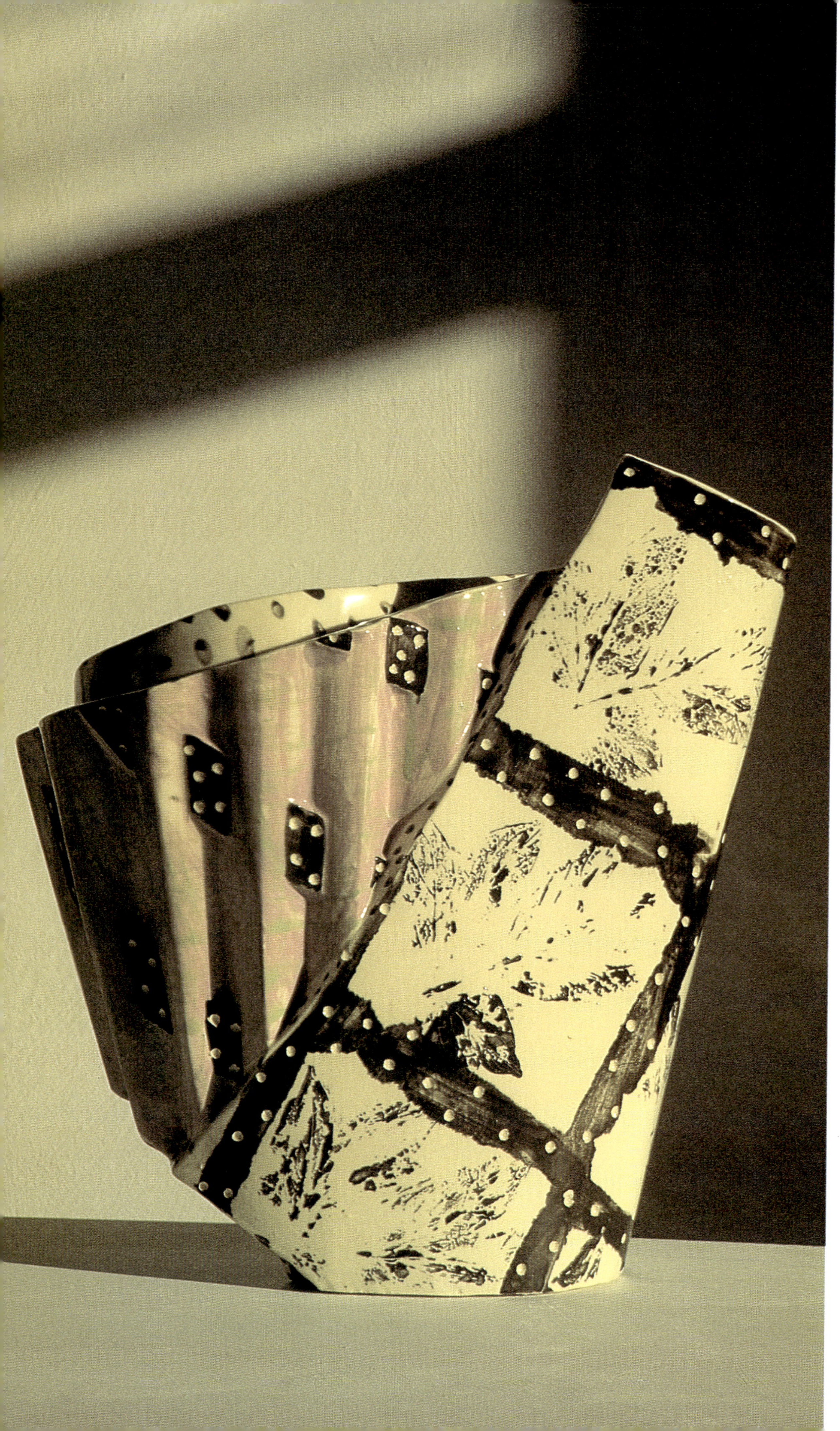

opposite

72 **Vase** 1995

Slip cast earthenware
Clear glaze, coloured slips and underglaze
H. 24 cm; 9.5 in
Photograph: David Cripps

73 **Jug and Mug** 1990s

Stoneware glazes, coloured slips, slip cast, clear glaze
Photograph: David Cripps

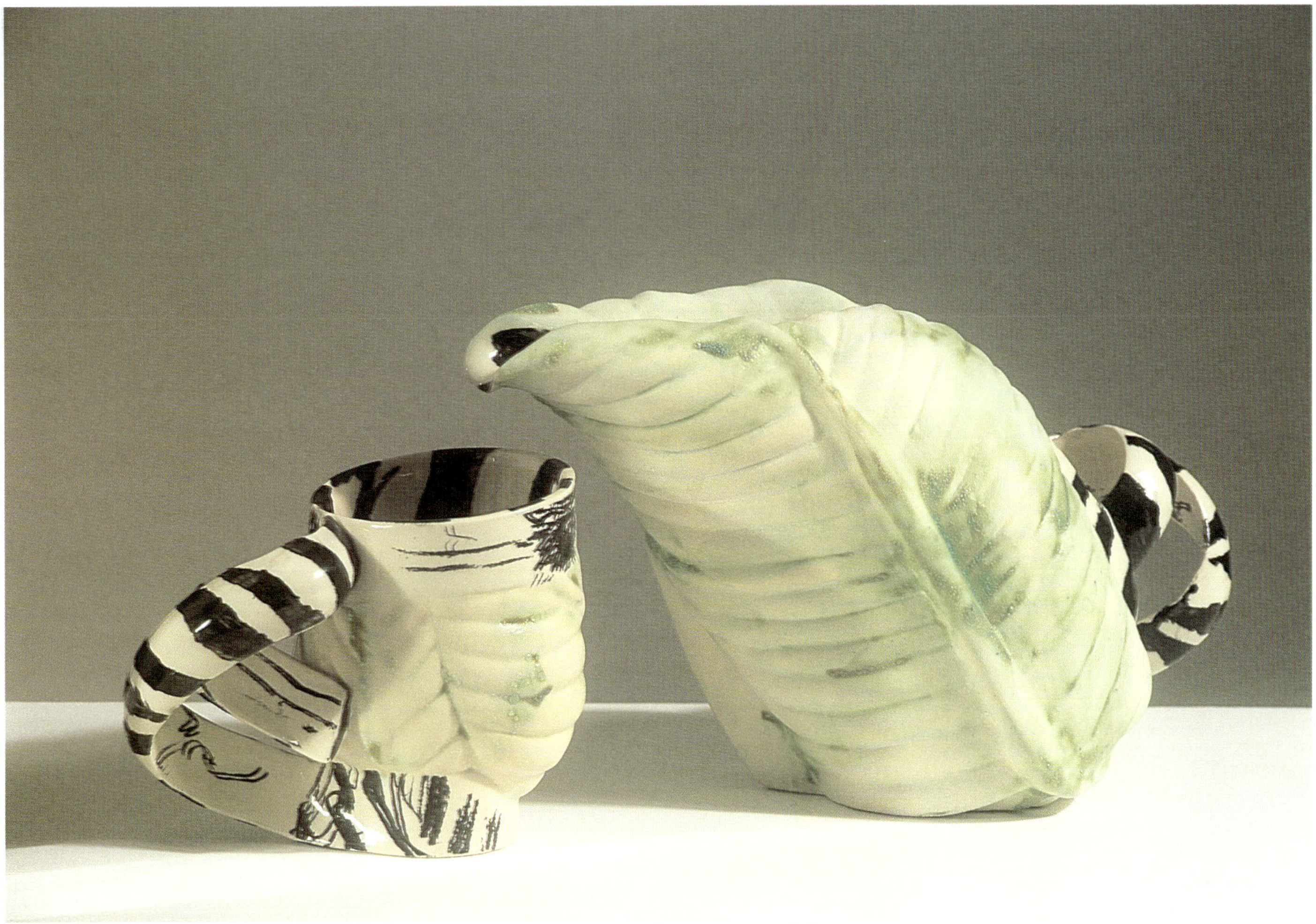

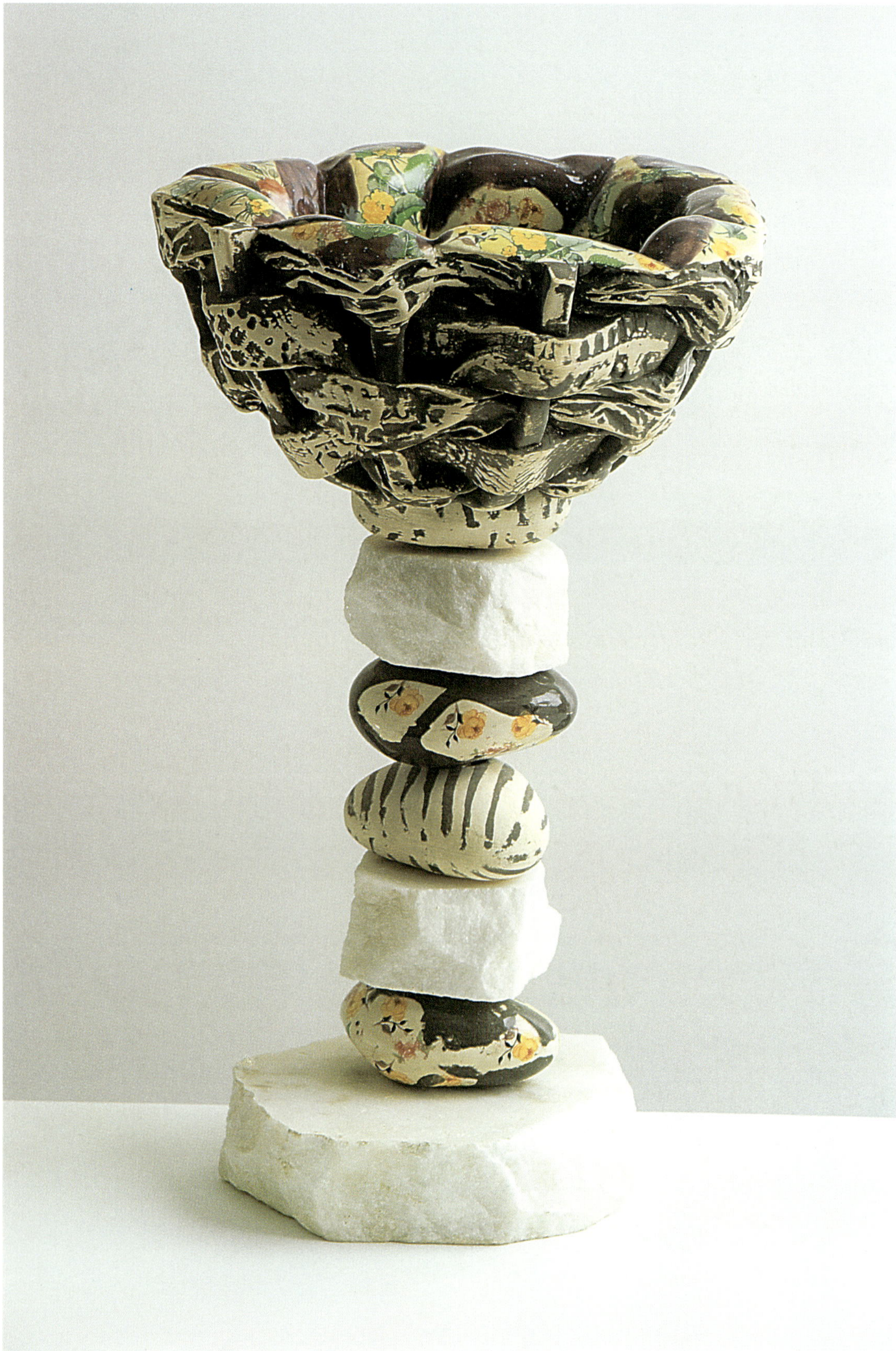

opposite

74 **Fruit Bowl** 1996

One-off, slip cast, marble, bolted metal rod, clear glaze, coloured slips, transfers
34 x 20 cm; 13.25 x 7.75 in
Collection: Pat Barnes
Photograph: David Cripps

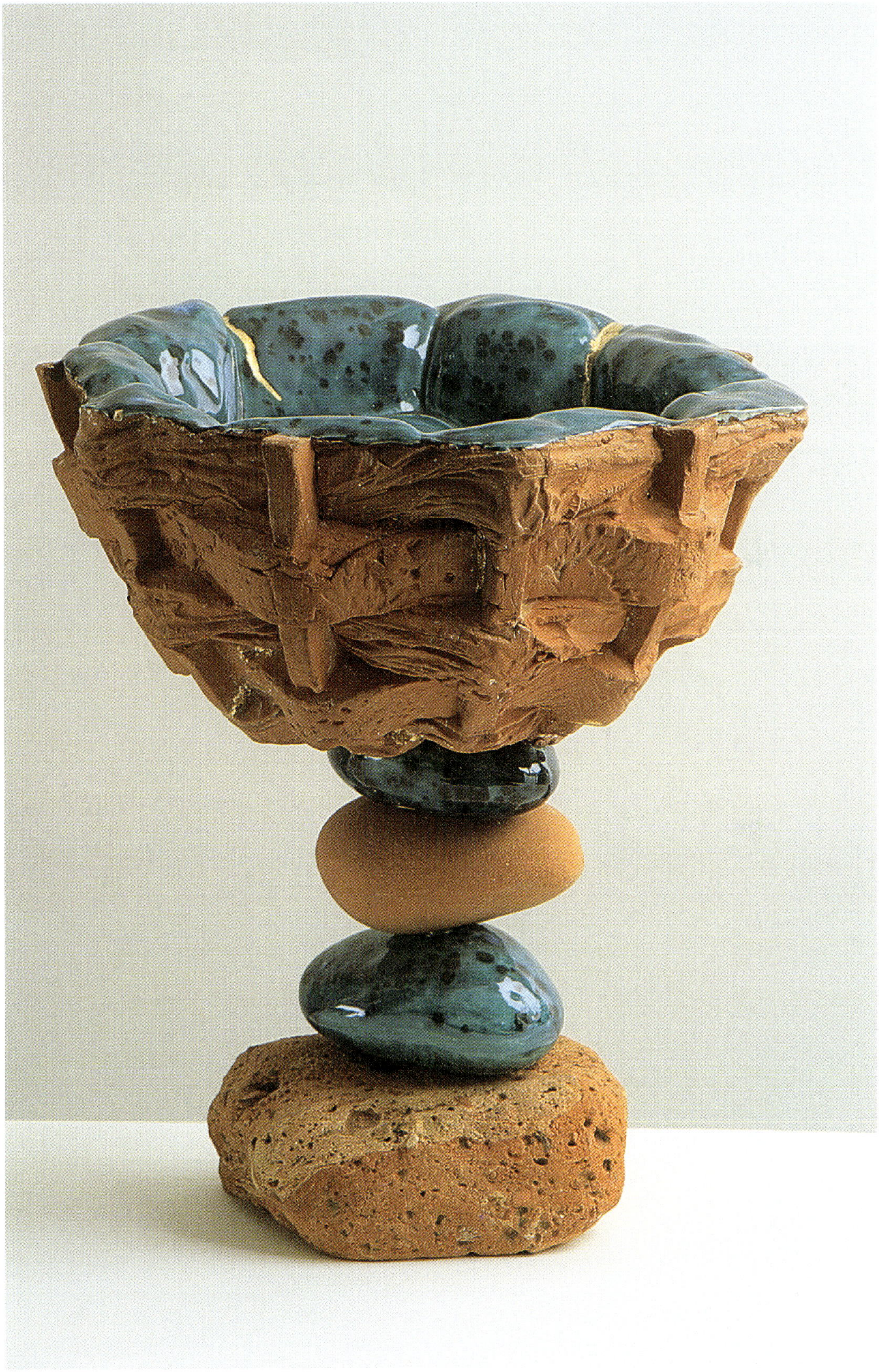

75 **Fruit Bowl** 1997

One-off, salvaged water-worn brick, bolted metal rod, press-moulded terracotta, slip cast earthenware, glaze and gold leaf
23 x 20 cm; 9 x 7.75 in
Collection: Glenys Barton
Photograph: David Cripps

76 **Jug and Mugs** 1997

Slip cast

Stoneware glazes and enamel

H. of jug 23 cm; 9 in

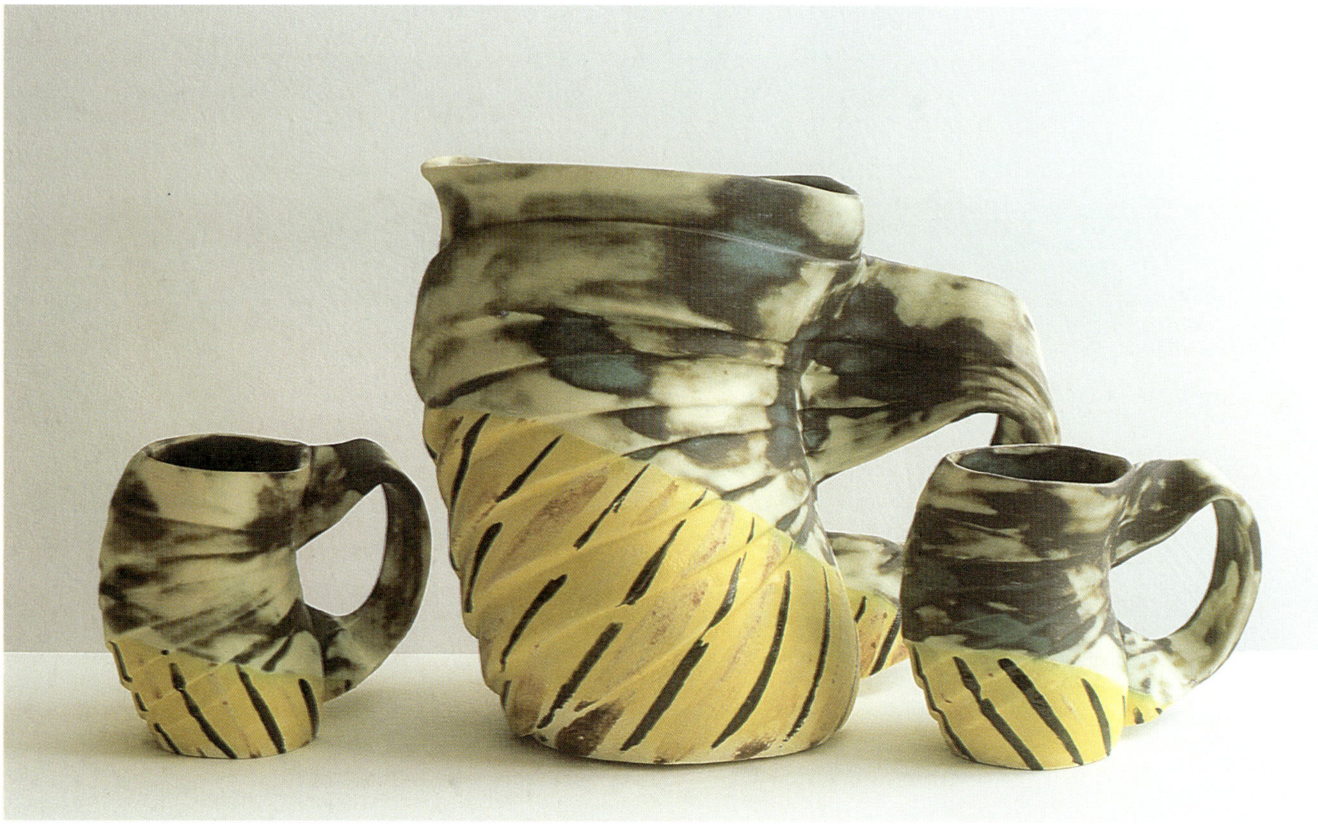

77 **Vase** 1997
Slip cast
One-off, stoneware glazes,
coloured slips, transfers
H. 40 cm; 15.75 in
Collection: the Artist
Photograph: David Cripps

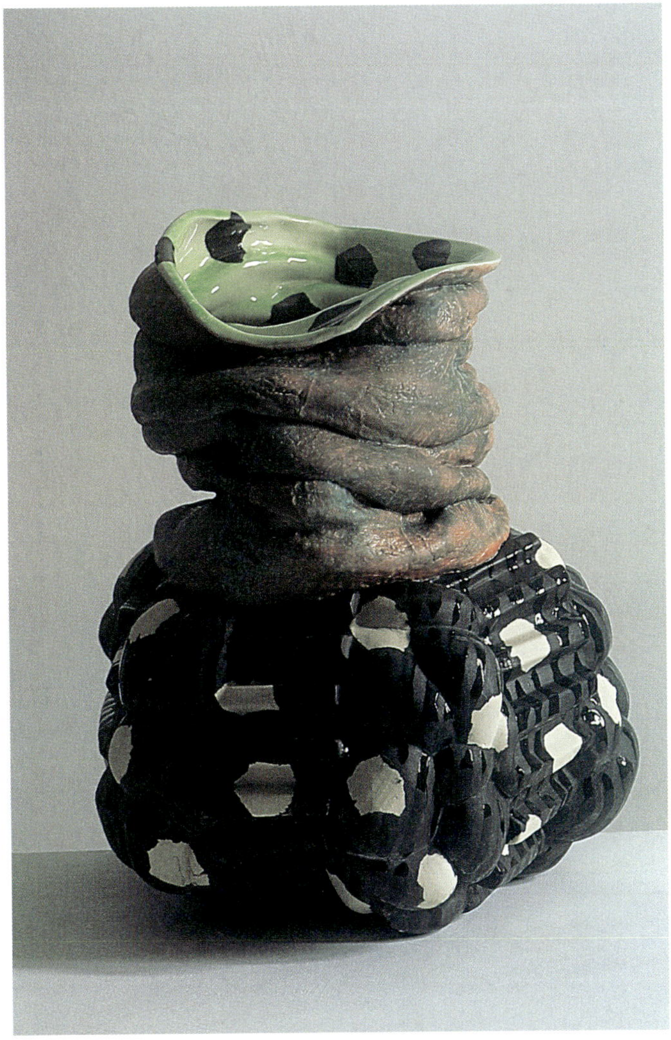

82

78 **Barcelona Vase** 1998

One-off, press-mould terracotta base bolted to slip cast vase, stoneware glazes, transfers, underglaze colour
Collection: Mark Grainer
Photograph: David Cripps

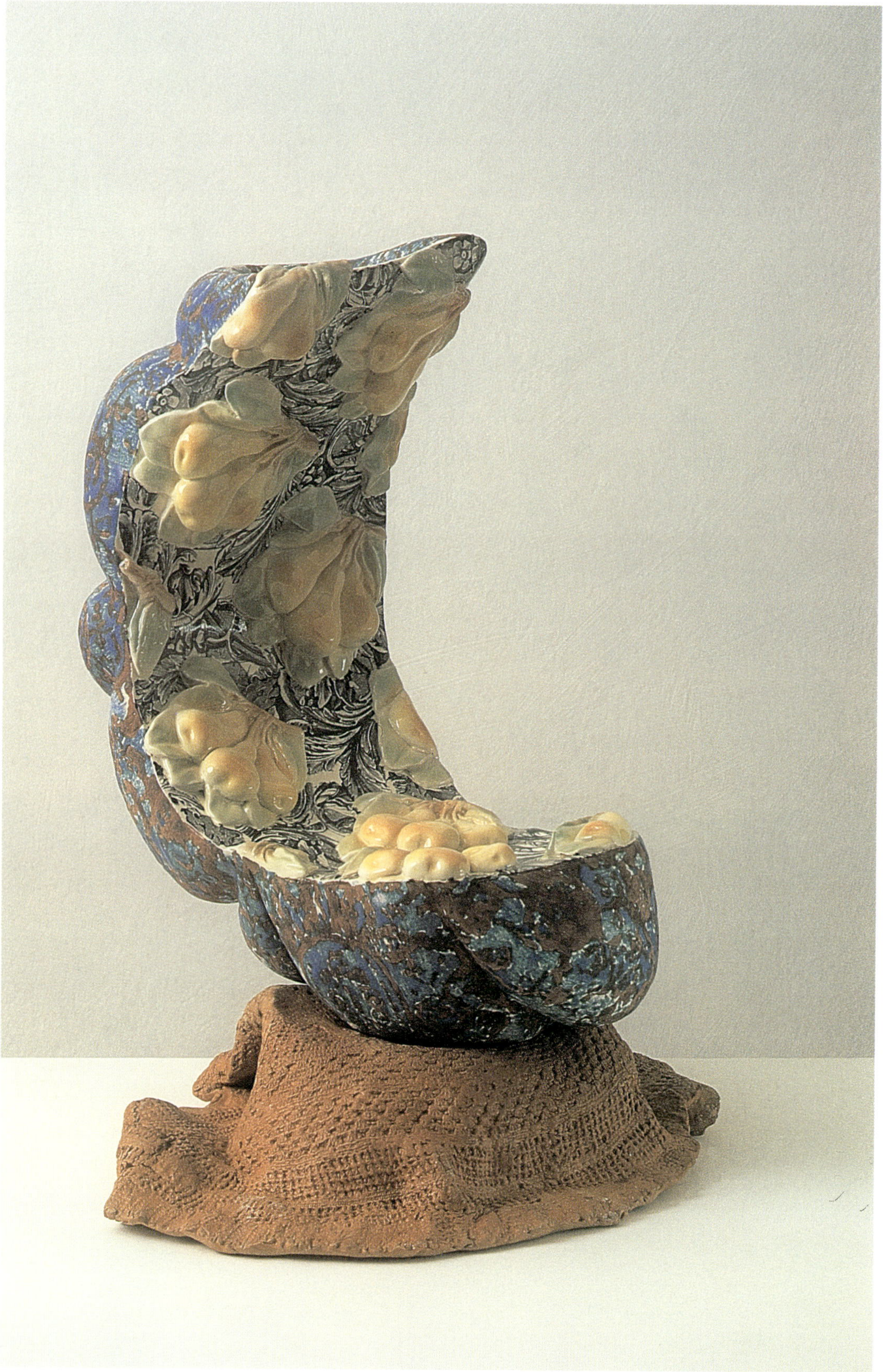

79 **Rudbeckia Dish** 1999
One-off, press-moulded terracotta
base bolted to slip cast bowl,
stoneware glazes, transfers,
underglaze colour, clear glaze
28 x 28 cm; 11 x 11 in
Collection: Ed Wolf
Photograph: David Cripps

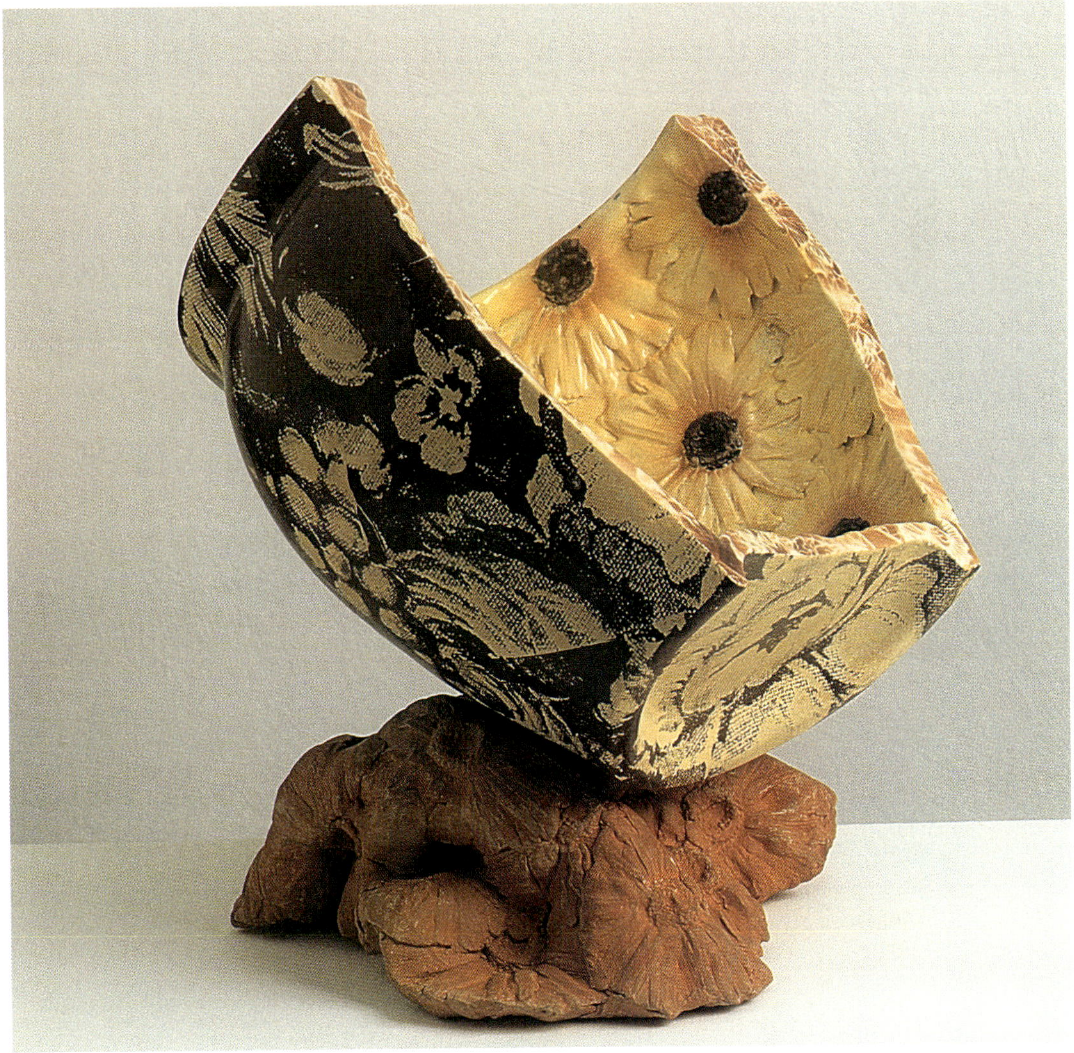

80 **Teapot Dish** (front view) 1999
One-off, slip cast, assembled, clear glaze, underglaze colour, transfers
33 x 23 cm; 13 x 9 in
Collection: Crafts Council

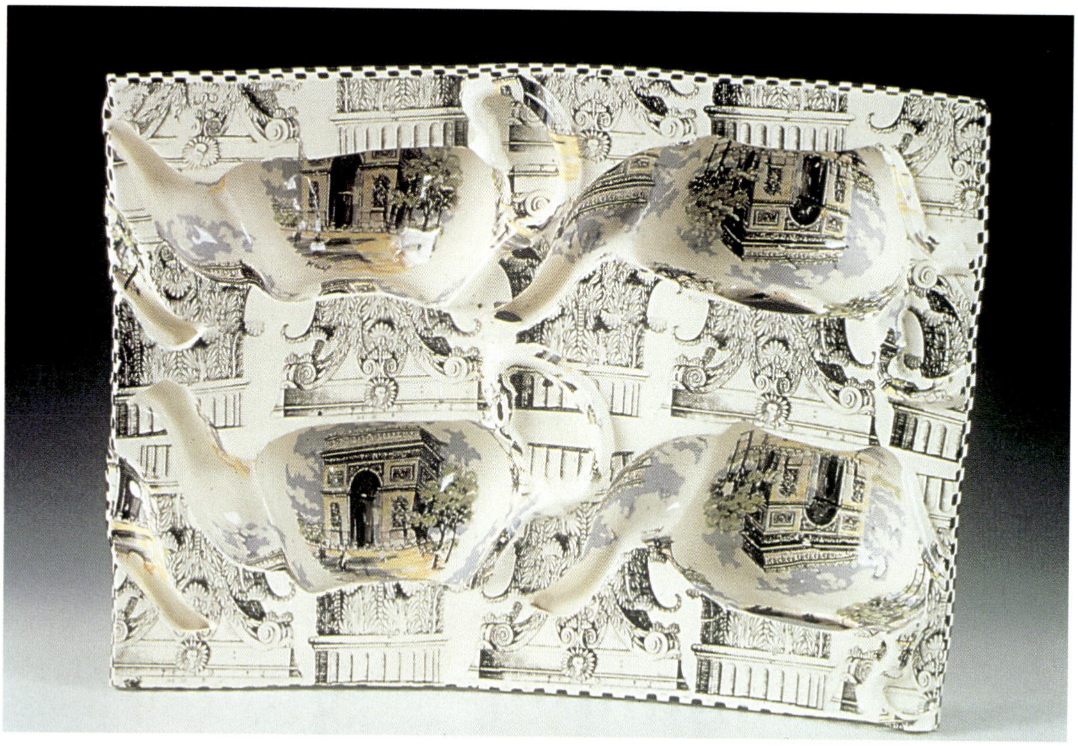

81 **Teapot Dish** (back view) 1999
One-off, slip cast, assembled, clear glaze, underglaze colour, transfers
33 x 23 cm; 13 x 9 in
Collection: Crafts Council
(The glaze is in different colours on the back and front of this work)

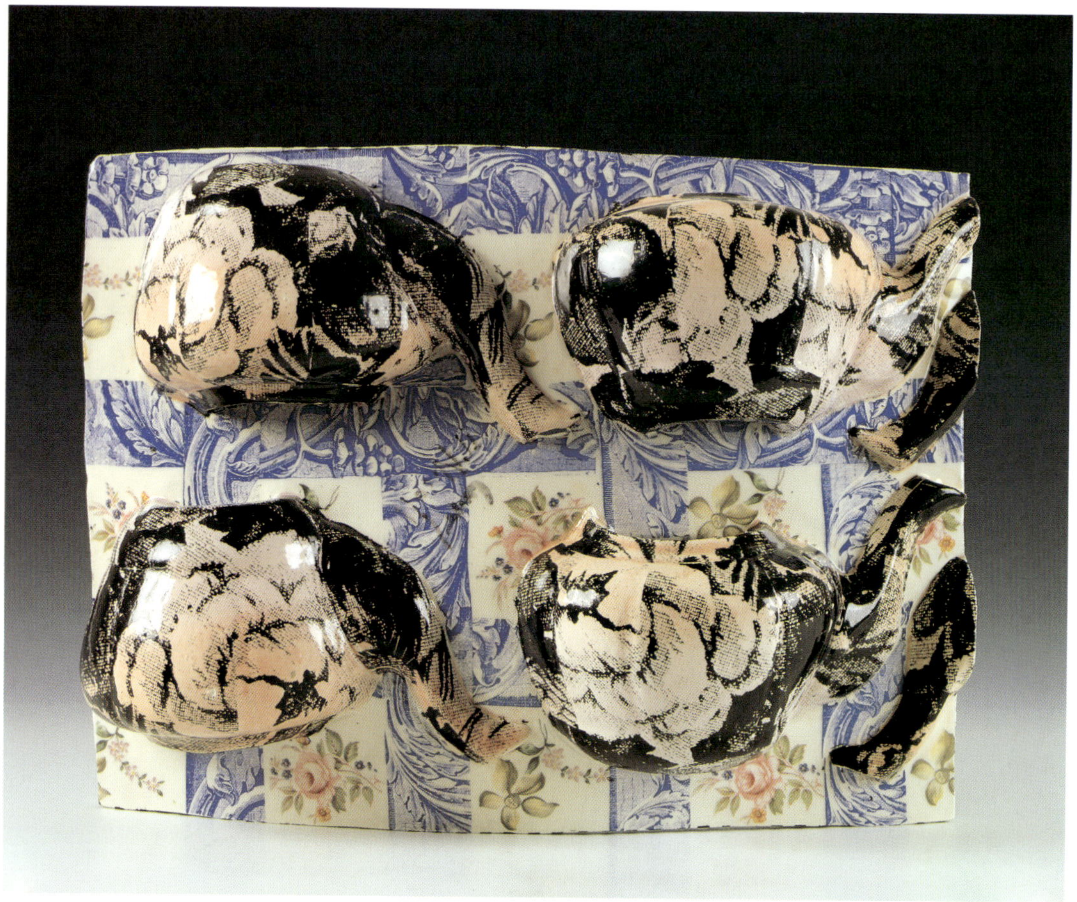

opposite
82 **Teacups** 1990s
Slip cast
Clear glaze, coloured slips, transfers
H. 15 cm; 5.75 in

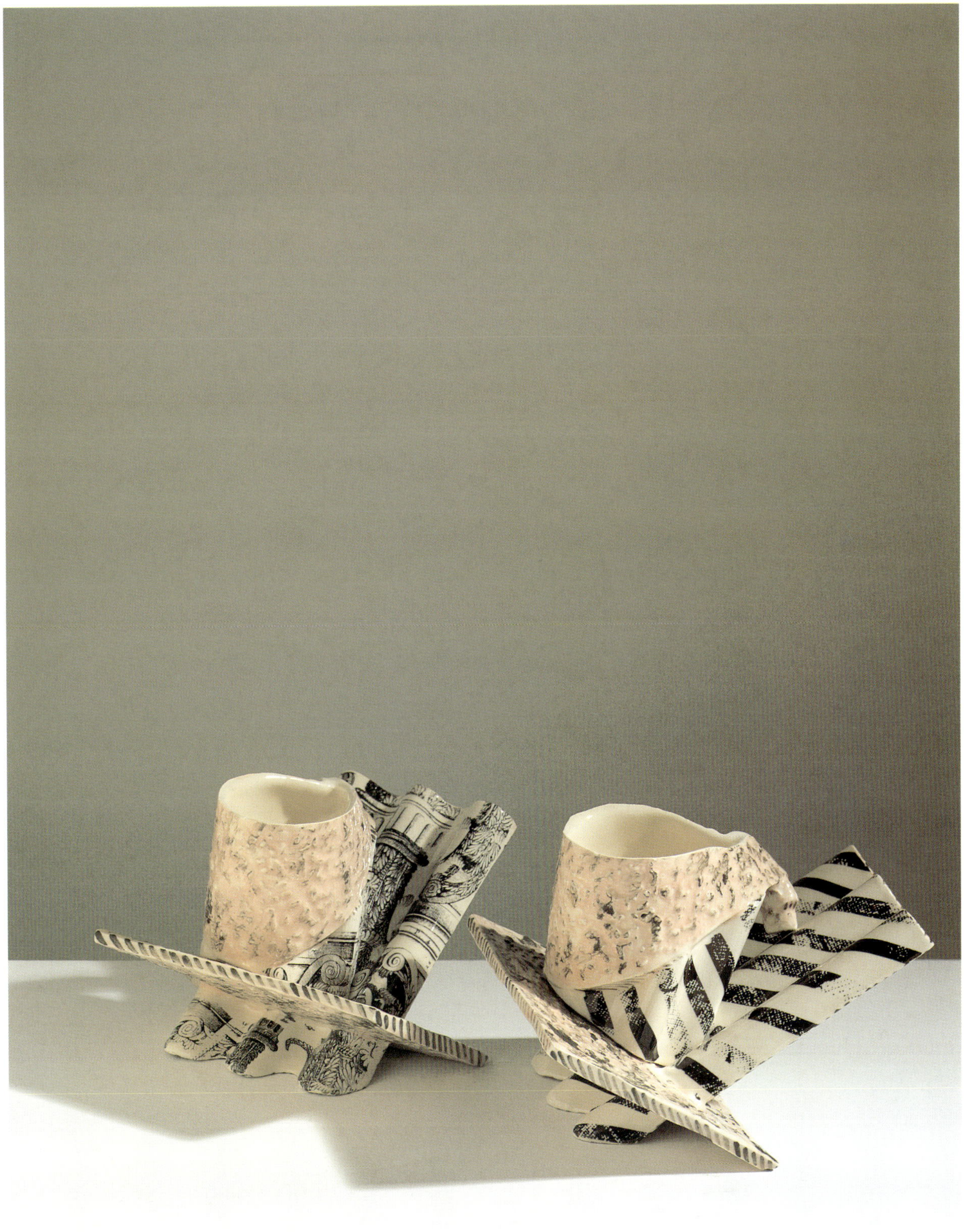

opposite
83 **Giraffe Bowl Holder** 2000
One-off, made from mould cast from teak giraffe, slip cast, clear glaze, transfers, junk shop glass bowl
H. 23 cm; 9 in
Collection: Andrew and Diana Mayfield
Photograph: David Cripps

McNicoll's work from the late 1990s onwards can be firmly positioned in what might be described as the 'consumption paradigm' in art practice. Unsurprisingly there is a political element to this kind of work. Sometimes this has taken sensational form, as when the artist Michael Landy oversaw the destruction of all his worldly goods at the 'event' *Breakdown*, held – aptly enough – in a defunct Oxford Street branch of the store C&A in 2001. Sometimes the point is made more quietly, as when the First Nation Canadian artist Brian Junger cuts up Nike Air trainers, using their distinctive markings to fashion simulacra of North-West Coast Aboriginal Art.

The latest phase of McNicoll's work explores the world of consumption through the re-presentation of a series of resonant objects and images. She favours mass consumption souvenirs picked up in junk shops. They send out blunted or scrambled messages – so we have a carved lion or giraffe signifying Africa (83), and by virtue of the medium, African tribal sculpture, a ceramic shire horse standing for a lost pastoral Englishness (93), a 1960s mantelpiece Brancusi in the form of a teak elongated bird (85). For surface decoration McNicoll now almost exclusively uses the commercial transfers made available by the ceramics industry, also characterised by low-definition, all-purpose imagery. These are collaged with her own researches – photographs, drawings and, most recently, modelled figures based on 'types' she has observed while on her personal Situationalist-inspired *dèrive* through the city. She still uses pattern, but it now tends to be created entirely from her encyclopaedic range of transfers.[30] Of course she continues to slip cast and assemble but in the context of the wider art world the 'notions of derivation, borrowing and replicating inherent in casting'[31] have acquired a new significance. Using this loaded material inevitably produces a species of social comment, underlined on occasion by the complex tongue-in-cheek titles she gives some of her pieces, such as *The Arrival of Christianity in the New World*, *Post-Colonial Images of Humanity* and *Petrochemical Cultures*.

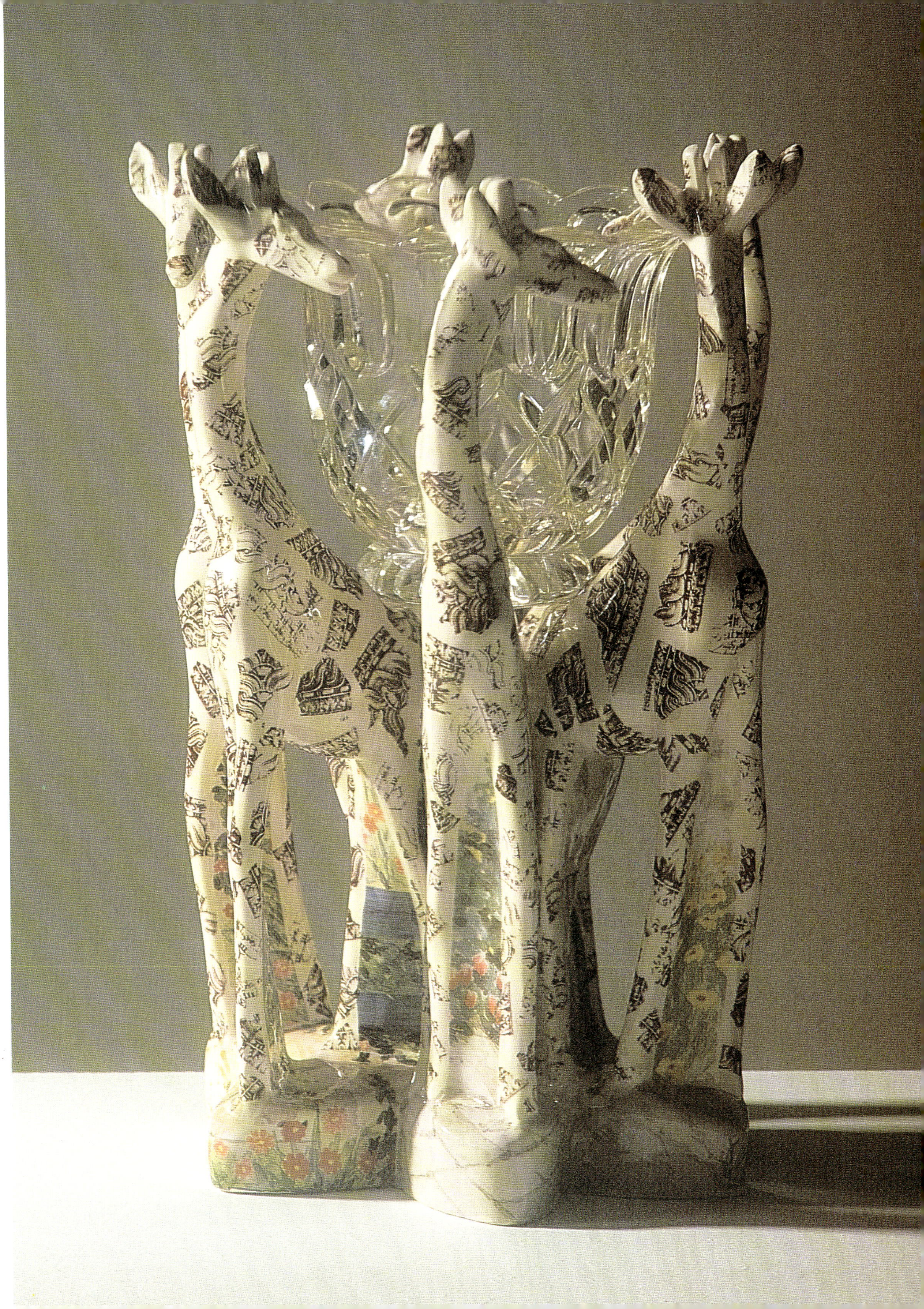

84 **Deer Vase Holder** 2000
One-off, mould made from commercial stag at bay, slip cast, clear glaze and transfers, junk shop vase
H. (excluding vase) 15 cm; 5.75 in
Collection: the Artist
Photograph: David Cripps

85 **Bird Vase Holder** 2000
One-off, made from mould cast from teak bird, slip cast, clear glaze and transfers, junk shop vase
H. 28 cm; 11 in
Collection: the Artist
Photograph: David Cripps

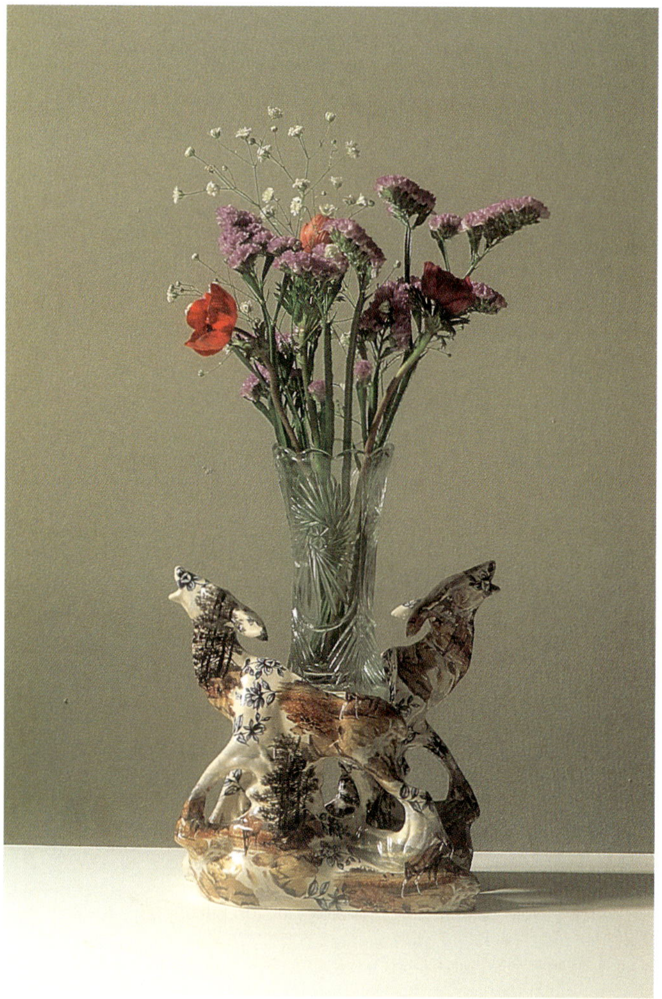

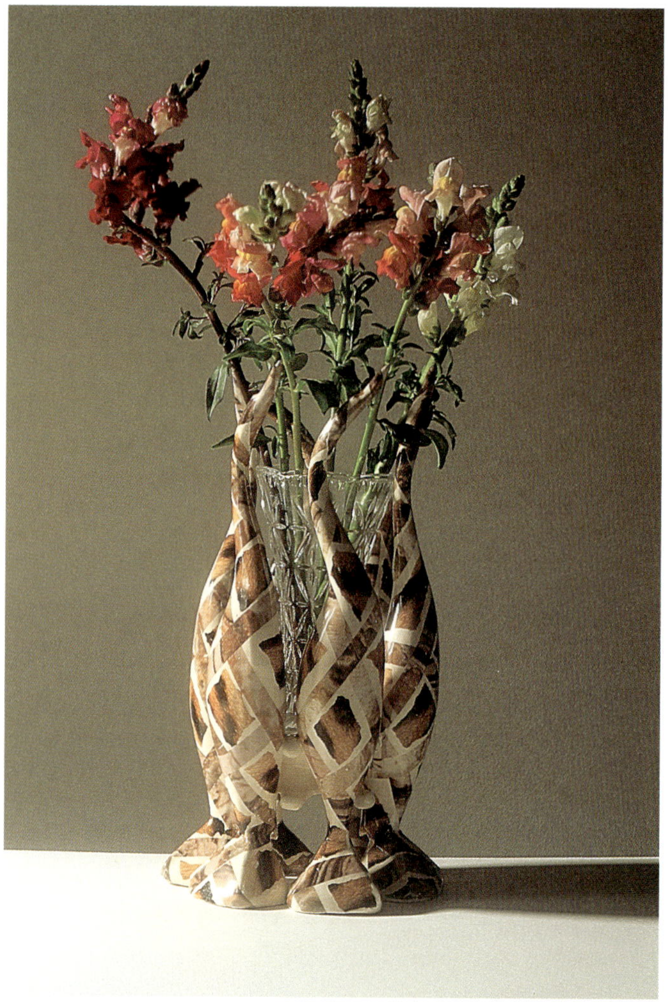

Many of her more recent pieces deal with cultural stereotypes, which she challenges through an inter-textual use of imagery. Thus in her 2000 *Moschino Girl Bowl* (87) a black girl, wearing a dress patterned with a repeated name of a fashion brand, wanders across a commercial transfer of a rural scene. *Moschino Girl Bowl* examines all sorts of ambiguous coded binaries – the urban black woman in a country setting, the branded clothing that may be counterfeit, the cottage garden that nods in the direction of Impressionism, filtered through countless amateur renderings and ersatz translations.

Other pieces make their point more stridently. In *Post-Colonial Images of Humanity* (86) the turbaned 'native' is cast in triplicate and set to supporting a bowl made up of a new world order of chunky Subbuteo figures. *Petrochemical Cultures* (100) introduces a figure of a small tubby middle manager spotted at Houston Airport and modelled from memory by McNicoll. Cast in triplicate he bears a bowl on his head and the surface of the piece is covered with a wealth of contradictory imagery – early American landscape, World War II soldiers, galleons sailing to the new world, oil rigs and so on. The Houston businessman is a new development, one of a group of figures-types directly modelled by McNicoll. Her decision to allow this element of expressive making was inspired by a reacquaintance with Tang figurines in 2001.

A receptivity to new influences and an ability to reappraise earlier discoveries has characterised McNicoll's career as a ceramicist. As an artist she has kept the faith by espousing the daring, anarchic openness to ideas that was in the air all those years ago at Leeds.[32] As a result, her life and work honours the spirit of the letter she received in her student days and which she has carefully kept: '*the incredible keeps coming true so frequently these days that one can barely stand the pace*'.

86 **Post-Colonial Images of Humanity** 2001
One-off, cast from a mould made from a 1950s figure from Ceylon and a Subbuteo figure, slip cast, stoneware glaze, clear glaze, transfers
H. 26 cm; 10.25 in
Collection: National Museum of Wales, Cardiff
Photograph: David Cripps

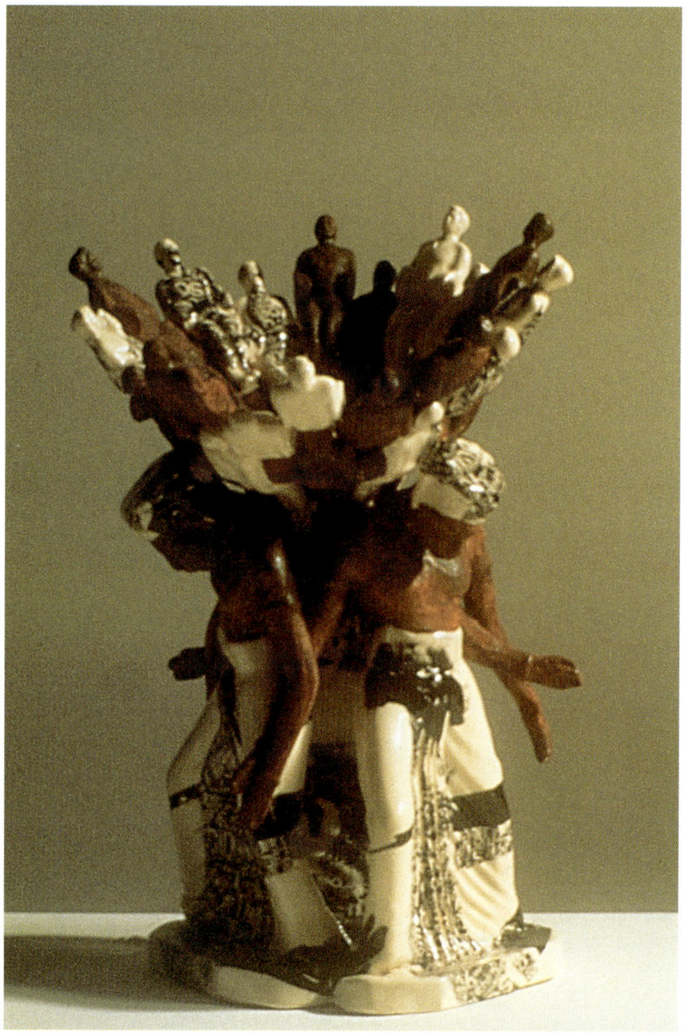

Notes

1 Programme, *Northern Festival of Ceramics, 9–11 September 1994,* Northern Potters Association.
2 All unattributed quotations in the text are from taped conversations between Carol McNicoll and the author, August 2002. Unattributed quotations at the beginning of sections are taken from McNicoll's personal archive.
3 *Carol McNicoll, Knick-Knacks*, exhibition catalogue, Yorkshire Sculpture Park, Wakefield, 2000.
4 See Tony Earnshaw, *Flowers East*, exhibition catalogue, London, 2000 for information on this anarchist artist.
5 National Advisory Council of Art Education, *First Report of the National Advisory Council on Art Education,* 1960, p.4.
6 For a reactionary response to the *Second Coldstream Report* see Peter Fuller, 'The necessity of art education' in *The Naked Artist*, Writers and Readers Publishing Cooperative, London, 1983, p.30. In the same year as the publication of this book of essays Fuller was to dismiss McNicoll's work as 'expensive, pretentious clap-trap'. See The Orchard Gallery, Londonderry, *Fifty Five Pots and Three Opinions*, 1983.
7 For background see King's College, University of Durham, *The Developing Process*, 1959.
8 See Tanya Harrod, *The Crafts in Britain in the Twentieth Century*, Yale University Press, New Haven, 1999, p.373, note 20.
9 Roger Coleman, *The Art of Work: An Epitaph to Skill*, Pluto Press, London, 1988, pp.126–30. Coleman taught at Leeds from 1967 to 1970. 'The Welfare State' is still operational. See John Fox, *Eyes on Stalks*, Methuen, London, 2002. 'YOW!' took place in 1968–9.
10 This was included in her Leeds degree show. Her submission was much admired by the Fine School's External Examiner, the painter Patrick Heron. See Janet Street-Porter, 'Tea-time for non-conformists', *Crafts*, vol.47, pp 32–5, November/December 1980.
11 Richard Deacon, 'Carol McNicoll: An appreciation' in *Carol McNicoll: Ceramics*, exhibition catalogue, Crafts Council, London, 1985.
12 Coleman dealt with the problem by turning to political action and then to artisanal work. He now directs the Helen Hamlyn Research Centre at the Royal College of Art.
13 Brian Eno was on the verge of becoming famous, one of the creators of 'glam-rock', a knowing, tongue-in-cheek reinvention of rock and roll. In 1970, however, he was a fiercely intelligent ex-art student turned cultural activist and experimental musician.

14 Jon Savage, *England's Dreaming: Sex Pistols and Punk Rock*, Faber & Faber, London, 1991, p.76.

15 Brian Eno's description of the strategies of Andrew Logan in his essay for *Andrew Logan: Magic Moments*, Ruthin Craft Centre, Ruthin, 1998.

16 See Jasia Reichardt's nervous attempts to characterise Andrew Logan's 'Total Art' in *Andrew Logan: The Artistic Adventure*, Museum of Modern Art, Oxford, 1991.

17 Peter York, 'Them', *Harpers & Queen*, October 1976, reprinted in *Style Wars*, Sidgwick & Jackson, London, 1980. York is hard to characterise and easy to dismiss. But as a journalist, often working in collaboration with Ann Barr, he provided easily the keenest insights into 1970s and 1980s social groupings.

18 Conversation with Michele Hanson, August 2002.

19 For an insightful contemporary assessment see Terence Maloon, 'Notes on style in the seventies', *Artscribe*, no.12, June 1978.

20 *Daily Mirror*, Tuesday 12 June 1973.

21 See Commonwealth Institute, *Artist Craftsmen of 401½ and Fosseway House Workshops 1970–1980*, 1980.

22 William Feaver, 'China, my China', *The Financial Times*, Monday 16 December 1974.

23 Robert Rosenblum, *Cubism and Twentieth Century Art*, Harry N. Abrams, Inc, New York, 1976, p.13.

24 See Rozsika Parker and Griselda Pollock, *Framing Feminism: Art and the Woman's Movement 1970–1985*, Pandora/Harper Collins, London, 1987, p.18 and p.163. Joanna Walton lost her life in the Lockerbie plane crash of 1988.

25 See Mole Leigh, 'Chronomanual craft: Time investment as a value in contemporary Western craft', *Journal of Design History*, vol.15, no.1, 2002, pp 33–45.

26 See Tanya Harrod, 'Bridging the divide', *Crafts*, no.80, May/June 1986.

27 Her original flat in the building was completed in 1983 and sold in 1995 when she converted half her basement studio into a second flat.

28 See Marilyn Strathern, *The Gender of the Gift*, University of California Press, Berkeley, 1988, p.178.

29 For a much fuller account of this phenomenon see Tanya Harrod, 'House-trained objects: Notes towards writing an alternative history of modern art' in Colin Painter (ed.), *Contemporary Art and the Home*, Berg, Oxford/New York, 2002.

30 In the summer of 2002 she carried her interest in pattern a step further when *Pattern Crazy* opened at the Crafts Council. This highly successful exhibition was curated by McNicoll and Jacqui Poncelet who commissioned an eclectic body of work from designers, fine artists and makers.

31 Richard Deacon, op.cit.

32 Writing of her submission to the 2001 Jerwood Prize, Edward Lucie Smith wrote: 'I found I responded most spontaneously to the work of McNicoll, because it is tirelessly inventive. My reaction to it, even when I don't much like a particular object, is to say: "Whatever will she think of next?"' *Crafts*, no.174, January/February 2002, p.52.

87 **Moschino Girl Bowl** 2000
One-off, slip cast elements, assembled, stoneware glazes, clear glaze, transfers
H. 30 cm; 11.75 in
Collection: Mark Grainer
Photograph: David Cripps

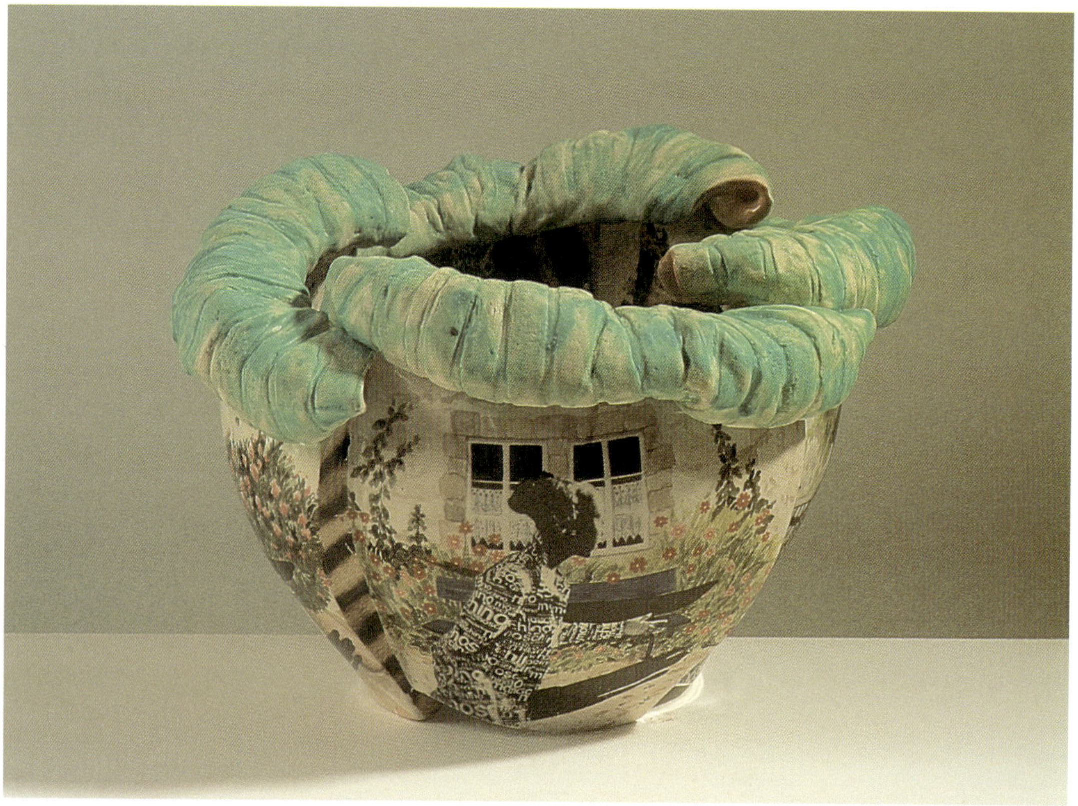

88 **From Chicago to Galveston** 2000
One-off, slip cast elements, assembled, stoneware glazes, clear glaze, transfers
H. 30 cm; 11.75 in
Collection: Susanna Heron
Photograph: David Cripps

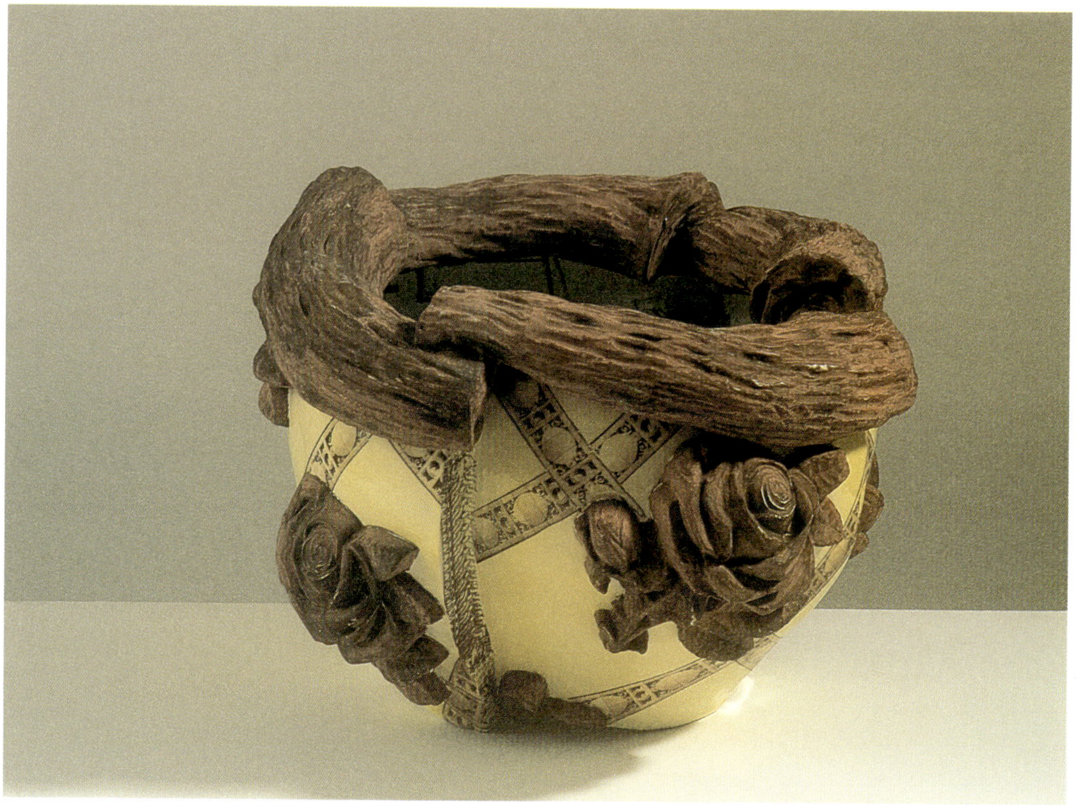

89 **Reflections** 1999

One-off, made from mould cast from commercial stag at bay, slip cast, stoneware glazes and transfers
H. 30 cm; 11.75 in
Collection: National Museums and Galleries of Merseyside
Photograph: David Cripps

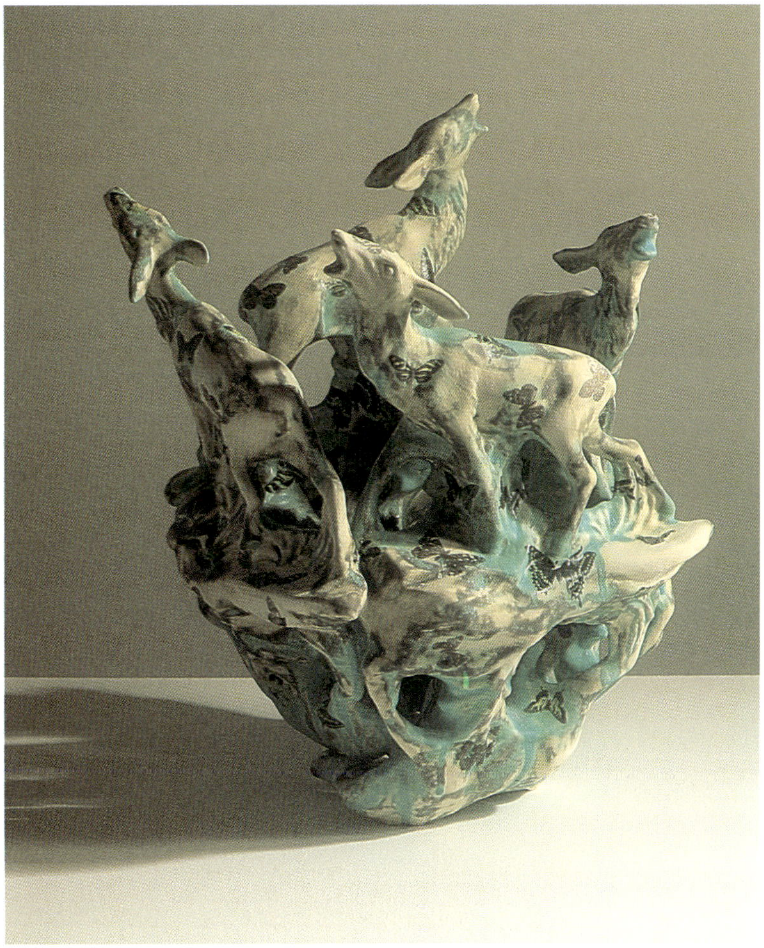

90 **Coliseum Bowl** 1999

One-off, made from mould cast from teak lion made for tourist market in Africa, slip cast, clear glaze and transfers
H. 18 cm; 7 in
Photograph: David Cripps

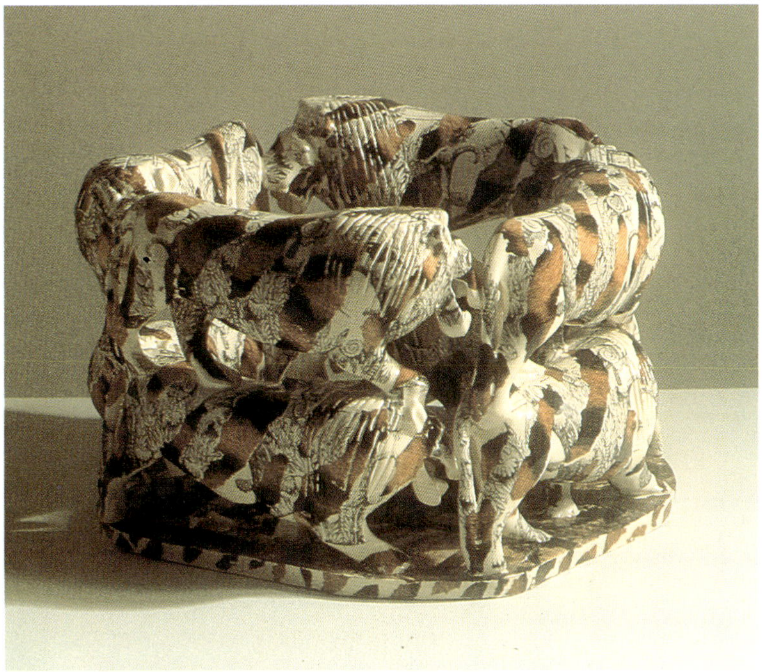

91 Interior of Carol McNicoll's 1995 flat, Apollo Works

Photograph: David Cripps

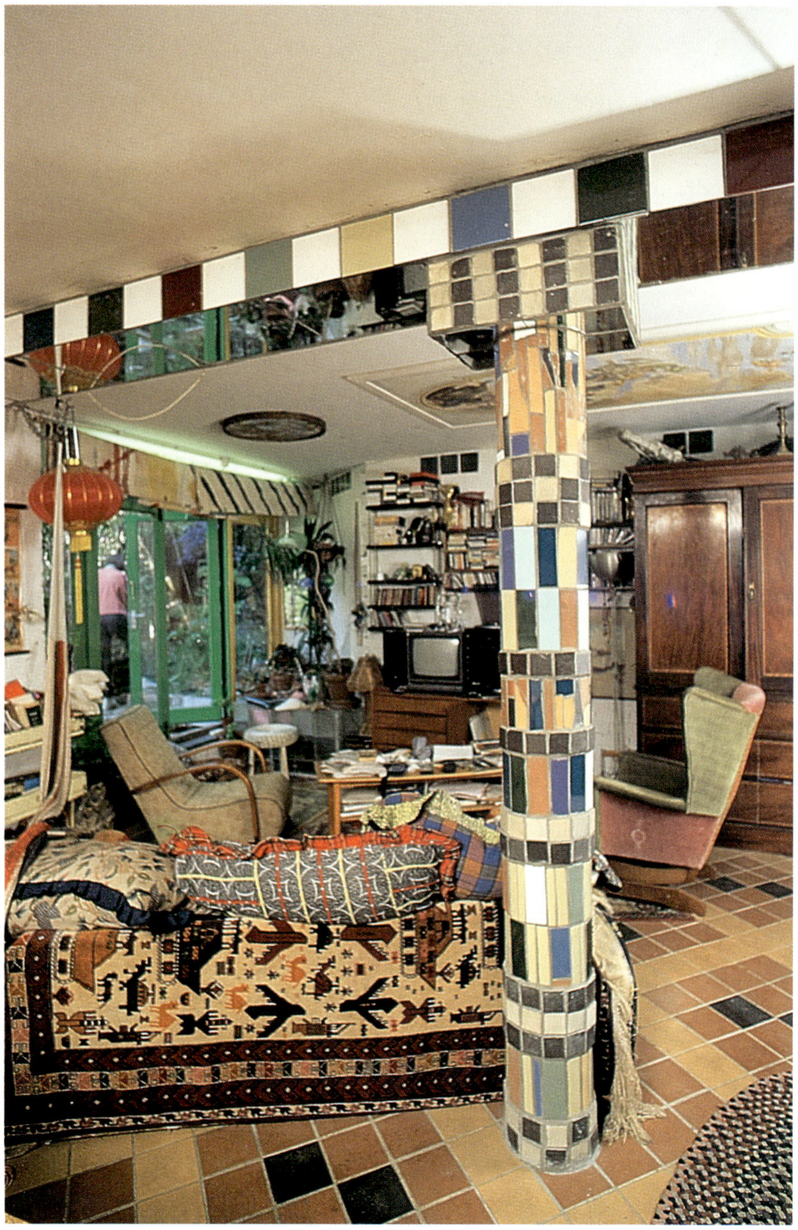

'Say It On Pots!'
A conversation with Carol McNicoll

RoseLee Goldberg

In the early 1970s at the Royal College of Art, Carol McNicoll maintained a provocative presence on the fourth floor, in the ceramics department. She made three-legged teapots with an inverted mouse for a lid, and stacks of cups and saucers that could not be separated. She made vases that looked like the wrapping paper that holds flowers together when bought on the run from a street vendor, or plates with *Chips, Chops and Peas* painted on their surfaces. She printed fabric patterns of a designer friend on an entire table-top collection and wheeled a square foot of 'mobile lawn' through the college's corridors.

With her signature red hair and green glasses, in check pants or flowing skirts, she seemed to alight from floor to floor, department to department (film, graphic design, jewellery, painting, sculpture), with the authority of a Queen at a mad hatter's tea party; she appeared determined to keep all whom she met on their toes, with her lively questions and her expectations to be always surprised and entertained by them. One look at the studio where she worked made it clear that she was not a ceramicist at heart; no earthenware bowls thrown on spinning wheels, no delicately wrought paintings on fine porcelain surfaces; rather, ceramic concoctions that were above all witty and filled with ideas. Ceramics for her was a pliable medium for talking about a broad cross-section of ideas and sensibilities.

RLG: How did you become a ceramicist?

CM: I never started out to be a ceramicist. I was studying fine arts at Leeds Polytechnic (from 1967 to 1970) and there just happened to be a ceramics department. It was a time when anything could be art, which was great, but I couldn't see the point of making art that didn't have a function. I started making ceramics because it was something that could be used. But I was also making films. One of them was called *Musical*, which was a send up of musicals. A group of us went to see *The Sound of Music* and thought it was such a hoot. So we collaged all the essential themes that a musical should have – a battle scene, a love scene, a runaway elephant – and we used students at the local art school to create a cast of thousands. The movie included a battle on either side of the River Nidd at Knaresborough, a conductor on a bridge, blackened 'natives' in canoes chasing the hero and heroine in a boat, all shot on 16mm with magnetic sound.

So becoming a ceramicist was kind of accidental. When I applied to the Royal College of Art, I applied to both the film and the ceramics department. I was accepted into the ceramics department, but if I'd got into the film department I might have become a film-maker. I didn't feel strongly about any medium at the time, just as long as I was making something useful or entertaining.

RLG: Was there anyone in particular teaching at Leeds who made the school so interesting for you?

CM: Patrick Hughes was teaching there. Lots of vaguely conceptual, performance art type artists would show up – Glen Williams, Robin Page, Tony Earnshaw, Jeff Nuttal or Ben [the French Fluxus artist] and Cornelius Cardew with his Scratch Music Orchestra. We thought no one was doing anything as interesting as we were doing up there in the north of England! There was a lot of performance art going on and we had a sense that anything close to theatre was interesting. The most boring thing you could do was paint. At Leeds we saw ourselves as being at the cutting edge.

I only made a few things in ceramics while I was at Leeds. A pair of hands holding a cup was one of them. The great thing was that the ceramics department was in the fine art department. You could do anything; write poetry, make clothes, anything could be considered as art at that point in Leeds. There was no sense that some things were art and some weren't.

RLG: What other influences – films, people, music – were important at this time?

CM: That was when I met Brian [Eno]. He had been a student at Winchester and he knew a friend of mine, Rob Neeley, a printer who'd been a year above me. Rob and others, including Brian, had gone down to London to start an artistic commune. They'd taken over a house in Camberwell and had started a band (this was before Roxy Music). They saw themselves as a kind of alternative group, living together and remaking the world. Art and life were going to be combined in this glorious whole. People would paint, some would make music and everyone would live together and recreate society all in one go in six months in Camberwell! I would come down to London to see Brian and I remember that he and I were very into games. We played a lot of mah-jong. It was also the time when there were a lot of drugs around. Reichian therapy was strong. And then there was music of course. Through Brian, I found out about John Cage. One of the things that I think Cage said – 'if you make a mistake, repeat it' – always stuck in my mind. I've been doing it ever since. In London we spent a lot of time trailing up and down Tottenham Court Road looking at electronics shops. We also spent a lot of time in uncomfortable spaces looking at performance art. When I moved to London in 1970 I moved in with him.

RLG: How did you come to work with Zandra Rhodes?

It was also through Rob that I met Zandra. He did her screen printing. He'd shown her my cup and saucer with hands and she'd ordered a set, even before I met her. One day somebody in her studio had stormed out in a huff and she needed someone to work with her. I'd made clothes with my mother and had worked in the theatre as an assistant wardrobe mistress, so it was easy for me to step in and help out. I worked for her, printing or sewing, off and on for years. I also made commissions for her. One of the earliest was a dinner service that I made at the Royal College of Art. We did it together in that she provided the decoration – we made a print at the college of one of her fantastic textiles – and then I used the print on ceramic cushions. It was very Zandra. Cushions for plates. I was making these extravagant pots for her and she'd give outrageous parties and everyone ate off my tableware. Then the whole spread would appear in magazines. It all seemed terribly glamorous.

McNicoll's conversation about growing up in the suburbs of Birmingham, in Moseley and Solihull, the only child of Scottish engineer David McNicoll and Irish nurse Brigit O'Keefe, who had also trained as a dressmaker and who passed away when McNicoll was only 13, provides a network of leads to her earliest influences and later eclectic tastes. Her father's interest in oriental rugs and his collection of engraved brass and carved furniture, which he brought back from India; her mother's fascination with Catholic ritual and the lives of saints; their combined obsession with making things; her 'Baroque' view of Europe as imagined from inside cavernous Birmingham cathedrals; her delight in the romantic Pre-Raphaelite collection in the city's art gallery.

In London McNicoll joined a vibrant, cross-pollinated world of fashion, photography, music, art, film and performance. By the early 1970s Carnaby Street had given way to the King's Road, Mary Quant to Biba's, and Pop Art (Richard Hamilton, Luccio Pozzi, Richard Blake) to Conceptual Art and Living Sculpture (Art and Language, Richard Long, Gilbert and George). For those prepared to negotiate the distances between London's far-flung cultural hubs and artists' homes and studios – from the ICA on the Mall, the Hayward Gallery and British Film Institute on the South Bank, and the Royal College of Art in Central Kensington to Notting Hill Gate, Maida Vale or Islington – a marvellous subculture of constantly shifting artistic experimentation was to be found. McNicoll travelled from one to the other with an ever expanding circle of innovative and energetic friends: performers Polly Eltes and Anne Bean of the Moodies, painter Duggie Fields, photographer and fashion journalist Tim and Janet Street-Porter, architect Piers Gough, sculptors Richard Deacon and Andrew Logan, and fellow ceramicists Jacqueline Poncelet and Alison Britton. She made costumes for Roxy Music (notably Brian Eno's iconic feathered jacket) and images of her work appeared on record sleeves and in a commercial for Maxell tapes. McNicoll not only revelled in the sincerity of so much individual and collective activity, she embodied it. At the RCA, in studio, dining room or bar, she herself was a spontaneous event. The college became an extension of her diverse scene when she invited her friends to lecture or spend the day, both to maintain her own level of creativity and to counteract the hierarchies between art and craft that she inevitably found there.

CM: It's difficult to imagine the excitement of London in the 1970s. There was this unbelievable scene of rock and roll, fashion, photography. One scene blended into another. There was still a belief in old-fashioned ideas like socialism. Feminism was just beginning. We felt we were creating this wonderful new way of life.

RLG: Can you talk about the crossover between rock and roll and ceramics?

CM: Yes, populism was the crossover. One of the discussions at the house in Camberwell was the idea that the only valid art form was a popular form, that the esoteric was not interesting. The goal was to manage to create something that was popular and that could also be intellectually and artistically interesting. That's what I was trying to do in my ceramics – make something that lots of people would want but that was saying something. And that was kind of where Roxy Music came from – this idea that you could do something really popular but also musically/artistically interesting.

RLG: How would you describe the distinct phases of your work?

CM: All my work in the 1970s was functional. It was all about product. I made a lot and I was very successful. I was absolutely opposed to making one-off objects or precious things that were art. This was also the period when there was a rediscovery of work by Clarice Cliff. Pre-war, hand-painted tableware made in editions in Stoke-on-Trent, which had all disappeared during the war. Then there was a moment when I was getting bored with production, which partly coincided with having my son Bekett, which in retrospect I now realise made it much more difficult to churn out the quantity of material that I was doing (especially since I'd decided to be the complete earth mother and do absolutely total ethnic child-rearing).

RLG: Were you producing everything yourself?

CM: Oh yes, I was making loads of things – I'd go into the studio and make 50 plates. At the beginning that was an exciting idea, to be able to make so many plates myself and then to sell everything. After a bit, the sight of 50 plates made me feel sick. Around that time I also started designing things that could be industrially produced. I didn't realise that you can't do both. You can't churn out material for 10 pence and then still do work for £10. Once you do things for industry, you start undercutting your own market.

RLG: So in response to the overload you returned to making one-off pieces.

CM: That combination of the boredom of producing in large quantities, having a child and understanding the market, led me to start making 'one offs' again. It was the 1980s and my contemporaries were making their names with one-off, rather pretentious objects. These were being bought for large amounts of money by a whole new group of people who collected ceramics. I got seduced into that a bit and the whole Crafts Council idea of the precious object.

But in the 1990s I went to India and saw a really living decorative art tradition. I decided that all this stuff that we were making in England was nonsense and that I wasn't going to do it any more. I went back to making things in editions only.

McNicoll also returned to an earlier interest in figuration and to pattern-work, which was absolute taboo in the 1970s – 'The worst thing anyone could say was that you were being decorative' she says – and she introduced an entirely new way of working with photography. Some of these developments are the result of a mature artist feeling at liberty to indulge immediate passions without concern for critical viewpoints of peers or public – 'partly I've got so old that I can do whatever I like' McNicoll quipped – and some are due to advancing technologies. Making transfers from digital photographs, for example, was financially prohibitive until a few years ago. Changing the consistency of clay by adding paper, McNicoll explains, allows her to make complicated collages and 'absolute copies' as well.

Importantly, she also now infuses the work with obliquely political content. For example, one of her latest objects comprises three small reclining figures of women dressed in suits – 'the way they dress in the city'– supporting a bowl. The interior of the bowl has a check pattern of clashing imagery, of oil rigs, fragments of a Mexican church, and a woman holding a gun, taken from a mural on a Chicago building. 'It's a meditation,' McNicoll says, 'on the basis of our wealth – guns, Christianity and oil.'

RLG: Your work has become very dreamy again.

CM: The work has gone back to where it started in a funny sort of way. When I first started I just made what I wanted, because I wasn't in any way part of the ceramic world. And I just made what I made. And then I gradually got seduced into being part of it – and it's like I've now come out the other side of it. And I again feel like I can make whatever I like.

RLG: You now have the experience and the maturity to understand your *métier* and to use it in any way you choose. And the confidence too.

CM: The other thing for me with the work I'm making now, is that I always felt that art wasn't really an appropriate medium for saying political things. I always thought there were other better ways of expressing yourself politically. Now that I realise that actually one doesn't have a voice, certainly in this country, there is no political party that I can support. We will go to war with Iraq in my name, whether I want us to or not. So I started to think I may as well say it on pots!

Recent work

92 **Wild West Bowl** 2000
One-off, made from mould cast from china shire horse, slip cast, clear glaze, transfers
H. 20 cm; 7.75 in
Collection: Mark Grainer
Photograph: David Cripps

opposite
93 **Teapot Vase** 2000
One-off, made from mould cast from china shire horse and commercial teapot, slip cast, clear glaze, transfers
H. 25 cm; 9.75 in
Collection: Ken Campbell
Photograph: David Cripps

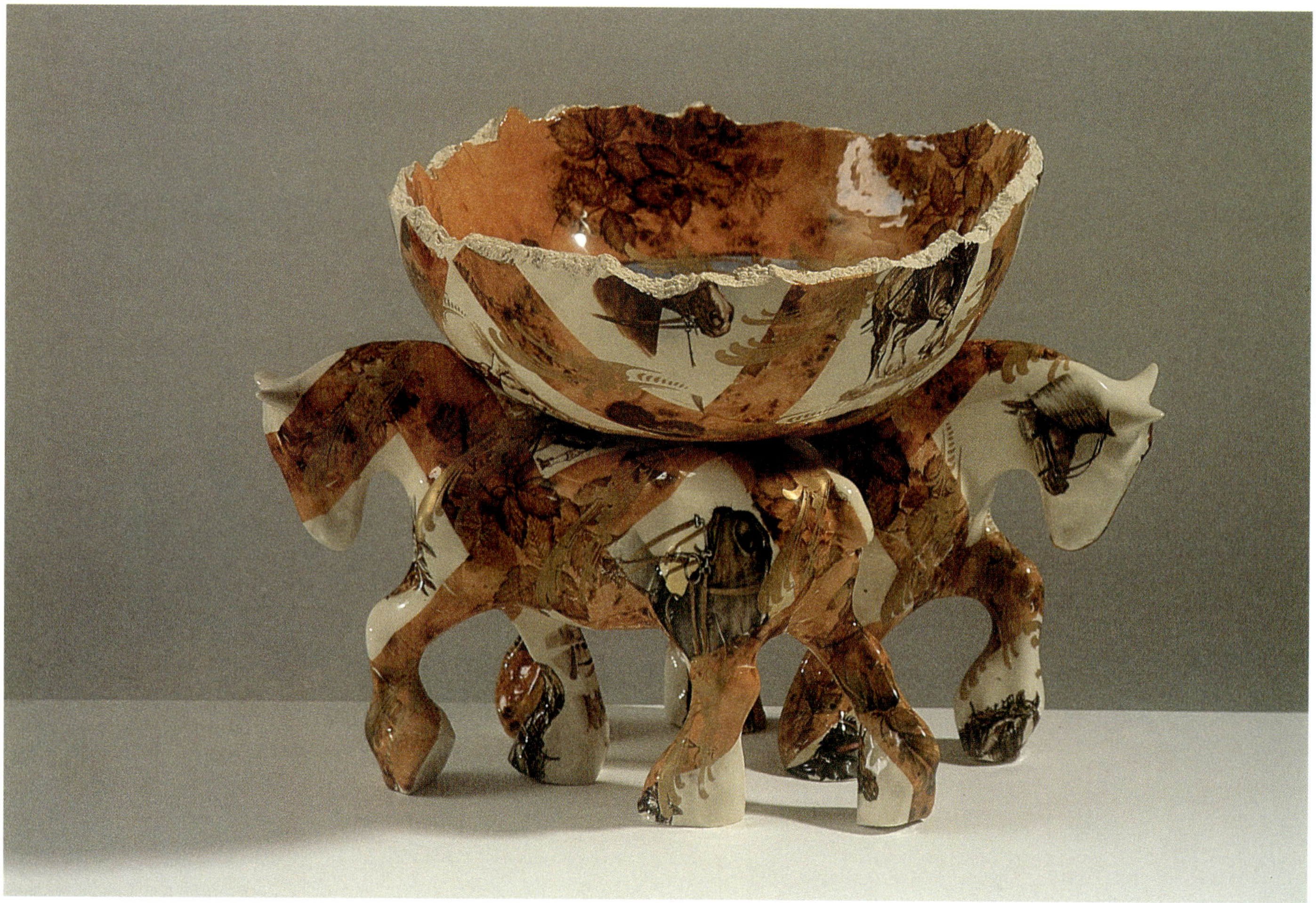

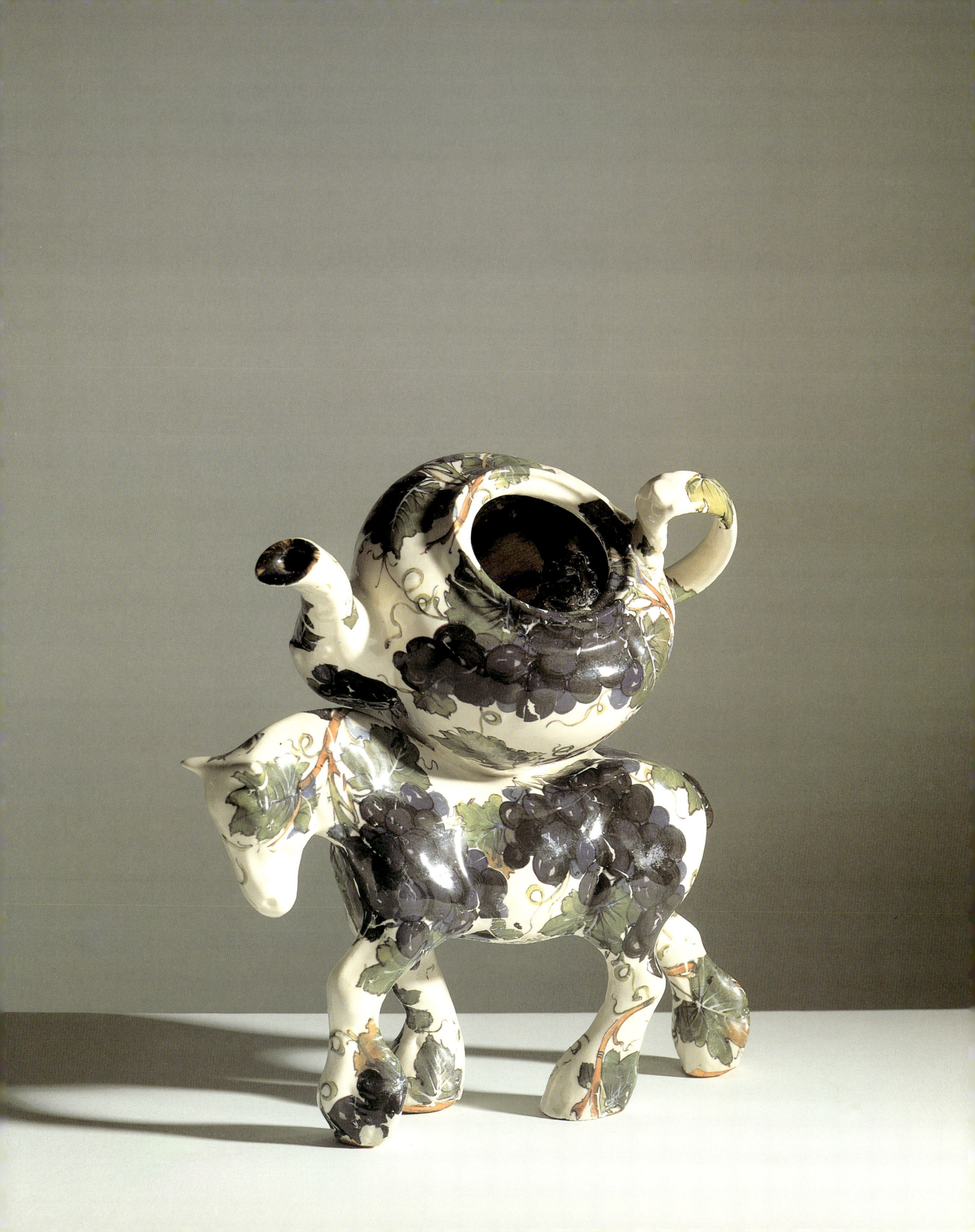

94 **Saucer Dish** 1999

One-off, made from mould cast from teak lion made for tourist market in Africa and commercial saucers, stoneware glaze, clear glaze, slip cast, underglaze colour, transfers
H. 18 cm; 7 in
Collection: Piers Gough
Photograph: David Cripps

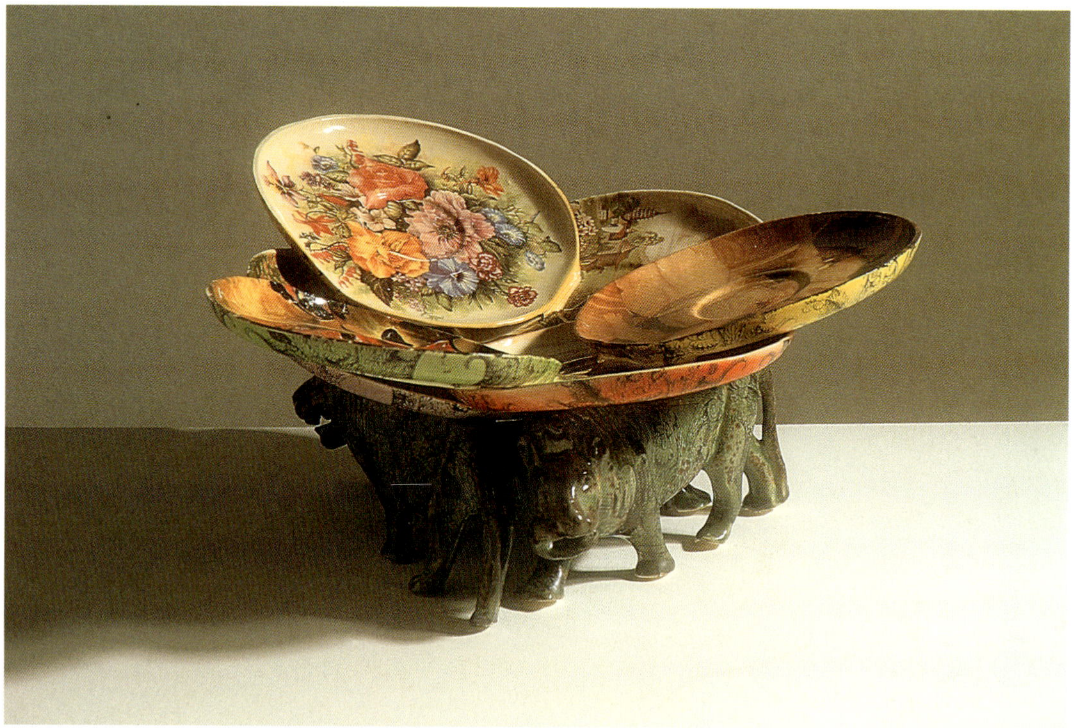

95 **Fruit Bowl** 2001

One-off, cast from mould made from teak buffalo, slip cast, reduced porcelain, underglaze transfers, on glaze transfers, clear glaze
Diam. 26 cm; 10.25 in
Collection: Shigaraki Museum, Japan

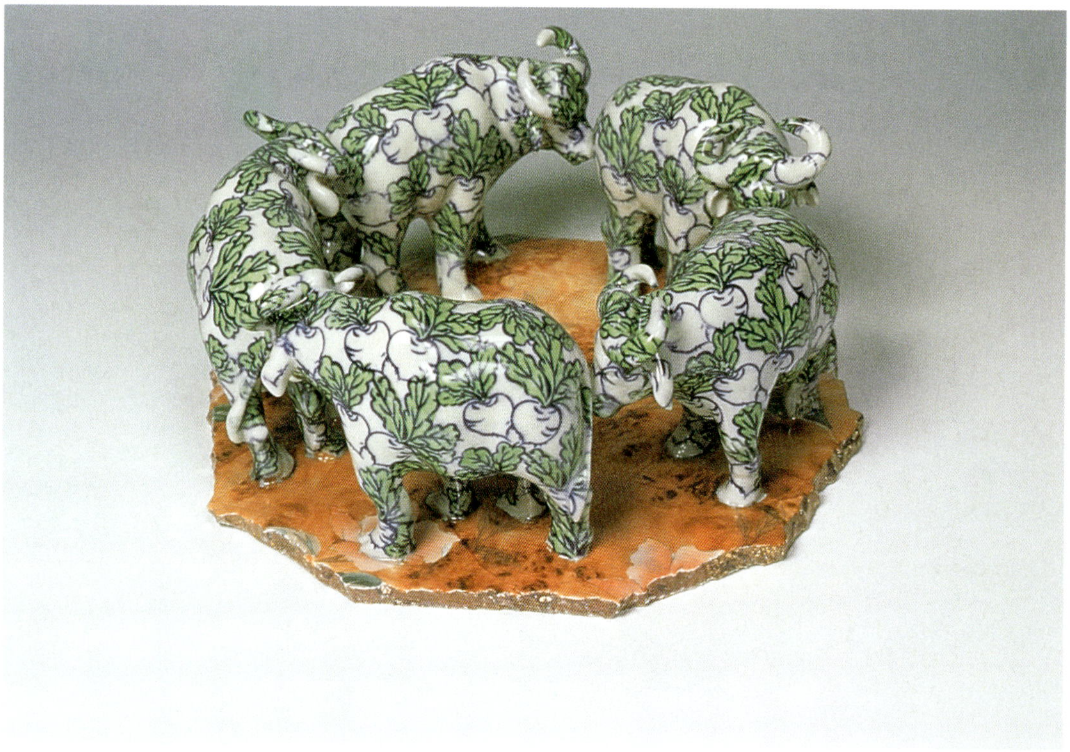

opposite

96 **Homage to Brancusi** 2001

One-off, mould made from a glass jug, slip cast, reduced porcelain, celadon glaze, transfers, aluminium base
H. 38 cm; 15 in
Collection: the Artist
Photograph: David Cripps

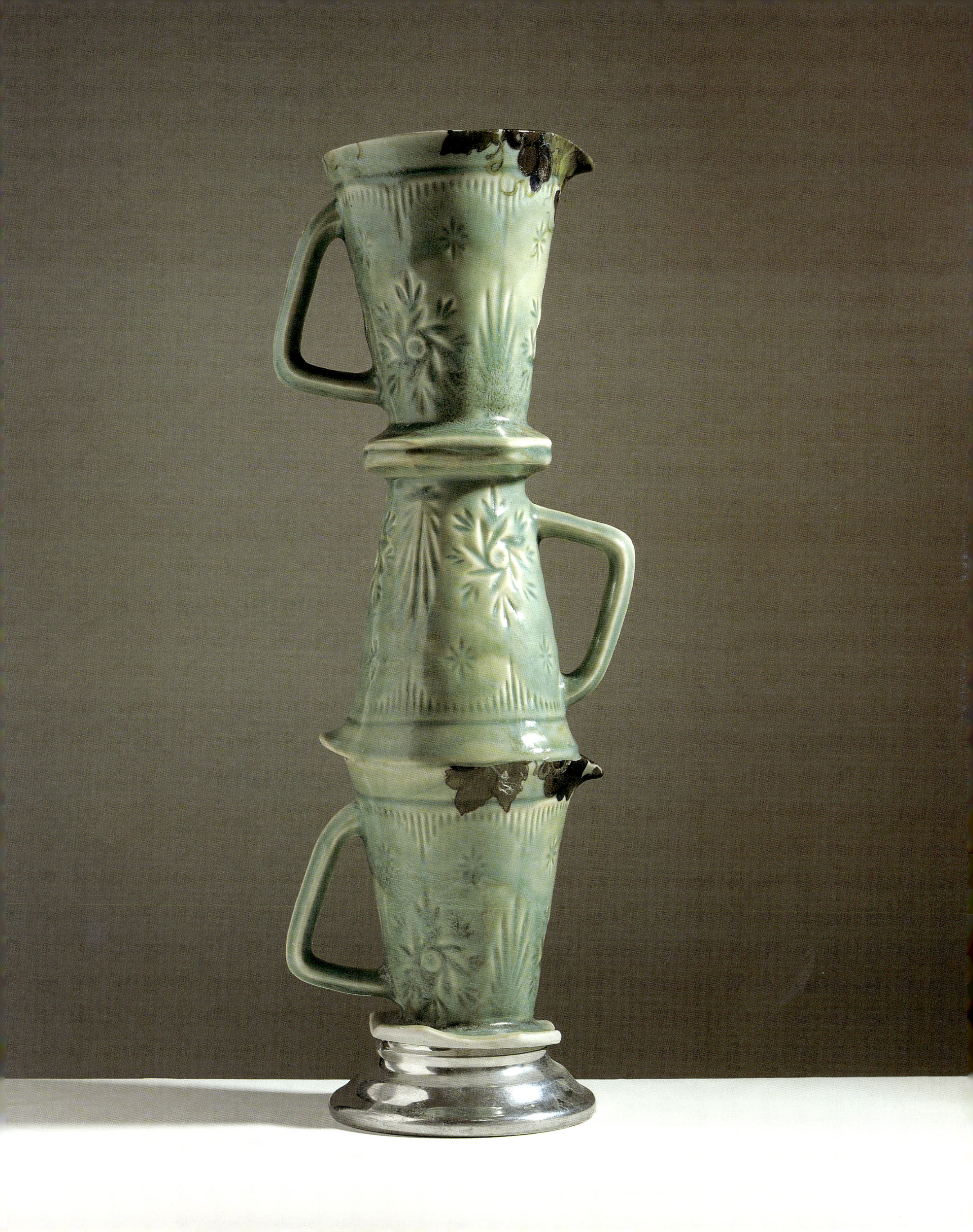

97 **Tea at the Miho Museum**
2001
One-off, mould made from a figure modelled by the artist and a commercial Chinese teapot, slip cast, stoneware glaze and transfers
H. 30 cm; 11.75 in
Collection: the Artist

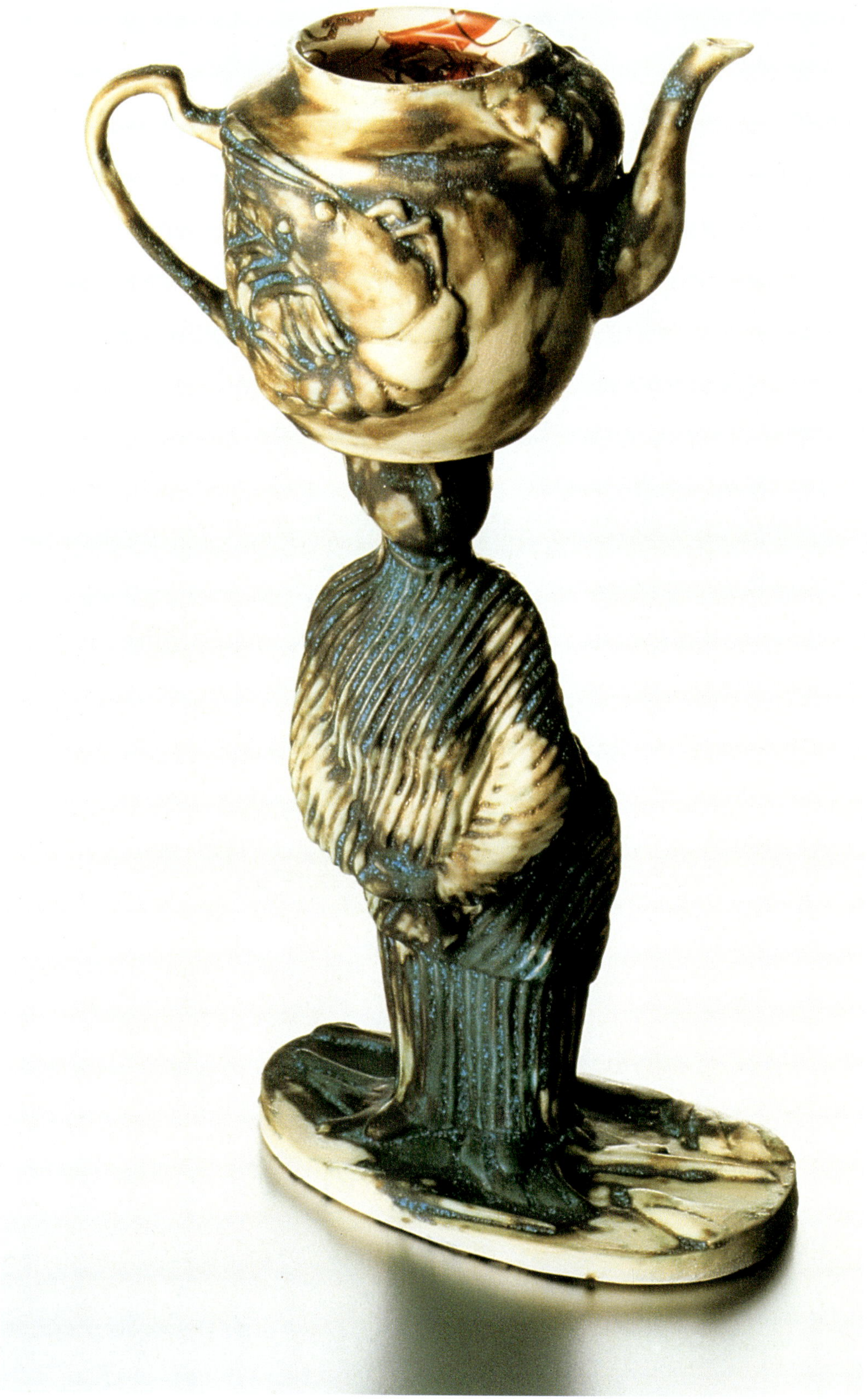

98 **North London Orientalism**
2001
One-off mould made from a figure modelled by the artist, slip cast, reduced porcelain, transfers, glass bowl
H. 22 x diam. 40 cm; 8.5 x 15.75 in
Private collection

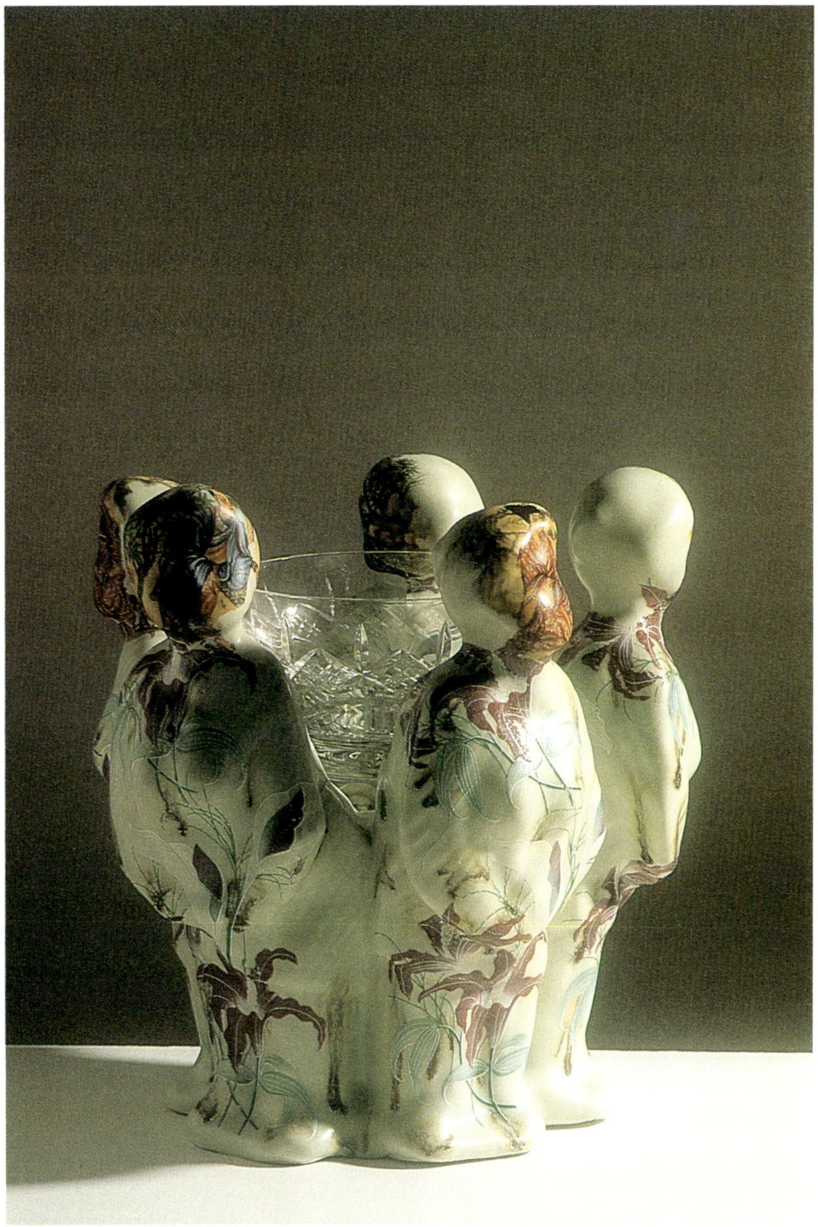

99 **Poodle Bowl Holder** 2001
One-off, mould made from a plastic poodle found in a flea market in the Midi, slip cast, reduced porcelain, transfers, junk shop bowl
Diam. 29 cm; 11.5 in
Collection: Jacqui Poncelet
Photograph: David Cripps

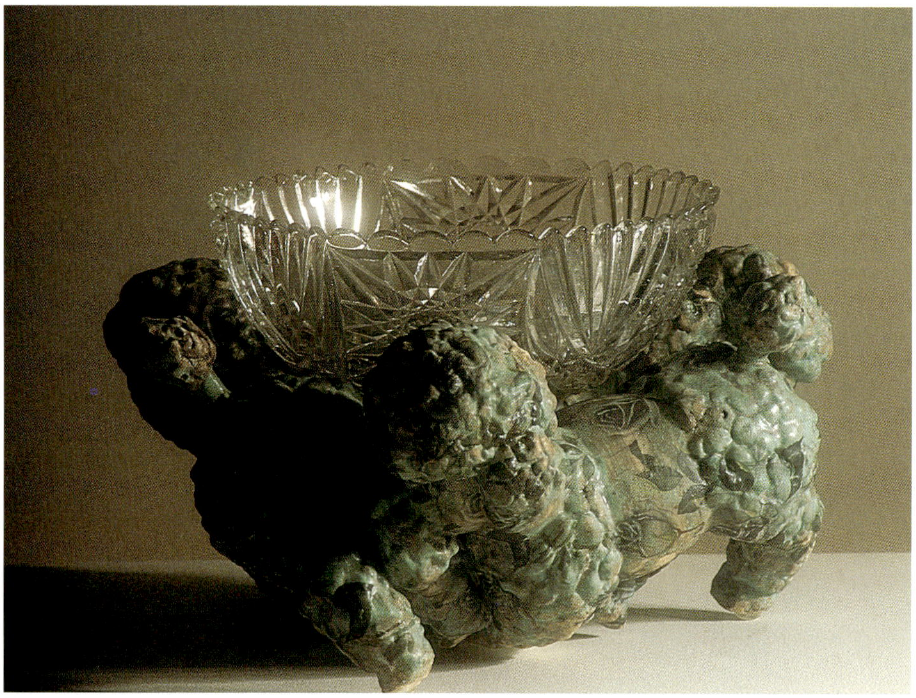

100 **Petrochemical Cultures** 2001
One-off, mould made from a figure modelled by the artist, slip cast, stoneware glaze, transfers
H. 30 cm; 11.75 in
Private collection
Photograph: David Cripps

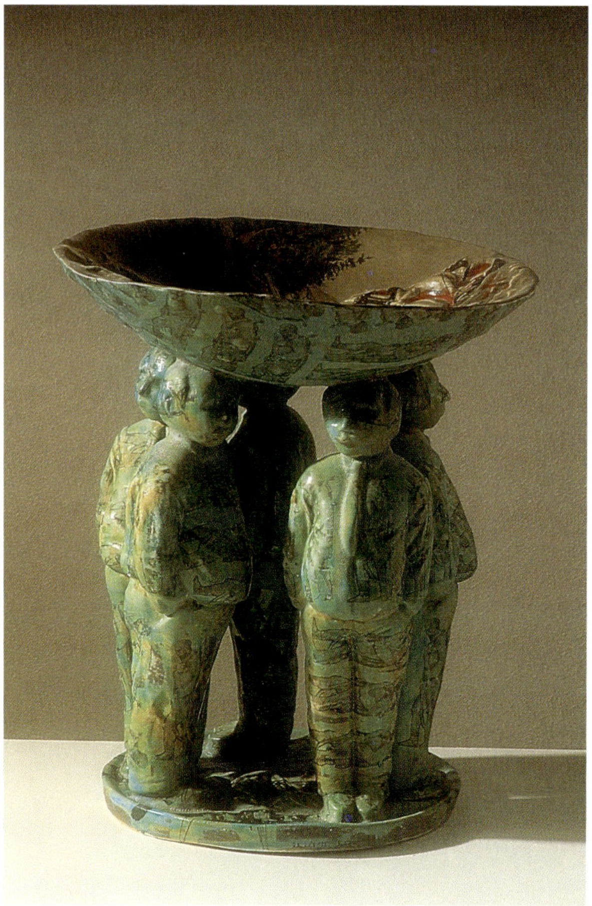

opposite
101 **Visions of Other Cultures** 2002
One-off, mould made from a figure modelled by the artist, clear glaze and transfers
H. 22 cm; 8.5 in
Collection: the Artist
Photograph: David Cripps

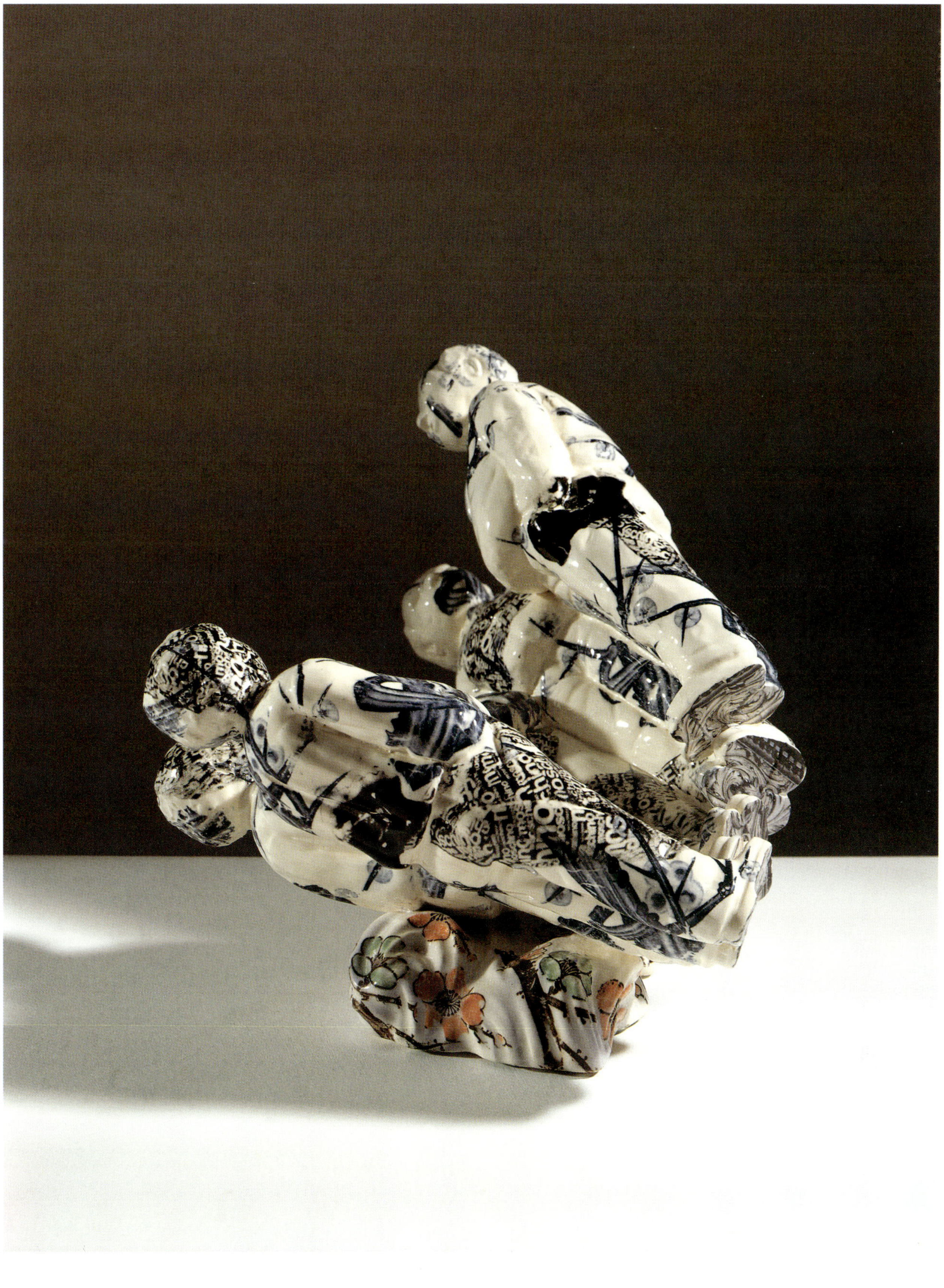

102 **City Dreams** 2002
One-off, mould made from a figure modelled by the artist, base cast from a cut glass bowl, slip cast, stoneware glaze, transfers
h. 28 cm; 11 in
Collection: the Artist
Photograph: David Cripps

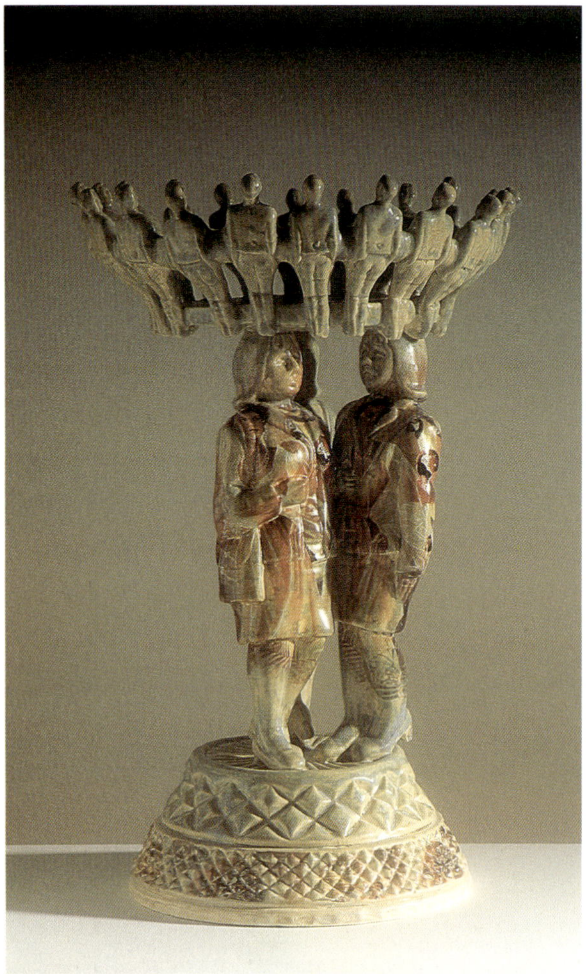

103 **Ladies Fruit Bowl** 2002
One-off, mould made from a figure modelled by the artist, slip cast, clear glaze, transfers, lustre
H. 22 cm; 8.5 in
Collection: the Artist
Photograph: David Cripps

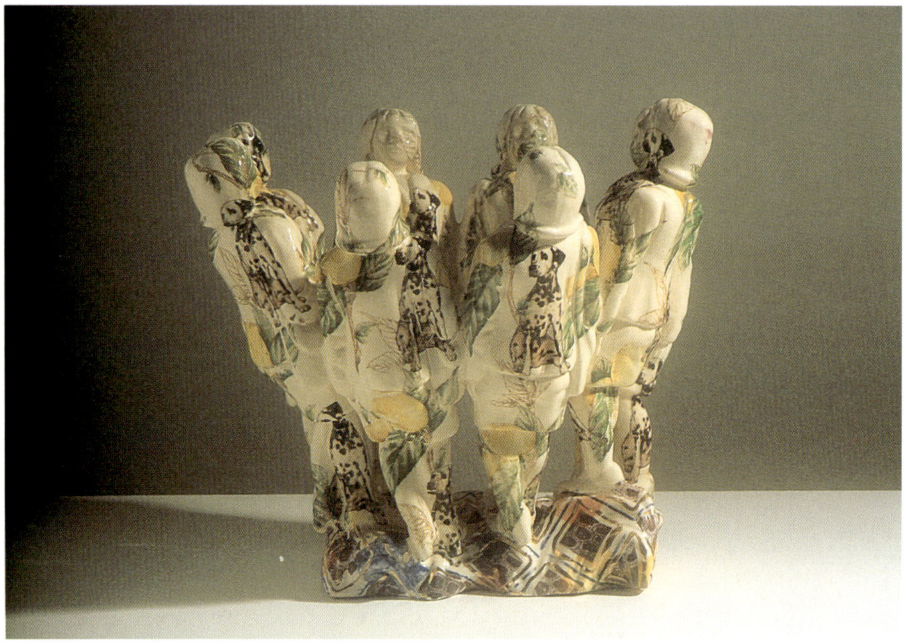

opposite
104 **Capitalist Dreams** 2002
One-off, mould made from figures modelled by the artist, slip cast, stoneware glaze, transfers
H. 22 cm; 8.5 in
Collection: the Artist
Photograph: David Cripps

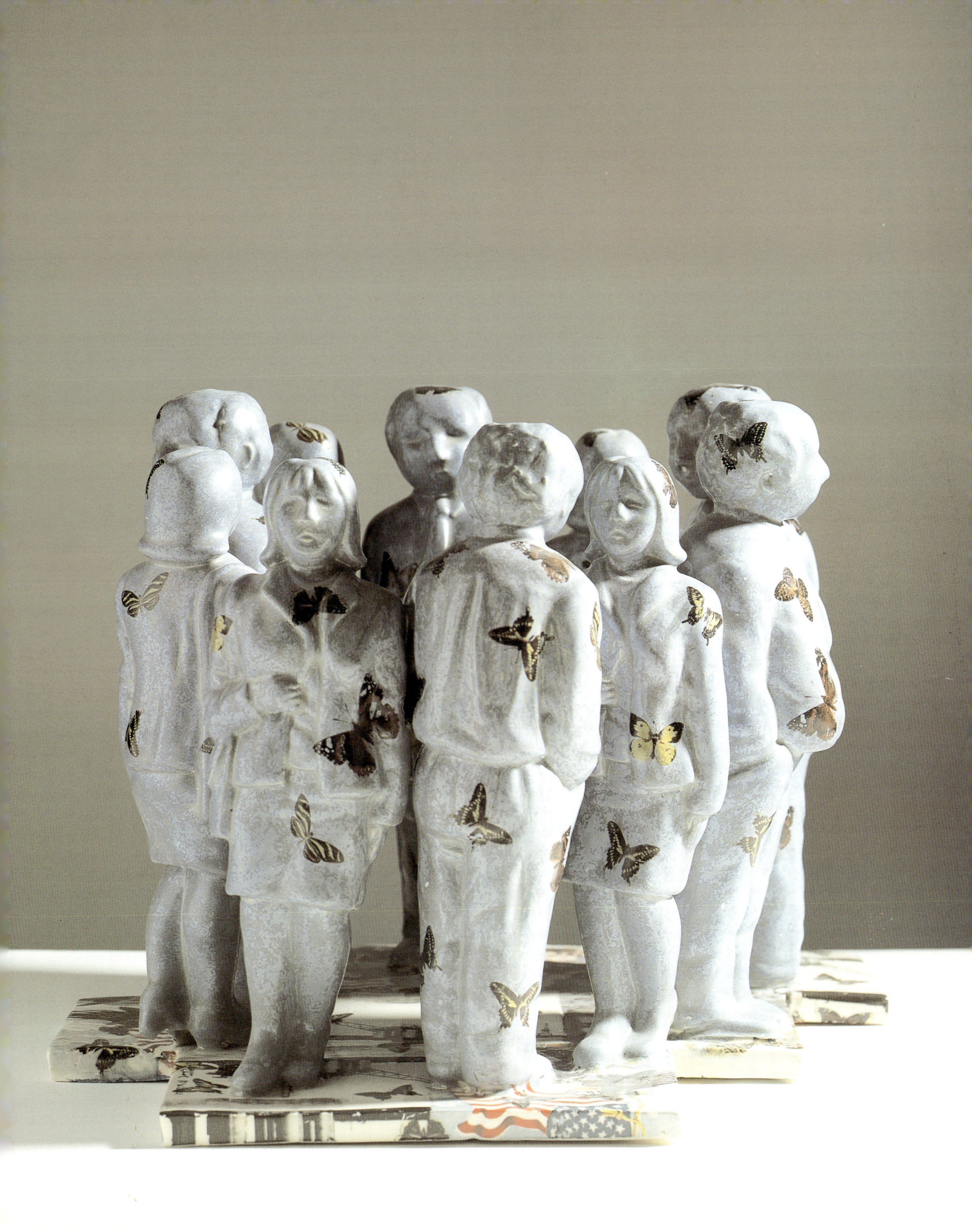

105 **Lunch Hour** 2002

One-off, mould made from a figure
modelled by the artist, slip cast,
stoneware glaze, transfers
Diam. 28 cm; 11 in
Collection: the Artist
Photograph: David Cripps

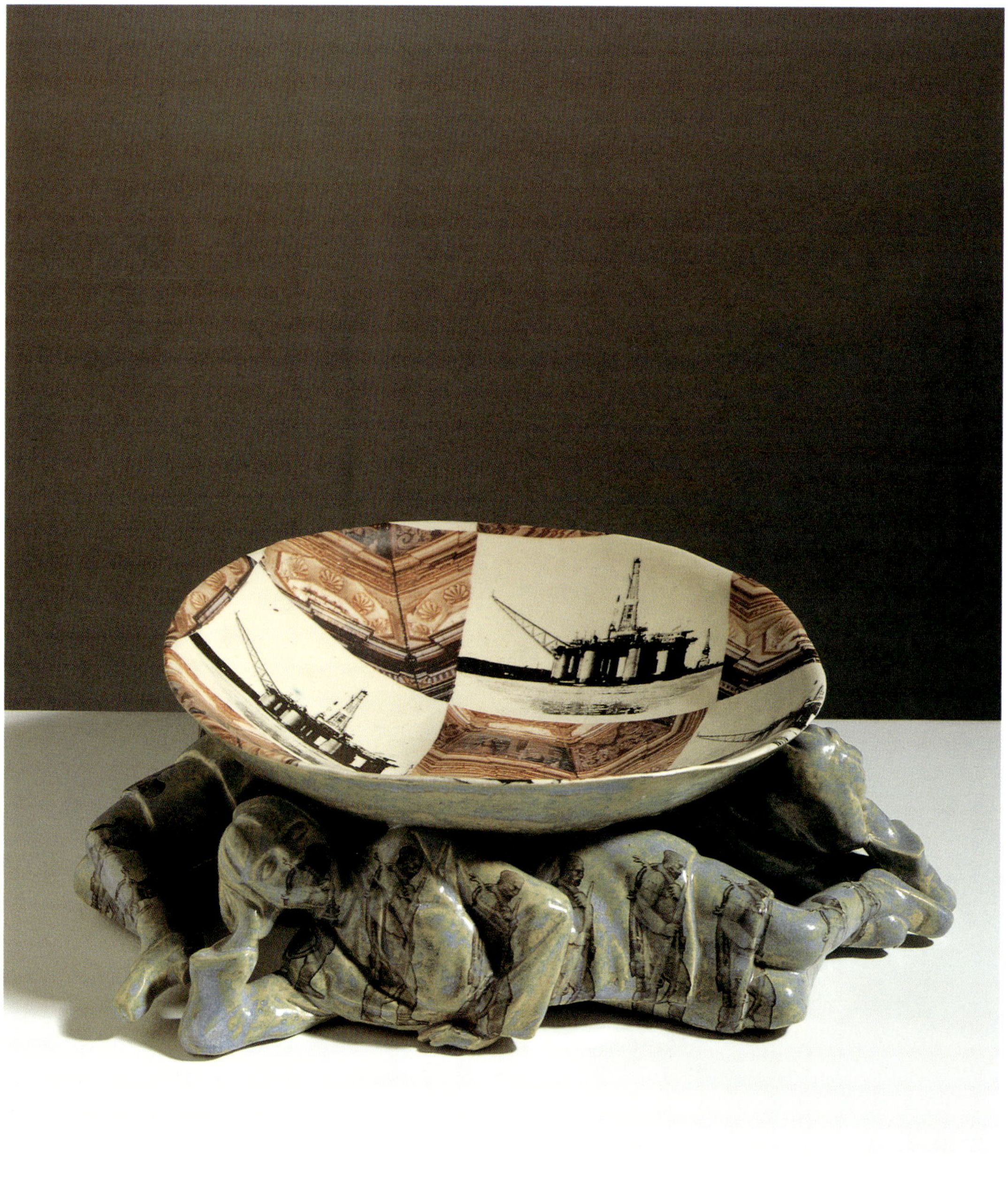

106 **Inflourescence** 2002
One-off mould made from a figure modelled by the artist, bowl cast from a cut glass bowl, slip cast, stoneware glaze transfers
H. 19 x diam. 40 cm; 7.5 x 15.75 in
Collection: the Artist
Photograph: David Cripps

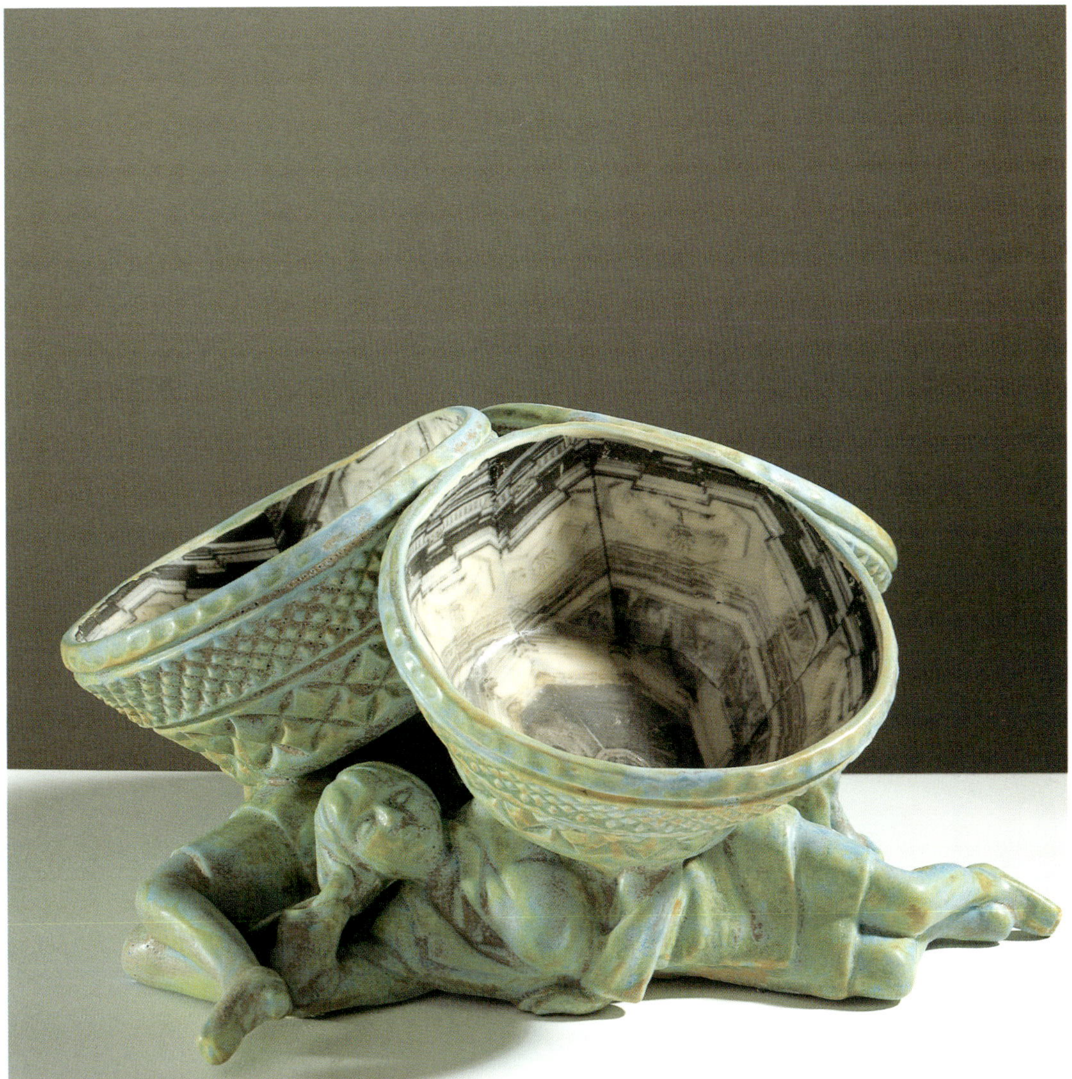

107 **Pair of Jugs** 2002

One-off, mould made from a figure modelled by the artist and glass jugs, slip cast, stoneware glaze, transfers
H. 32 cm; 12.5 in
Collection: the Artist
Photograph: David Cripps

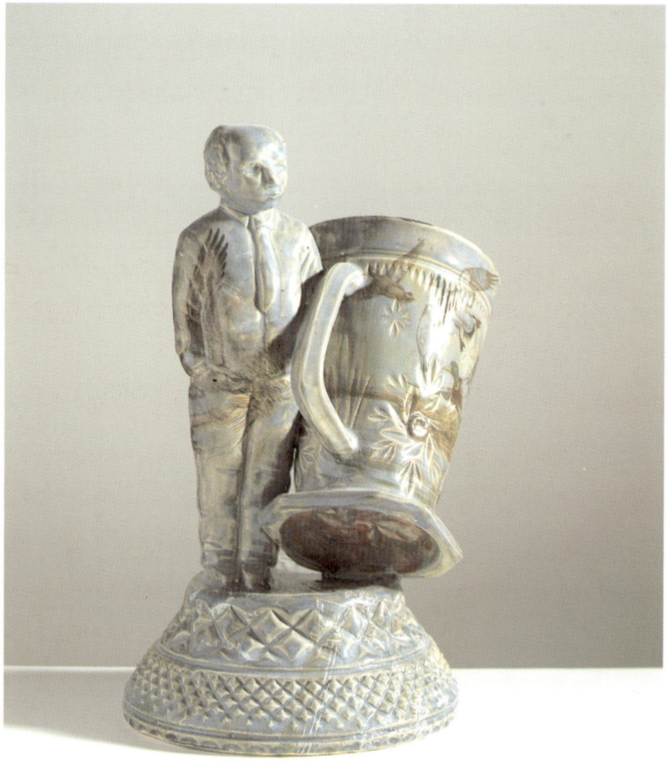

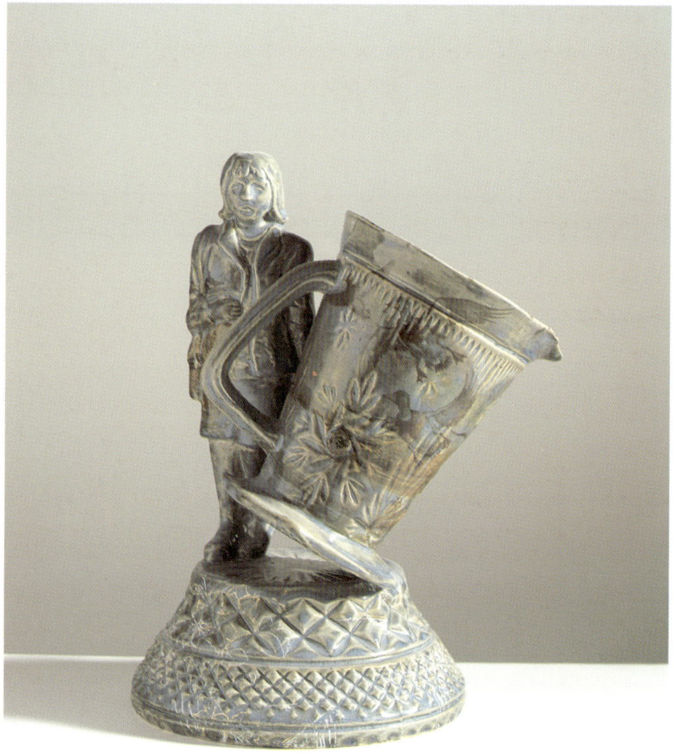

Glossary

Celadon glaze
High-fired, glossy, pale turquoise glaze, originally from China.

Clear glaze
Transparent glaze.

Faience
A French term for earthenware.

Fired cloth
Fabric impregnated with clay. When fired the fabric burns out leaving the clay looking like fabric.

Free-blown glass
Glass blown without using a mould to form it.

Onglaze enamel
Colour applied to the glaze after firing. Enamel is fired at a much lower temperature (normally about 800°C) than the glaze.

Oribe ware
Type of Japanese ceramic ware first produced in Mino Province (now Gifu Province) between 1568 and 1603. Oribe ware was made both for the tea ceremony and for everyday use, and is characterised by being decorated with a combination of areas of coloured glaze and areas of pattern.

Press-moulded terracotta
Press-moulding is a technique whereby plastic clay is pressed into a plaster mould to create a shape or texture. Terracotta is unglazed red clay.

Reduced porcelain
Porcelain fired to around 1280°C in an atmosphere with a low oxygen content, causing oxygen to be removed from the glaze compounds. In this type of firing the clay starts to melt and beautiful and somewhat unpredictable glaze effects can result.

Sgraffito
Drawing produced by scratching through a layer of coloured clay to reveal the base colour.

Silk-screening
A method of printing using a screen of fine mesh.

Slip
A mixture of clay and water.

Slip casting
A method of casting widely used in the ceramic industry. Slip, made fluid by the addition of deflocculants, is poured into plaster moulds. The plaster absorbs water from the surface of the slip touching the mould, forming a solid layer of clay. The excess slip is poured out leaving a hollow cast, which can be removed by opening the mould.

Stoneware glaze
Glaze fired at a high temperature, normally over 1200°C.

Transfers
Method of applying imagery using images printed on to special paper and painted with a transparent coating. When the transfers are soaked in water the image floats off on the coating and this can be applied to glazed ware and fired. There is an enormous range of commercially made transfers available.

Underglaze
Colour applied on to the fired clay and glazed over.

Chronology

1943 Born Birmingham, England

1956–61 Convent of the Holy Child Jesus, Edgbaston, Birmingham

1966–7 Pre-Diploma, Solihull College of Technology, Solihull

1967–70 Studied Fine Art at Leeds Polytechnic (Diploma in Art and Design, Fine Art, First Class Honours)

1970 Awarded Princess of Wales Scholarship to study at Royal College of Art

1970–3 Studied ceramics at Royal College of Art (MA Ceramics)

1980–4 Designed giftware collection for Rising Hawk Pottery

1980–Present Designed giftware collection for Axis Diffusion

1986–2001 Lecturer at Camberwell School of Arts and Crafts, London

1983 Designed giftware collection for Warehouse Designs

1985–6 Designed giftware collection for Next Interiors

1988 Visiting lecturer at National University, University of the Andes, Bogota, Colombia

1990 Ran workshops on 'Form and Function' at Banff Centre, Banff, Canada

1990 'Business and the arts' award trophies for the 1990 ABSA/Daily Telegraph Award for Business and the Arts

1992 Designed glass collection for Victoria Glass, London

1993 Ran lectures, demonstrations and workshops for ceramics weekends at Aberystwyth Arts Centre, Aberystwyth, Wales

1994 Ran lectures, demonstrations and workshops for Northern Festival of Ceramics, Northern Potters Association, Middlesbrough

1996 Ran one-week series of lectures and workshops, Robert Gordon University, Aberdeen, Scotland

1997 'Obscure objects of desire? Reviewing the crafts in the twentieth century', University of East Anglia, Norwich, conference paper published by the Crafts Council

2001 Artist in Residence for six weeks at Shigaraki Ceramic Sculpture Park, Japan, funded by the Japan Council as part of their medium term visitors' programme in commemoration of the Okinawa/Kyushu Summit 2000

2002 Co-curated *Pattern Crazy* with Jaqui Poncelet, Crafts Council Gallery, London

2003 Two week residency, Ceramics and Glass Department, De Montfort University, Leicester as part of *Show5* – Carol McNicoll

Selected exhibitions

One/two-person exhibitions

1974 *China, My China*, Royal College of Arts Gallery, London
1975 Two-person show, Thumb Gallery, London
1976 Axis Gallery, Paris
1978 Axis Gallery, Paris
1980 Francis Kyle Gallery, London
1983 Crafts Council Shop, Victoria and Albert Museum, London
1985 *Carol McNicoll Ceramics*, Crafts Council Gallery, London
1987 New shop-opening show, Axis, Paris
1989 Crafts Council Shop, London
1990 The Oxford Gallery, Oxford
1994 *Carol McNicoll*, Osiris Gallery, Brussels, Belgium
1994 *Carol McNicoll and Phil Rogers*, Paul Rice Gallery, London
2000 *Carol McNicoll, Knick-Knacks*, Yorkshire Sculpture Park, Wakefield

Group exhibitions

1969 *Northern Young Contemporaries*, Manchester, England
1981 *British Ceramics and Textiles*, Knokke Heist, Belgium
1982 *The Maker's Eye*, Crafts Council Gallery, London
1984 *Artist Potters Now*, Museum of Oxford, Oxford, England
1985 *Fast Forward*, ICA, London, England
1986 *Potted History*, Gardner Centre, Brighton, England
1987 *British Crafts*, Hamburg Museum, Hamburg, Germany
1988 *Six Ways*, Anatole Orient Gallery, London
1988 Gallery Kapelhuis, Amersfort, Holland
1989 *L'Europe des Ceramics*, Centre Culturel de L'Yonne, Auxerre and touring to Madrid, Budapest, Strasbourg and campagne Ardennes
1989 *Fifth Biennial de Chateauroux*, Les cordeliers, Musée Bertrand, Chateauroux, France
1989 *Off The Wheel*, Whitworth Art Gallery, Manchester
1990 *Great British Design*, Tokyo and touring to Osaka, Sapporo and Hiroshima, Japan
1990 *Lucie Rie, Hans Coper and Their Pupils*, Sainsbury Centre for the Visual Arts, Norwich, and touring to Cambridge, England
1990 *British Ceramics in Norway*, Horland Kunster Sentrum Nondes, Nordenfjeldske Indestiral Arts Museum, the Art Museum, Bergen, Trondheim and Oslo, Norway
1991 *Aspects of Sculpture*, Heidelberg and Munich, Germany
1991 *The Abstract Vessel*, Oriel Gallery, Cardiff and touring

1991 *British Ceramics*, Santa Fe and New York, United States

1991 *Colours of Earth*, British Council, New Delhi, Varanasi, Calcutta, Bombay, Madras and Bangalore, India

1992 *Colours of Earth*, British Council, touring to Kuching, Penang, Kuala Lumpur and Kota Kinabali

1993 *High Table*, MAC, Birmingham and touring

1993 *Form and Function*, Contemporary Applied Arts, London

1993 *The Raw and The Cooked*, Barbican Art Gallery, Glynn Vivian, MOMA and The Shigaraki Ceramic Cultural Park, London, Swansea, Oxford and Shigaraki, Great Britain and Japan

1993 *Visions of Craft 1973-93*, Crafts Council Gallery, London

1994 *Recent Purchases by the Contemporary Art Society*, Oldham Art Gallery, Crafts Council Craft and Design Gallery, Oldham and London

1995 *Out of this World: The Influence of Nature in Craft and Design*, Crafts Council Gallery, London and touring

1995 *Teapotmania*, Norwich Castle Museum and touring

1996 *Take it From Here: Purchases by the Contemporary Art Society, 1992-5*, Sunderland Museum and Art Gallery, City Library and Vardy Gallery, Sunderland

1996 *William Morris Revisited: Questioning the Legacy*, Whitworth Art Gallery, Manchester

1996 *Objects of Our Time*, Crafts Council Gallery, London

1997 *Carol McNicoll - Ceramics: Steven Newell - Glass*, Crafts Council Shop, London

1997 *The Contemporary Teapot*, Keramikmuseet Grimerhus, Middelfart, Denmark

1997 *Time for Tea*, British Council, international tour

1998 *The Pleasure of Peace*, Sainsbury Centre for the Visual Arts, Norwich and touring venues

1998 *Decadence*, Crafts Council Gallery, London

1999 *Twenty-Fifth Anniversary Showcase Exhibition*, Crafts Council Shop at the Victoria and Albert Museum, London

1999 *Barrett Marsden at Galerie Binnen*, Galerie Binnen, Amsterdam, Holland

1999 *541 Vases, Pots, Sculptures and Services*, Stedelijk Museum, Amsterdam, Holland

2000 *British Ceramics 2000.dk*, Keramikmuseet Grimmerhus, Middlefart, Denmark

2003 *Show5* - Carol McNicoll, Retrospective, The City Gallery, Leicester

Public collections

Australia

National Gallery of Victoria, Melbourne

Holland

Boymans Museum, Rotterdam
Dordrecht Museum, Dordrecht
Stedelijk Museum, Amsterdam
Museum Het Princess Hoff, Leeuivarden

United Kingdom

Bedfordshire Schools Art Collection, Bedford
Birmingham Museum and Art Gallery, Birmingham
Bolton Museum, Bolton
Bradford Art Galleries and Museums, Bradford, West Yorkshire
British Craft Council, London
Cleveland Craft Centre, Middlesbrough
Contemporary Arts Society, London
Fitzwilliam Museum, Cambridge
Glasgow City Art Gallery, Glasgow
Harris Museum and Art Gallery, Preston, Lancashire
Hove Museum, Hove, Sussex
New Walk Museum and Art Gallery, Leicester
Norwich Castle Museum, Norwich
Oldham Art Gallery, Oldham
Paisley Art Gallery, Paisley
Shipley City Art Gallery, Shipley, Yorkshire
Ulster Museum, Belfast
Victoria and Albert Museum, London

Selected bibliography

Artist Potters Now, exh.cat., Museum of Oxford, Oxford, 1984

British Ceramics, exh.cat., Rhodos/Keramikmuseet Grimmerhus, Denmark, 2000

British Council Manchester, exh.cat., The British Council, Manchester, 1992

Britton, Alison and Margetts, Martina, *The Raw and the Cooked: New Work in Clay in Britain*, exh.cat., Museum of Modern Art, Oxford, 1993

'Carol McNicoll ceramics 1972–85', *Gallery News*, Aberystwyth Arts Centre, Aberystwyth, 1986

Carol McNicoll, Knick-Knacks, exh.cat., Yorkshire Sculpture Park, Wakefield, 2000

Colours of Earth, exh.cat., British Council, London, 1991

Colours of Earth, exh.cat., British Council, London, 1992

Dormer, Peter, *The New Ceramics*, Thames & Hudson, London, 1982

Dormer, Peter (ed.), *Fast Forward*, exh.cat., Institute of Contemporary Arts, London, 1985

Gough, Piers, 'Carol McNicoll review', *Craft*, no.78 (Jan/Feb), 1986

Harrod, Tanya (ed.), *British Ceramics*, exh.cat., Museum Het Kruithuis, Hertogenbosh, Holland, 1985

Harrod, Tanya (ed.), *Potted History*, exh.cat., Gardner Centre, Brighton, 1986

Harrod, Tanya, 'Bridging the divide', *Craft*, no.80 (May/June), 1986

Harrod, Tanya, *The Crafts in Britain in the Twentieth Century*, 1999

Harrod, Tanya, 'Carol McNicoll', *International Journal of Ceramics and Glass*, no.2 (Feb/Mar), 1986

Harrod, Tanya, 'Review', *Craft*, no.100 (Sept/Oct), 1989

Harrod, Tanya, 'Sources of inspiration', *Crafts*, (Nov/Dec), 1999

High Table, British Studio Pottery of the 1980s, exh.cat., Craftspace Touring, Birmingham, 1994

High Table, British Studio Pottery of the 1990s, exh.cat., Craftspace Touring, Birmingham, 1993

Hill, Rosemary, 'Six of the best', *Craft*, no.116 (Sept/Oct), 1990

Huston, John, *The Abstract Vessel*, Bellew Publishing/ Welsh Arts Council, London, 1991

Lewinstein, Eileen, 'Carol McNicoll, slip caster extraordinary', *Ceramic Review*, no.117 (May/June), 1989

Lucie-Smith, Edward, 'The raw and the cooked', *Ceramic Review*, no.143 (Sept/Oct), 1993

Margetts, Martina, *Visions of Craft*, exh.cat., Crafts Council, London, 1993

McNicoll, Carol, 'Carol McNicoll', *London Potters Newsletter*, no.138 (Dec/Jan), 1994

Obscure Objects of Desire, Conference Proceedings, Crafts Council, London, 1997

Out of This World: The Influence of Nature in Craft and Design 1880–1995, exh.cat., Crafts Council, London, 1995

Pim, Henry, 'Carol McNicoll ceramics', *Ceramic Review*, no.97 (Jan/Feb), 1986

Reid, Christopher, 'A culture of doodles', *Craft*, no.64 (Sept/Oct), 1983

Rose, Andrea, *Time for Tea*, exh.cat., British Council, London, 1997

'Solo show', *Arts Report*, no.53 (June), West Midlands Arts Association, 1986

Teapotmania: The Story of the British Craft Teapot and Teacosy, exh.cat., Norfolk Museums Service, Norwich, 1995

Three English Ceramicists, exh.cat., Keramish Werksentrum Heusden, Holland, 1982

Twenty-Five Years: Crafts Council Shop at the Victoria and Albert Museum, exh.cat., Crafts Council, London, 1999

Watson, Oliver, *British Studio Pottery, The Victoria and Albert Collection*, Phaidon/Christie's, Oxford, 1990

Watson, Oliver and Deacon, Richard (eds), *Carol McNicoll Ceramics,* exh.cat., Crafts Council, London, 1985

'What next', *Craft*, no.77 (Nov/Dec), 1985

Wright, Philip, 'A view from the south', *Craftwork*, no.11 (Spring), 1986

Broadcasts

Beautiful Things, TV programme, BBC Wales, 1997

Acknowledgements

I would like first to thank Tanya Harrod for not only contributing one of the two essays but also for being willing to help me deal with what was to me the insurmountable problem of organising my history; without her help this book could not have happened. I would like also to thank Mark Prest my curator and the Crafts Council for giving me this unique opportunity. I would like to thank David Cripps who for many years has recorded my work, and whose photos form the visual nucleus of this book. I am grateful to RoseLee Goldberg who restructured her life in order to find the time to write for me.

I am grateful to all the collectors who kindly allowed Mark and myself access to their collections and lent work for photography, particularly Pat Barnes, Ed Wolf, Zandra Rhodes and Piers Gough.

I have a group of close friends whose advice and support preserved my sanity throughout this project. I will always be in their debt.

Finally I would like to thank my son Beckett Vester for always being available for an entertaining argument.

Carol McNicoll

Index of works